Kapiert! 1

William Rowlinson

Oxford University Press

Oxford University Press, Walton Street, Oxford OX2 6DP
Oxford New York Toronto
Delhi Bombay Calcutta Madras Karachi
Petaling Jaya Singapore Hong Kong Tokyo
Nairobi Dar es Salaam Cape Town
Melbourne Auckland

and associated companies in
Beirut Berlin Ibadan Nicosia

Oxford is a trade mark of Oxford University Press

First published 1983
Reprinted 1984, 1985, 1986
ISBN 0 19 832496 0

Typeset by Rowland Phototypesetting Ltd
Bury St Edmunds, Suffolk
Printed in Hong Kong

Acknowledgements

The author wishes to thank Lilo Lehnigk and Gisela Schladebach for their precise and critical reading of the manuscript, and Kathleen Williams, Head of Modern Languages at Silverdale Comprehensive School, Sheffield, for her constructive advice and helpful suggestions. Once again the author would like to thank the Oxford University Press production team for their now-customary help, patience, and encouragement.

Photographs are by the author.
Illustrations are by Peter Edwards.

Kapiert! is complete in two parts. Each part comprises:
pupils' book
teacher's edition
presentation tape/cassette

Preface

Kapiert! is a two-part German course with textbooks and tapes/cassettes leading towards GCSE examinations. In format and approach it parallels the author's French course **tout compris**. The large number of short units allows the two parts of the course to be used over two, three or even four years and still give the pupils a real sense of progress; the generally adult approach also makes the course suitable for older school beginners and adults.

The course is based on a grammatical syllabus with language in situation and language as function (e.g. expressing surprise, regret, liking; offering; thanking . . .) also determining content. Especially in the early stages a carefully graded one-step-at-a-time approach has been used, with new structures introduced with known vocabulary and vice versa: at this stage exercises within a unit are also sequentially graded. Though the grammar syllabus is a generally accepted one, teachers will note that some areas (the genitive, for instance) get much less stress than has often been the case. Frequently in the past the early years of German have been made unnecessarily complicated by attention to the exception and the rare at the expense of practice-time with the everyday and useful.

All four skills – aural comprehension, speaking, reading, writing – are taught by the course. Though it is up to the individual teacher to decide what stress he or she puts on each of these, it is assumed that the first two will form the basis of most learning in the initial stages.

Many exercises and activities are marked for pairwork. There is a growing realisation of the value of this technique in language classrooms to give pupils practice in oral interchange. It is, indeed, difficult to practise this skill effectively in normal-sized language classes without pairwork: nor can the language laboratory provide the face-to-face exchange of language that pairwork can. Before handing over an exercise to pairs, though, it is vital in these early stages that it be first worked through thoroughly with the whole class to make sure that pairs know what they are doing and how to do it accurately.

Pairwork should not continue too long – short bursts are most effective.

The fifty-six units of part one are grouped in fours, with every fourth unit a revision unit. The revision units aside, units follow no set pattern, variety and novelty being used to generate and keep interest. The revision units review the grammar and list the vocabulary of the previous three units, and also contain six or seven revision exercises based on the main grammar points. These revision exercises are largely, though not entirely, intended as written work.

Part one covers a wide range of everyday situations, mainly those a tourist would encounter, and the commonest language functions. It includes most of the basic morphology of the language, normal main-clause syntax and the present tense of strong and weak verbs. Towards the end of part one the simplest form of the perfect, . . . *haben . . . past participle*, is introduced. This is revised, then developed more fully in part two, where the first few units provide an overlap with part one and avoid the 'step' often found in courses at this point.

Early units of part one concentrate on dialogue material; narrative is introduced from unit 33. Aural comprehension is used from the very beginning, with the material of the comprehension dialogue printed a page or two later. Reading comprehension is developed gradually, and the textbook should be supplemented, from about unit 40 onwards, by a period each week or fortnight devoted to silent reading. A selection of short readers is needed for this: the author's reader-pack **Lies mal Deutsch! 1** is entirely suitable – as are a number of other collections of short readers at a basic level.

English is used in the course for scene setting, to give reality and (sometimes) humour to exercises, for the instructions to activities and for the explanation of grammar. From time to time pupils are asked to answer questions or give summaries in English, affording the teacher feedback on how well material has been understood. For all this English seems necessary; it is hoped, however, that the format of the course will ensure that most work in most lessons is in German.

There is a good deal of background offered in passing on the two Germanies, Austria and Switzerland. Some teachers will wish to use these starting points to develop further background work in class. The hundred or so photographs in part one were taken with their civilization or language content in mind (there are quite a number of exercises based on 'notice language') and the drawings, as well as their humour, also have quite a large civilization content.

The tape/cassette to part one is recorded by German actors and consists entirely of presentation material. Though many of the exercises in the course can be used in the language laboratory, most teachers now find it almost as convenient and very much cheaper to record these themselves or have their German assistant do so. It would, however, be rather more difficult for a teacher to record the dialogues, scenes, and narratives of the presentation material as effectively as professional actors can.

The teacher's notes for the course form a separate section of the teacher's edition of **Kapiert!**, which is then followed by the text of the pupil's book. This practice has been adopted since most teachers like to teach in the classroom using the same text as their pupils. The teacher's notes explain briefly the point of each section of material and how it may be used and exploited. They are not intended to be prescriptive – the teacher knows better than any course author his own strengths and his pupils' capacities and interests. Not all activities marked for pairwork need be done in pairs, not all exercises marked as suitable for writing should be written. The teacher's notes are suggestions only: the wise teacher will choose, reject, adapt on the basis of the needs of the pupils in front of him.

The following signs are used in the text:

material appearing on the presentation tape;

material suitable for pairwork.

The numbers in the German–English vocabulary at the end of the book refer to the unit in which a German word in a particular meaning is first introduced.

W.R.
Sheffield 1982

Contents

Introducing German-speaking Europe

This is Germany. Actually, it's West Germany, the Federal Republic of Germany, **die Bundesrepublik Deutschland (BRD)**. It's what we usually mean when we talk about Germany. You can see from the map where the biggest towns lie.

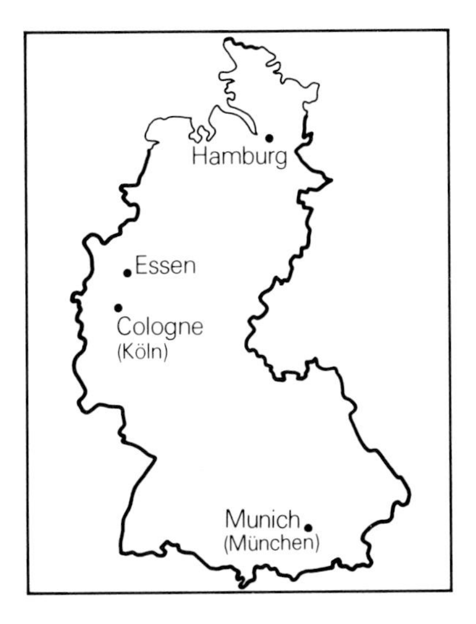

But there is another Germany, East Germany, the German Democratic Republic, **die Deutsche Demokratische Republik (DDR)**. It's a Communist state, part of the Eastern bloc, and it's much smaller than West Germany. (West Germany has 60 million inhabitants, East Germany has 17 million.)

There are two other major European countries that speak German too. Austria, **Österreich**, which has 7½ million inhabitants, and Switzerland, **die Schweiz**, about 70% of whose 6½ million inhabitants speak German.

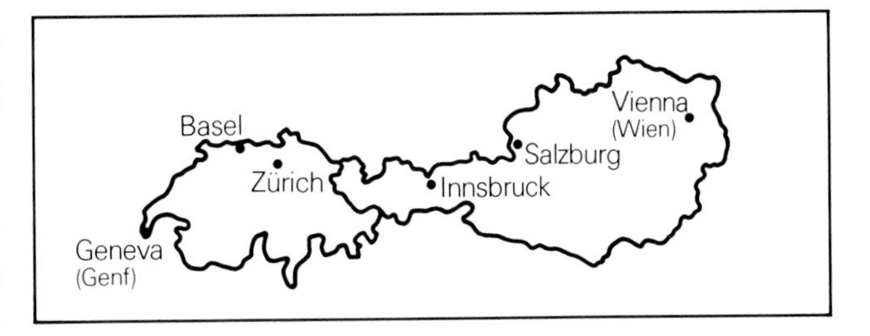

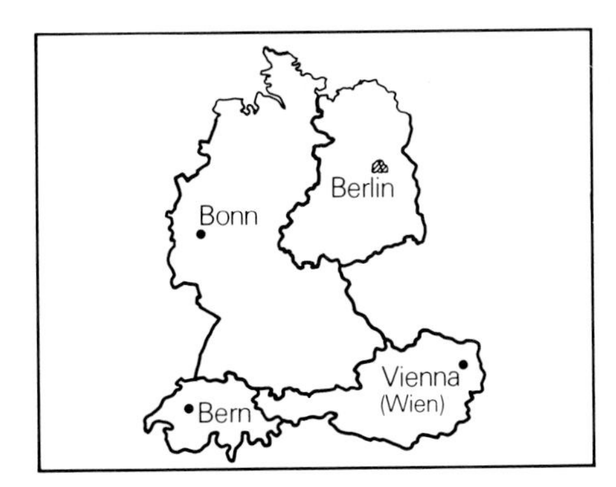

The capitals of these countries are **Bonn** (West Germany), **Berlin** (East Germany), **Bern** (Switzerland) and Vienna, **Wien** (Austria). To be precise, the capital of the DDR is *East* Berlin, since West Berlin is a free city not forming part of the territory of the DDR and with close ties with West Germany. This division of both Germany and Berlin came about after the 1939–45 war.

All these countries have formed part of one or other of the various 'Germanies' that have existed – the Hohenstaufen Empire, Bismarck's German Empire, Hitler's Third Reich, and many others. There are no clear-cut boundaries to define a German state apart from the North Sea and the Baltic coasts, which is one reason for the tremendous territorial changes in Germany throughout history.

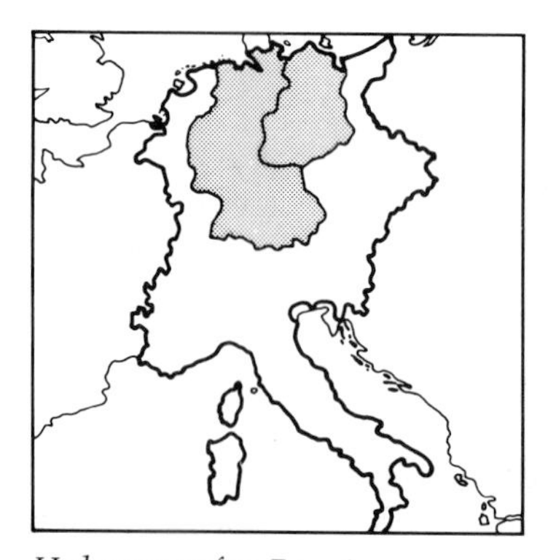
Hohenstaufen Empire, 12th century

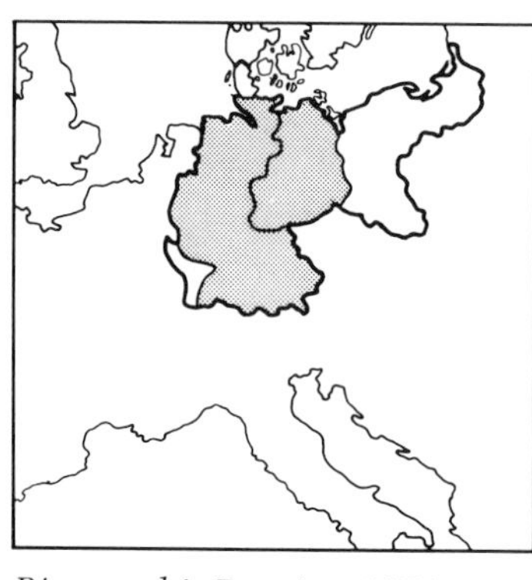
Bismarck's Empire, 1871

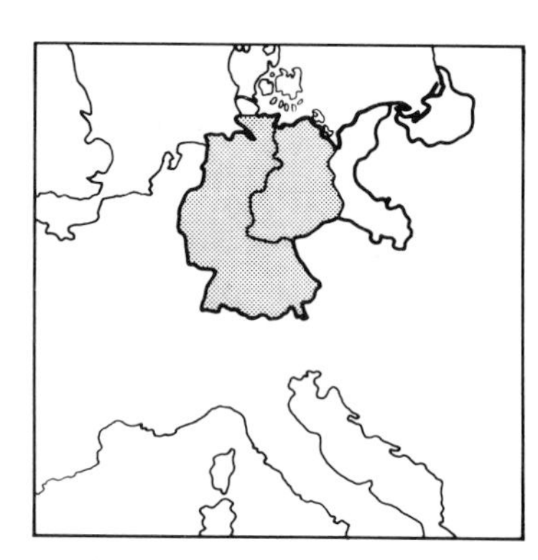
Hitler's Third Reich, 1937

The dialects of the German language vary considerably from one area to another and there is no one form that everyone accepts as standard. North German speech is very different from that of Austria, mostly in pronunciation but also in the use of different words and phrases. Switzerland has its own version of German which even Germans find difficult to understand, though most Swiss speak a comprehensible form of standard German as well. In general we shall be learning the German of North-central Germany, but you will meet and eventually be expected to recognize language from other parts of German-speaking Europe.

Countries bordering on the two Germanies, Austria, and Switzerland

UNIT 1

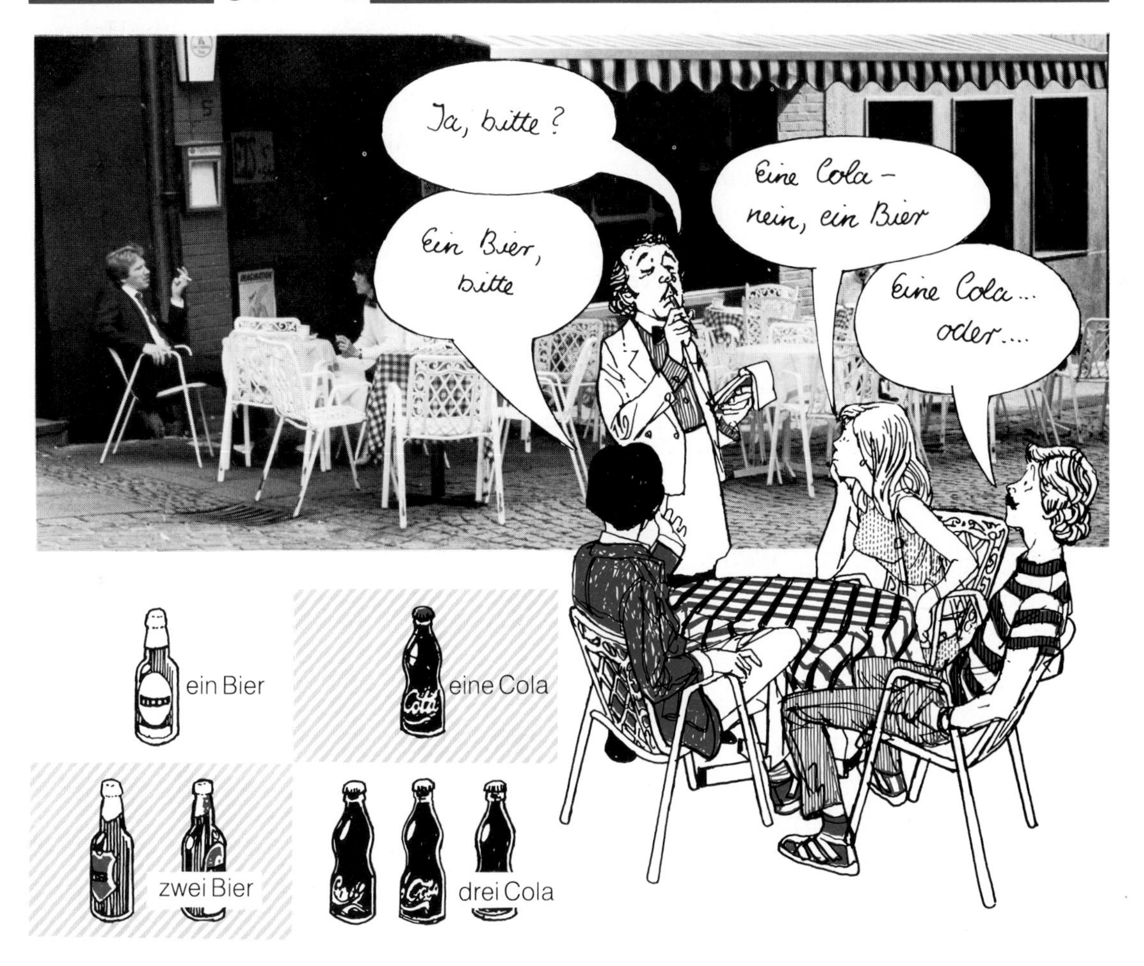

1 Ein Bier, zwei Bier, drei Bier

The scene involves a waiter in a pub taking an order for drinks. Listen to the dialogue twice, then answer these questions:

1. What does the first boy order?
2. What does the girl then start to order?
3. What does she change her mind to?
4. What does she think the waiter has written down as her order?
5. What does the second boy order to start with?
6. Why is the waiter cross?
7. What is the final order?

ja yes
bitte please
und and
für Sie for you
nein no
also so
doch after all
oder or

2 Turn over and listen to the dialogue again with the text in front of you.

Ein Bier, zwei Bier, drei Bier

Waiter	Ja, bitte?
Hans	Ein Bier, bitte.
Waiter	Ein Bier. Ja, und für Sie?
Anne	Eine Cola. Nein, ein Bier.
Waiter	Also zwei Bier.
Anne	Nein, e i n Bier, bitte.
Waiter	Also ein Bier und eine Cola?
Anne	Nein, ein Bier.
Waiter (to Hans)	Und für Sie?
Hans	Ein Bier!
Waiter	Also doch zwei Bier! Und für Sie?
Klaus-Dieter	Eine Cola.
Waiter	Also, für Sie ein Bier und für Sie ein Bier und für Sie eine Cola, ja? Zwei Bier und eine Cola.
Klaus-Dieter	Ja . . . oder . . . nein, ein Bier, bitte.
Waiter (tearing up order slip)	Drei Bier also?
All three	Ja ja, bitte, drei Bier!

3 With the teacher playing the waiter and the whole class the customers, order drinks. See how much you can confuse the waiter by changing your mind.

4 Answer these questions from various waiters. Use the text to help you invent your answers.

1 Für Sie eine Cola, ja?
2 Und für Sie?
3 Zwei Bier für Sie?
4 Ein Bier oder eine Cola?
5 Für Sie ein Bier und eine Cola, ja?
6 Drei Cola?
7 Zwei Bier oder zwei Cola?
8 Ja, bitte?

UNIT 2

 **1** **Was trinkst du?**

Mother is asking the children and their father what they would like to drink with lunch. She gets unexpected answers. Listen to the dialogue twice, then answer these questions.

1 What does mother expect Adrian to drink?
2 What does he drink?
3 What does she offer Dieter?
4 What does he want?
5 What does mother expect Renate to have?
6 What does she ask for?
7 What choice does mother offer father?
8 What does he choose?

was what
ich trinke I am drinking
du trinkst you are drinking
auch also; as well
heute today
Vati (*familiar*) father
wie immer as always

2 Turn over and listen to the dialogue again with the text in front of you.

1 Was trinkst du?

Mother	Was trinkst du, Adrian? Eine Cola?
Adrian	Nein, ein Bier.
Mother	Und du, Dieter, trinkst du ein Glas Milch?
Dieter	Nein, ich trinke auch ein Bier.
Mother	Renate, du trinkst Limonade, ja?
Renate	Nein, ich trinke heute auch Bier.
Mother	Du auch Bier! Und du, Vati, was trinkst du heute, Bier oder Wein?
Father (virtuous)	Ich? Ich trinke ein Glas Wasser – wie immer!

3 One member of each pair decides on what he is going to drink and writes it down. The other member then sees how many questions he needs to guess it. Then change round. The member of each pair who guesses the other member's drink in the fewest questions wins. If you guess quickly, have another round!

Pattern — Was trinkst du heute? Ein Glas Bier?
— Nein.
— Ein Glas ...... ?
......
— Ein Glas Cola?
— Ja, ich trinke ein Glas Cola.

4 Write out these sentences, choosing the right words to make each refer correctly to the text. Refer back if necessary!

1 Trinkst du [ein Bier / ein Glas Limonade], Dieter? — Nein!

2 Du trinkst [Milch / ein Glas Bier], Renate, ja? — Ja!

3 Vati, trinkst du [Bier oder Wein / Wasser] ? — Ja!

4 Trinkst du [eine Cola / Bier], Adrian? — Nein!

And what about *you*?

5 Und was trinkst d u ? — Ich trinke [Bier / Wein / Limonade / Milch / Wasser / Cola] !

5 Listen to the dialogue again with your books closed, and see if you can give each person's answer to mother before you hear it.

UNIT 3

Ein Bier, bitte!

1 Listen carefully to the dialogue, following the text in your books.

Bertold	Was trinkst du?
Michael	Ich? Ich trinke Bier. Du auch?
Bertold	Bier? Ach nein! Nicht Bier! . . .
Michael	Ein Bier, bitte.
Bar-girl	Eine Mark, bitte.
Bertold	Eine Limonade, bitte.
Bar-girl	Tja, die Limonade ist leider alle.
Bertold	Also . . . ein Glas Rotwein.
Bar-girl	Der Rotwein ist leider auch alle.
Bertold	Und der Weißwein?
Bar-girl	Auch der Weißwein!
Bertold	Also, eine Cola, bitte.
Bar-girl	Die Cola . . .
Bertold	Ja ja . . . die Cola ist auch alle. Milch?
Bar-girl	Die Milch ist leider auch alle.
Bertold	Na, so was! Ich trinke ein Glas Wasser.
Bar-girl	Wasser ist nicht da.
Bertold	Bier ist aber da? Das Bier ist nicht alle?
Bar-girl	Nein, Bier ist da.
Bertold	Also, ein Bier, bitte.
Bar-girl	Eine Mark . . .
Michael	Was trinkst du?
Bertold	Bier.
Michael	D u trinkst Bier? Na, so was! Prost!

nicht not
die Mark Mark
tja yes, well . . .
ist is **ist alle** (*colloq.*) has run out
der Rotwein red wine
der Weißwein white wine

leider unfortunately
na, so was! would you believe it!
da there
aber though
prost! cheers!

2 **Which is which?** Put the right name to each picture.

die Milch
das Wasser
der Rotwein
die Limonade
die Cola
das Bier

1 

2 

3 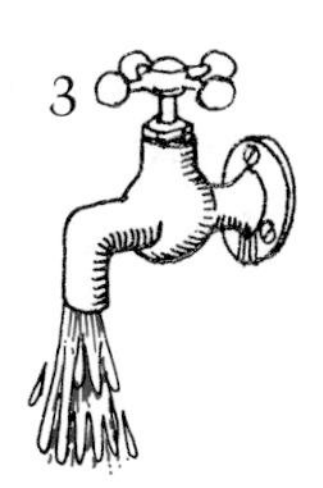

4 

5 

6 

3 Picture gallery

der Rotwein

ein Rotwein

die Limonade

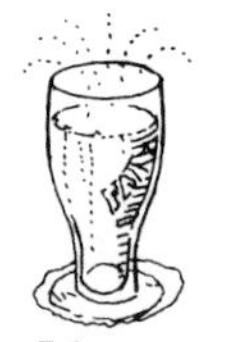
eine Limonade

das Bier

ein Bier

Label these pictures **ein (eine) ......** or **der (die, das) ......** according to which makes best sense.

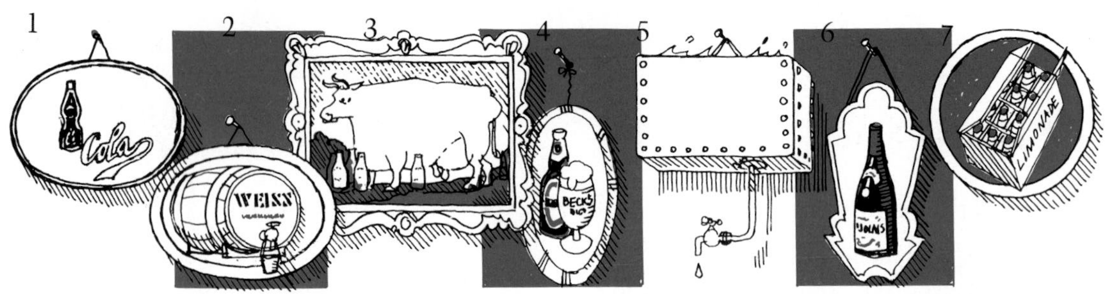

4 Be the out-of-everything barmaid! (You haven't even any beer)

Answer these orders.

1 Zwei Glas Limonade, bitte.
2 Ein Glas Rotwein, bitte.
3 Ist Weißwein da?
4 Ein Glas Milch, bitte.
5 Bitte, eine Cola.
6 Ein Glas Wasser, bitte.
7 Zwei Bier und eine Limonade, bitte.

5 There's not much left

vier Mark

fünf Mark

sechs Mark

In pairs: one member of the pair plays the customer, one the barman. The customer wants *two* drinks (one for his/her friend). The barman only has one or two things still available, so when the customer discovers what they are he has to take those. Play the scene through twice, exchanging roles. Barman – don't forget to tell the customer the *total* price.

Bier	2,00
Cola	1,00
Limonade	1,00
Milch	1,00
Rotwein	3,00
Weißwein	3,00

UNIT 4 REVISION

Grammar

1 Nouns in German have gender – they may be masculine, feminine, or neuter.

When Germans use *a* or *the* before a noun, they use **ein** or **der** for masculine nouns, **eine** or **die** for feminine nouns and **ein** or **das** for neuter nouns:

the . . .	der Rotwein	die Mark	das Glas
a . . .	ein Rotwein	eine Mark	ein Glas

Genders must be learnt with nouns, since there is no way of telling what a noun's gender may be. So don't learn **Bier**, learn **das Bier**. All nouns are written with a capital letter.

2 Questions are formed in German by simply inverting subject and verb, with a question word first if necessary:

Trinkst du Bier? Was trinkst du?

Questions can of course also be asked simply by making a statement in a questioning tone of voice:

Du trinkst ein Bier?

and **ja** can be added for emphasis:

Du trinkst ein Bier, ja?

3 ein Glas Bier – *a glass of beer*
zwei Glas Limonade – *two glasses of lemonade*

No word for *of* after expressions of quantity in German.

A
1 Trinkst du Cola? — Ja, ich trinke . . . . . .
2 Trinkst du Limonade? — Nein, ...
3 Trinkst du Wasser? — Ja, ...
4 Trinkst du Milch? — Nein, ...
5 Trinkst du Bier? — Ja, ...
6 Trinkst du Wein? — Nein, ...

B **ein** or **eine**?

1 

2 

3 

4 

5 

6

7 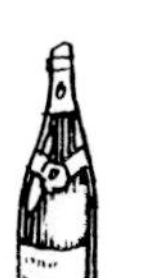

8

der Wein wine
der Rotwein red wine
der Weißwein white wine
Vati (*familiar*) father

die Milch milk
die Limonade lemonade
die Mark mark (*coin*)
die Cola cola

das Bier beer
das Glas glass
das Wasser water

ein(s) one
zwei two
drei three
vier four
fünf five
sechs six

ich trinke, du trinkst I, you drink
ist is

ja yes
nein no
bitte please
für for
also then
und and
was what
ich I
du you (*familiar*)
Sie you (*polite*)
heute today
wie as
immer always
ach oh
nicht not
tja yes, well
leider unfortunately
alle (*colloquial*) sold out
da there
aber though
das that
doch after all
prost! good health
na, so was! would you believe it!
oder or

C der, die, or das?

1

2
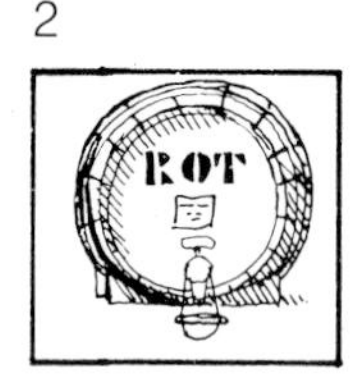

3

4

5

6

D Apologize (you haven't any!)

Ein Glas bitte! — Tja, der (die, das) ...... ist leider alle!

E Answer:

1 Trinkst du immer Wasser?
2 Trinkst du ein Glas Bier oder ein Glas Limonade?
3 Was trinkst du heute?
4 Du trinkst Milch?
5 Ist Cola da?

F Fit the questions to these answers:

1 Ich trinke ein Bier.
2 Das ist Rotwein.
3 Ja, bitte.
4 Nein, ich trinke ein Bier.
5 Leider nicht!
6 Nein, Limonade ist nicht da.
7 Nein, heute nicht.

Ist Bier da?
Trinkst du Wein?
Eine Cola?
Limonade ist da, ja?
Was ist das?
Trinkst du Milch?
Was trinkst du?

G Invent suitable captions for the balloons in these pictures:

UNIT 5

1 A Buying food

Stefan Was kaufst du hier, Mutter?
Mutter Ich weiß nicht . . .
Stefan Kaufst du Wurst?
Mutter Wurst? Nein. Käse vielleicht.
Stefan Ach ja. Kaufst du Edamer? Er ist gut, der Edamer!

du kaufst you buy
hier here
die Mutter mother
ich weiß I know
die Wurst sausage
der Käse cheese
vielleicht perhaps
der Edamer Edam cheese
gut good

B Buying presents

Katrin Was kaufst du für Mutter, Adrian?
Adrian Ich weiß nicht . . .
Katrin Kaufst du Seife?
Adrian Vielleicht.
Katrin Und für Vati?
Adrian Ja, was kaufe ich für Vati? Ein Hemd?
Katrin Ja, ein Hemd. Das Hemd dort vielleicht – es ist so schön!

die Seife soap
das Hemd shirt
dort there
schön nice

C Buying music

Hans Morgen, Peter.
Peter Morgen, Hans. Was kaufst du hier?
Hans Ich weiß nicht, eine Platte vielleicht. Und du?
Peter Ich kaufe eine Kassette für Renate.
Hans Für Renate?
Peter Ja, sie ist für Renate.

der Morgen (good) morning
die Platte record
die Kassette cassette

D Buying drinks

Klaus Du kaufst Bier, ja?
Bertold Ja. – Zwei Löwenbräu, bitte.
Klaus Und Wein?
Bertold Ja, Wein auch. – Zwei Niersteiner, bitte.
Klaus Kaufst du auch Cola?
Bertold Ich weiß nicht. Eine Flasche vielleicht.
Klaus Gut. – Auch eine Flasche Cola, bitte. – Und Schnaps?
Bertold Nein, Schnaps kaufe ich nicht. Ich habe nur zehn Mark!

das Löwenbräu *type of beer from Bavaria*
der Niersteiner *type of wine*
die Flasche bottle
der Schnaps brandy; spirits
ich habe I have
nur only
zehn ten

2 Who gets what?

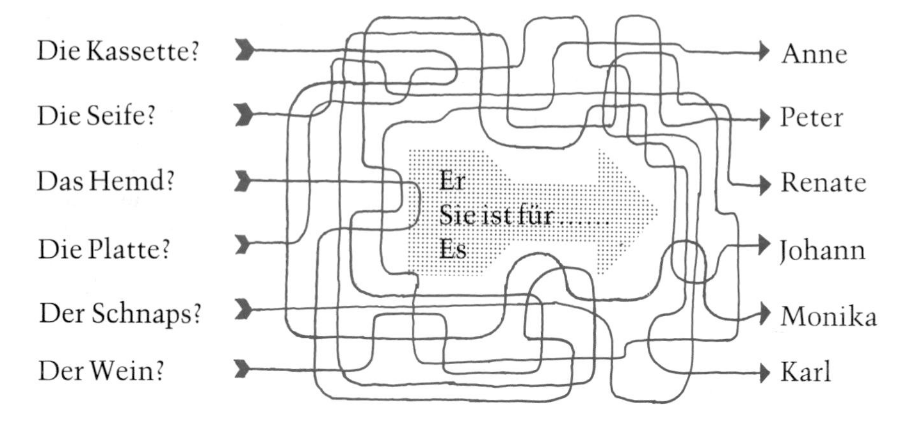

3 Er kauft, sie kauft

Answer these questions on the scenes in section 1, using **er** or **sie** in each answer:

1 Kauft Mutter Wurst?
2 Kauft Adrian Seife?
3 Was kauft er für Vati?
4 Was kauft Hans?
5 Was kauft Peter?
6 Ist die Platte für Renate?
7 Kauft Bertold Bier?
8 Was kauft er auch?
9 Hat er fünfzehn Mark?

4 Kaufst du  die Platte? Sie (er, es) ist gut (schön)!

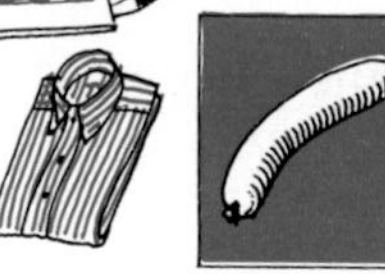

5
1 Was kaufst du für Uwe?
— Für Uwe kaufe ich Bier!
2 Und für Renate?
— Für Renate ......
3 Und für Mutter?
4 Und für Klaus-Dieter?
5 Und für Vater?
6 Und für Anne?

6 Hast du zwei Mark? — Nein, leider habe ich nur eine Mark.

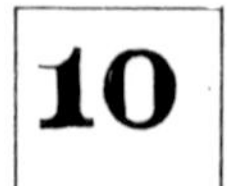

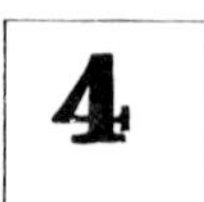

7 Trinkst du Rotwein? — Nein, Rotwein trinke ich nicht. Ich trinke ......

UNIT 6

1

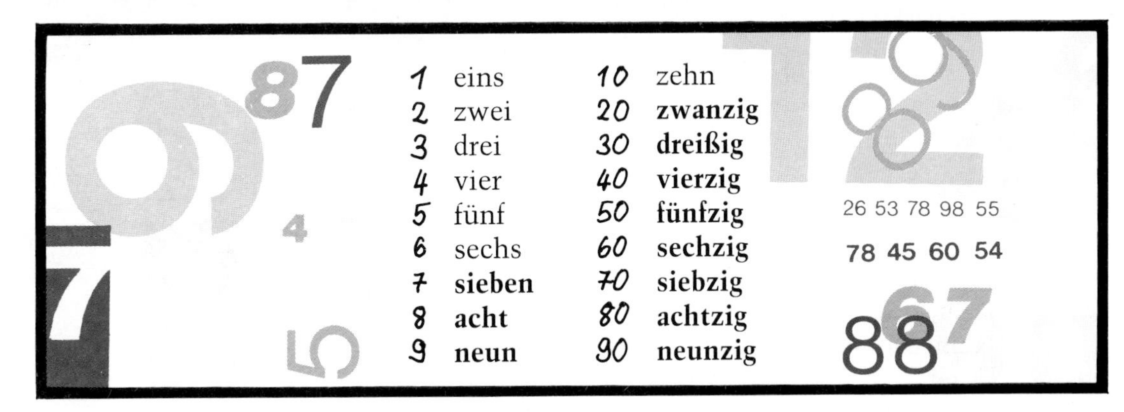

1	eins	10	zehn
2	zwei	20	**zwanzig**
3	drei	30	**dreißig**
4	vier	40	**vierzig**
5	fünf	50	**fünfzig**
6	sechs	60	**sechzig**
7	**sieben**	70	**siebzig**
8	**acht**	80	**achtzig**
9	**neun**	90	**neunzig**

2 Ich hätte gern ein Pfund Tomaten

Listen to the text and see if you can spot the German words for:

good morning
I should like
yes please
no thank you
that's all
good-bye.

3

Listen to the tape again and try to note down in English:

both things the customer is buying
how much of each he buys
what he has to pay
what size note he pays with
how much change he gets.

4

Das ist

eine Tomate

eine Banane

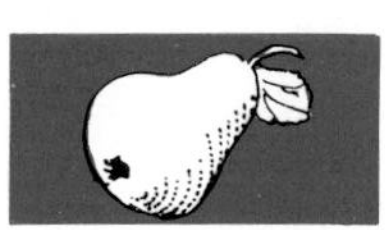
eine Birne

eine Pflaume

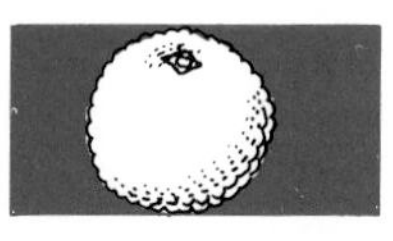
eine Orange

Das sind

Tomaten

Bananen

Birnen

Pflaumen

Orangen

5 — Guten Morgen!
— Guten Morgen!
— Ja, ich hätte gern

ein Pfund ein Kilo	Tomaten Bananen Birnen Pflaumen Orangen

— So, bitte schön. Sonst noch etwas?

— | Ja, bitte. Ich hätte gern ......
Nein, danke, das ist alles. |
|---|

— Das macht	eine zwei	Mark	zehn zwanzig	zusammen.

— Bitte schön.

— Zehn Mark, danke schön . . . und	acht sieben	Mark	neunzig achtzig	zurück, bitte.

— Danke schön.
— Bitte schön. Auf Wiedersehen!
— Auf Wiedersehen!

Changing the quantities and things in the boxes, use this pattern to buy yourself some fruit. The greengrocer may need to work out his sums on a piece of paper.

Here is an extension to the pattern in case he gets them wrong!

	das Kilo
Tomaten	DM 2,90
Bananen	DM 3,30
Birnen	DM 3,00
Pflaumen	DM 2,80
Orangen	DM 3,50

— Entschuldigung, nicht | sechs | Mark | neunzig | zurück, | sieben | Mark | zwanzig | !

— Ach ja, | sieben | Mark | zwanzig | . Entschuldigung. Bitte schön.

6 Renate wants to slim, Hans needs a present for his brother, Father loves cheese, Dieter adores pop music, Herr Bauer is teetotal, Ute likes juicy fruit and Susi the rather remarkable cat has just learned to talk. Who asks for what?

1 Ein Glas Limonade, bitte.
2 Ich hätte gern drei Pfund Käse.
3 Ich hätte gern die Pink-Floyd-Platte, bitte.
4 Zwei Kilo Orangen, bitte.
5 Eine Flasche Schnaps, bitte – sie ist für Rainer!
6 Ist Milch da, bitte?
7 Nur ein Glas Wasser, bitte.

UNIT 7

1

11	**elf**	16	**sechzehn**	21	**einundzwanzig**	32	zweiunddreißig
12	**zwölf**	17	**siebzehn**	22	zweiundzwanzig		...
13	dreizehn	18	achtzehn	23	dreiundzwanzig	41	einundvierzig
14	vierzehn	19	neunzehn		...		...
15	fünfzehn	20	zwanzig	31	einunddreißig	100	**hundert**

2

Frau Braun ist krank, und . . .

Herr Braun macht die Hausarbeit.

Was er macht:

Und wann:

Er putzt die Wohnung.

Um 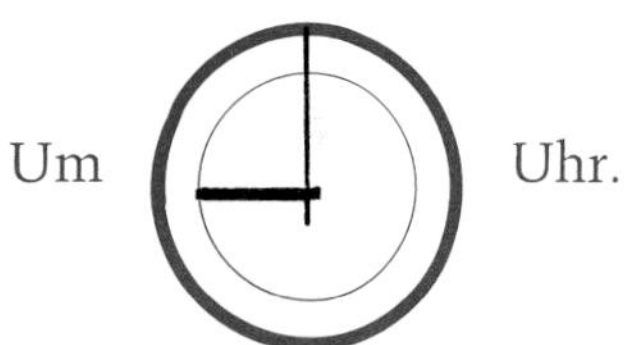 Uhr.

Er macht Mittagessen.

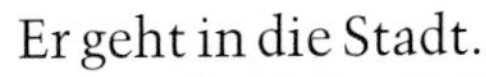

Er geht in die Stadt.

Er kauft Bananen, Wurst, Käse, Butter und Brot.

Er kommt zurück.

Er trinkt eine Tasse Kaffee.

Er macht Abendbrot.

Und um Uhr ist er sehr, sehr müde!

Now you recount Herr Braun's day, following this pattern:

Um ...... Uhr putzt er die Wohnung.
Um ...... Uhr ......
......

3 Wie spät ist es? 9·20 Es ist neun Uhr zwanzig.

1 8·00 2 2·10 3 10·05 4 5·05 5 11·07
6 4·17 7 7·29 8 3·35 9 6·15 10 12·01

4 Use two pencils as hands on this clockface and ask your partner time questions.

5 Wann gehst du in die Stadt? Um elf Uhr dreißig?
—Ja, um halb zwölf.
Und du, wann gehst du in die Stadt? Um . . . . . .
—Ja, um . . . . . .

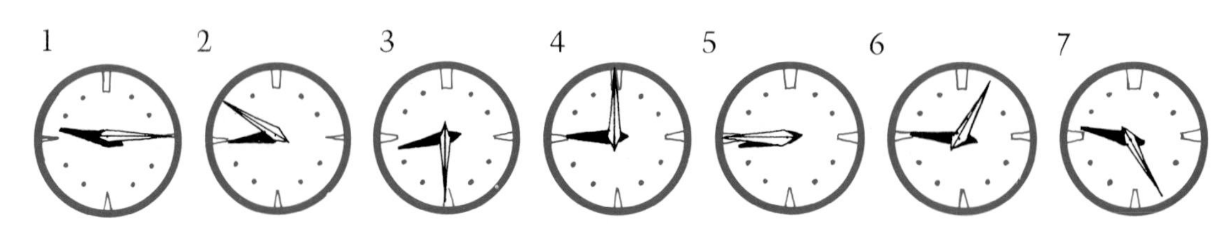

6 Dozy Donald's watch is always ten minutes slow.

What time is it really when his watch shows the times in section 5 above?

UNIT 8 REVISION

Grammar

1 Present singular of verbs

ich gehe — **ich** forms end in **-e**
du gehst — **du** forms end in **-st**
er, sie, es geht — **er** forms end in **-t**

2 Word order in statements

Das Hemd dort	ist	sehr schön.
Ich	kaufe	eine Kassette.
Schnaps	kaufe	ich nicht.
Leider	habe	ich nur eine Mark.
Um zwei Uhr	geht	er in die Stadt.

In a statement the verb *must* come in second place. In first place may be the subject (as in the first two examples above) or the object (as in the third example) or an adverb (as in the fourth example) or an adverb phrase (as in the last example), but the verb is always second. Notice that it is the second *idea*, not necessarily the second word. When the subject does not stand first in the sentence, it normally follows the verb. Putting something other than the subject first gives whatever is put first extra emphasis (as in the last three examples).

3 Plural of nouns: -n

eine Tomate — zwei Tomaten
eine Banane — drei Bananen

Many German nouns, including almost all those that end in **-e**, form their plural by adding **-n**. Nearly all feminine nouns form their plural in this way.

4 Numbers

0 null	13 dreizehn	40 vierzig
1 eins	14 vierzehn	50 fünfzig
2 zwei	15 fünfzehn	60 sechzig
3 drei	16 sechzehn	70 siebzig
4 vier	17 siebzehn	80 achtzig
5 fünf	18 achtzehn	90 neunzig
6 sechs	19 neunzehn	100 einhundert
7 sieben	20 zwanzig	101 einhunderteins
8 acht	21 einundzwanzig	. . .
9 neun	22 zweiundzwanzig	200 zweihundert
10 zehn	. . .	201 zweihunderteins
11 elf	30 dreißig	. . .
12 zwölf	31 einunddreißig	
	. . .	

der Käse cheese
der Morgen morning
der Schnaps brandy; spirits
der Herr gentleman; Mr
der Kaffee coffee

die Wurst sausage
die Mutter mother
die Seife soap
die Platte record
die Kassette cassette
die Flasche bottle
die Tomate tomato
die Banane banana
die Birne pear
die Pflaume plum
die Orange orange
die Frau woman; Mrs
die Hausarbeit housework
die Stadt town
die Butter butter
die Tasse cup
die Wohnung flat

das Abendbrot evening meal
das Hemd shirt
das Pfund pound
das Kilo kilo
das Mittagessen lunch
das Brot bread
das Viertel quarter

ich kaufe I buy
ich habe I have
ich mache I make
ich putze I clean
ich gehe I go
ich komme I come
ich weiß I know
ich hätte gern I should like

gut good
dort there
schön nice
hier here
nur only
er he
sie she
es it
so so
bitte (schön) there you are; don't mention it

5 Time

Clock time

Wie spät ist es?	Es ist	ein Uhr
(Wieviel Uhr ist es?)		fünf (Minuten) nach eins
		Viertel nach eins
		halb zwei (*half past one*)
		Viertel vor zwei
		zwei Uhr
	Es ist	fünf vor/nach zwölf
		Mittag/Mitternacht

A.m. and p.m. have no exact equivalents in German. The adverbs **vormittags** (*in the morning*), **nachmittags** (*in the afternoon*), **abends** (*in the evening*), and **nachts** (*at night*) are used where it is necessary to differentiate; otherwise the 24-hour clock is used.

24-hour clock (also used to read off digital times)

Es ist ein Uhr fünfzehn	dreizehn Uhr
ein Uhr dreißig	vierundzwanzig Uhr
ein Uhr fünfundvierzig	null Uhr eins

danke (schön) thank you
sonst noch etwas? anything else?
alles everything
zusammen together
zurück back
krank ill
wann? when?
um at
sehr very
müde tired
spät late
wie? how?
vor before
nach after
auf Wiedersehen goodbye
Entschuldigung! excuse me

A das ist? das sind?

B Wie spät ist es?

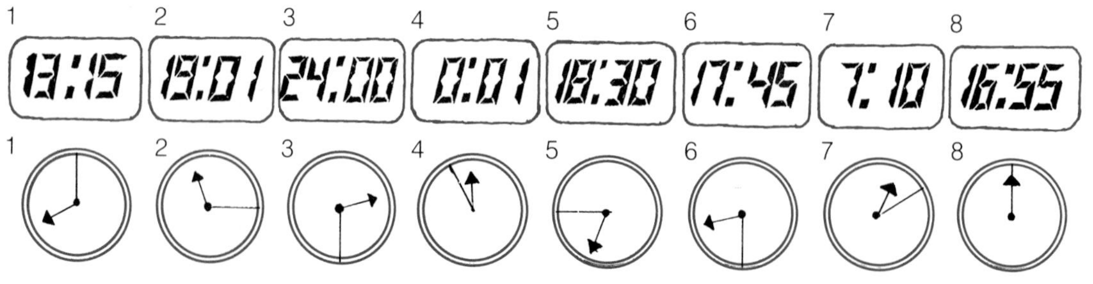

C
1 Renate trinkt eine Tasse Kaffee. — Ich ...... auch ......
2 Anne geht in die Stadt. — Du ...... auch ......
3 Ich komme nicht zurück. — Dieter ...... auch ......
4 Du kaufst eine Platte. — Klaus ...... auch ......
5 Peter macht nicht die Hausarbeit. — Du ...... auch ......
6 Vati putzt die Wohnung. — Die Wohnung ...... ich auch.

D Dreimal drei ist neun. Und . . .

7 × 7 =
8 × 8 =
4 × 4 =
2 × 13 =
5 × 10 =
7 × 11 =
12 × 3 =
17 × 5 =

E

1. Trinkst du Bier?
   — Nein, Bier trinke ich nicht.
2. Kommst du um zwei?
   — Nein, um ......
3. Hast du Käse?
4. Ist es spät?
5. Machst du die Hausarbeit?
6. Ist sie krank?
7. Geht er in die Stadt?
8. Ist es dort?
9. Hat sie die Kassette?

F Write out these labels in full:

zehn Mark fünfzig

1 

2 

3 

4 

5 

6 

7 

8 

G At the grocer's

Buy the shopping on your list from your partner.

Bananen	2 Stück: DM 1,50
Tomaten	Kilo: DM 3,00
Orangen	Kilo: DM 4,50
Pflaumen	Pfd: DM 3,10
Birnen	Kilo: DM 3,95
Wurst	Pfd: DM 4,00
Käse	Kilo: DM 7,80
Butter	Pfd: DM 4,50
Brot	Stück: DM 2,10
Rotwein	Flasche: DM 3,70

UNIT 9

1 Window shopping

Listen to the text, then answer these questions without turning to p. 32.

1 Why does the first woman have to tell the second woman the prices?
2 Which trousers is the second woman interested in? What do they cost?
3 Where in the window is the shirt she wants to know the price of? What is its price?
4 What does she ask about next? What does it cost?
5 What does she finally enquire about? Whereabouts in the window is it? Why do you think the other woman doesn't want to tell her?

2 You don't fool me!

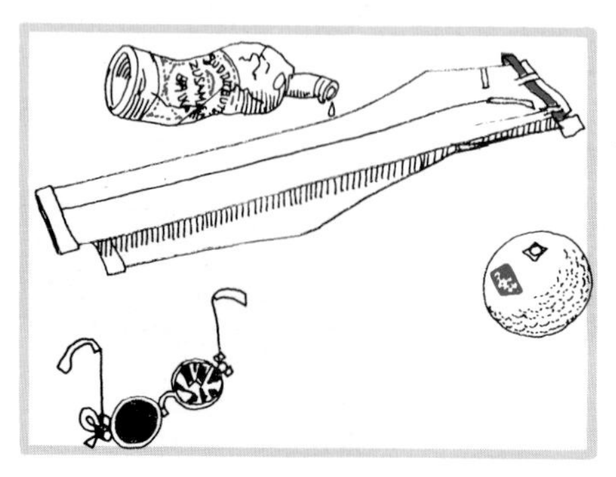

Welche Flasche ist besser?
—Die Flasche rechts!

Hose

Orange

Brille

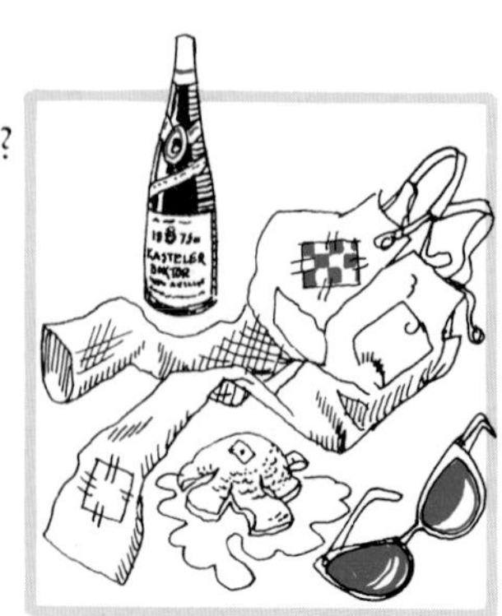

Und welcher Pullover?
Mantel
Käse
Wein

Und welches Hemd?
Brot
Glas
Haus

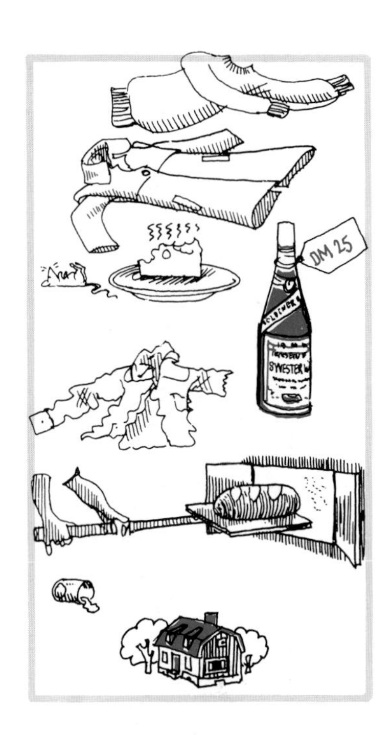

3 At the delicatessen

Point to the thing that you're talking about!

1 Der Rotwein	ist	gut.	— Welcher?	— Der Rotwein hinten links.
2 Die Wurst	sind		— Welche?	......
3 Die Bananen			— Welches?	
4 Der Kaffee				
5 Der Weißwein				
6 Das Bier				
7 Der Schnaps				

4 I just don't believe it!

1 Ich kaufe die Jeans.
— Sie kaufen die Jeans?!
2 Ich habe hundert Mark mit.
3 Ich mache Abendbrot.
4 Ich gehe in die Stadt.
5 Ich komme um Mitternacht zurück.
6 Ich putze die Wohnung.
7 Ich trinke ein Bier.
8 Ich kaufe drei Pfund Käse.
9 Ich weiß, was das kostet.

1 Window shopping

I. Frau Was kaufen Sie, Frau Brandt?
II. Frau Ich weiß nicht. Ich habe meine Brille nicht mit. Wieviel kostet die Hose?
I. Frau Welche Hose?
II. Frau Die Jeans hier vorne.
I. Frau Achtzig Mark.
II. Frau Oh! Das ist aber teuer. Und das Hemd, wieviel kostet das Hemd?
I. Frau Welches Hemd?
II. Frau Das Hemd dort rechts.
I. Frau Das kostet fünfzig Mark neunzig. Kaufen Sie das Hemd?
II. Frau Nein, das ist auch teuer. Wieviel kostet der Pullover?
I. Frau Welcher?
II. Frau Der Pullover dort links.
I. Frau Der kostet hundertzehn Mark.
II. Frau Hundertzehn Mark! Das ist sehr teuer. Und wieviel kostet der Mantel?
I. Frau Welcher Mantel? Der Mantel ganz hinten?
II. Frau Ja! Der ist s o schön! Wieviel kostet er?
I. Frau . . . Oh! Frau Brandt, ich sage es nicht!
II. Frau Aber ich habe meine Brille nicht mit!
I. Frau Ja, und es ist auch viel besser so – so wissen Sie nicht, wieviel der Mantel kostet!

meine my
mit with (me)
wieviel how much
welche which

teuer dear

ganz right

sagen say
aber but
viel much
besser better
so like that
wissen know

5

1 Wieviel kostet die Jeans?
2 Welches Hemd kostet fünfzig Mark neunzig?
3 Ist der Pullover links oder rechts?
4 Wieviel kostet er?
5 Wo ist der Mantel?
6 Ist er teuer?

UNIT 10

1 Was kaufen sie?

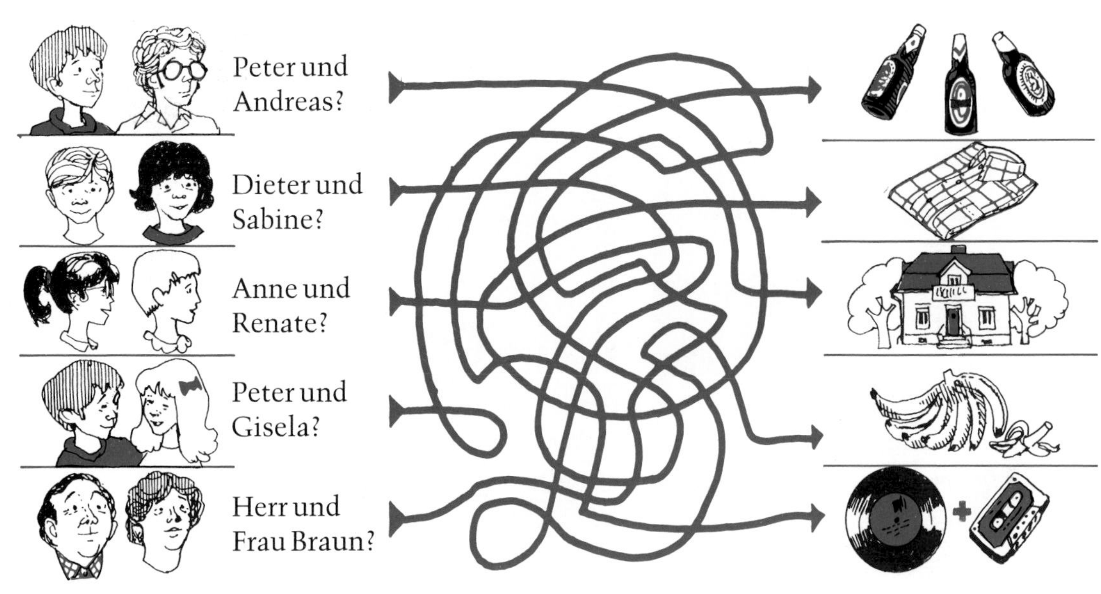

2 We drink anything that's going

—Was trinkt ihr? Bier? —Ja, Bier trinken wir gern!
—Du vielleicht, aber ich trinke lieber......

3 How nice! (it isn't really!)

1 Wir kommen heute zurück.
 —Ihr kommt heute zurück? Ach, wie schön!
2 Wir machen Abendbrot.
3 Wir haben sieben Wings-Platten.
4 Wir trinken immer Champagner.
5 Wir kaufen ein Auto.

4 Wir gehen in die Stadt, und wir kaufen . . .

One pair writes down something that they're going to buy in town – choose it from this list . . .

Individuals from the rest of the class guess what it is:

—Ihr kauft...... ?

— { Nein!
 { Ja, wir kaufen......

When the correct object is guessed the guesser and his/her partner write down what *they* are going to buy and guessing begins again.

Tomaten
ein Hemd
Schnaps
Orangen
die Jeans
Rotwein
Weißwein
eine Kassette
Pflaumen
Seife
Bananen
Käse
Cola
Milch
Wurst
Kaffee
Butter
Limonade

5 Guess the mime

In front of class pairs mime something you can express in German (drinking water, buying a shirt . . .). The rest of the class guess the mime, using: **– Ihr ......** **– Ja, wir ...... /–Nein, wir ...... nicht**. The one who guesses is on next with his or her partner.

6 Who's buying what?

1 Was kaufst du hier?

2 Was kauft Herr Braun hier?

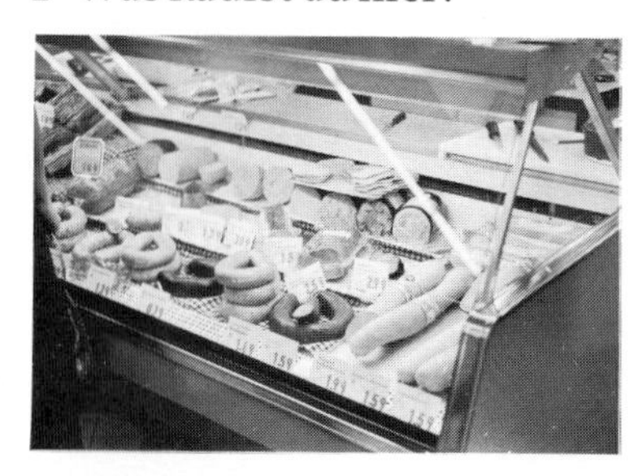

3 Was kauft ihr hier?

4 Was kaufen Herr und Frau Brandt hier?

5 Was kaufe ich hier?

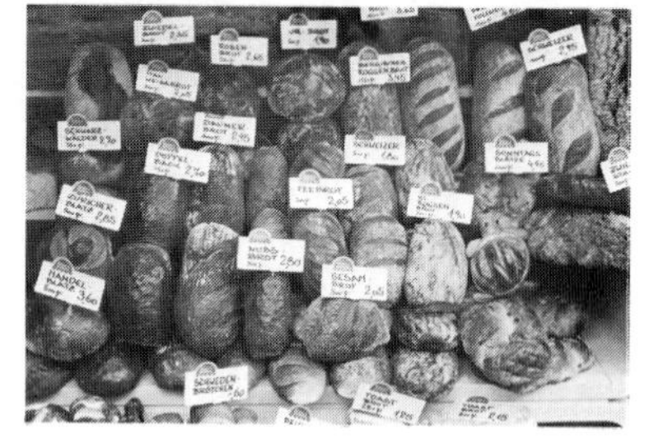

6 Was kaufen wir hier?

7 Oh yes you are!

1 Wir sind doch nicht krank?
—Doch, ihr seid krank!
2 Sie sind doch nicht zusammen? —Doch, wir ......
3 Das Bier ist doch nicht alle? —Doch, es ......
4 Ich bin doch nicht schön? —Doch, Sie ......
5 Du bist doch nicht müde? —Doch, ich ......
6 Die Platten ...... hier? —Doch, sie ......
7 Ihr ...... zurück? —Doch, wir ......
8 Frau Gerstenmeyer ...... da? —Doch, sie ......

UNIT 11

1

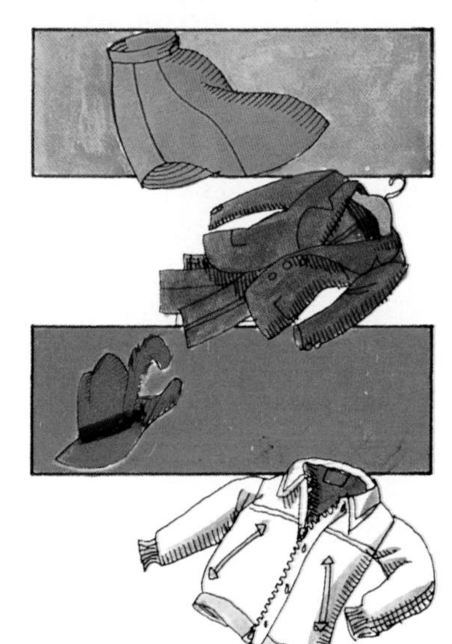

Das ist ein Rock. Er ist grün.

Das ist ein Anzug. Er ist braun.

Das ist ein Hut. Er ist rot.

Das ist eine Jacke. Sie ist weiß.

Das sind Röcke. Die Röcke sind blau.

Das sind Anzüge. Die Anzüge sind grau.

Das sind Hüte. Die Hüte sind gelb.

Das sind Jacken. Die Jacken sind schwarz.

2 At the cleaner's

Three customers are collecting clothes at the dry cleaner's. Without turning the page, listen to the scene twice, then answer these questions.

das Zettelchen ticket
viele many
das stimmt that's right

1. What is the first customer collecting?
2. What colour is it?
3. What does it cost?
4. What is the second customer collecting?
5. Is it green?
6. What is the number of her ticket?
7. What does the third customer want?
8. What colour is it?
9. Why is the shopkeeper surprised when he finds it?
10. How did the misunderstanding occur?

3 Welche Farbe?

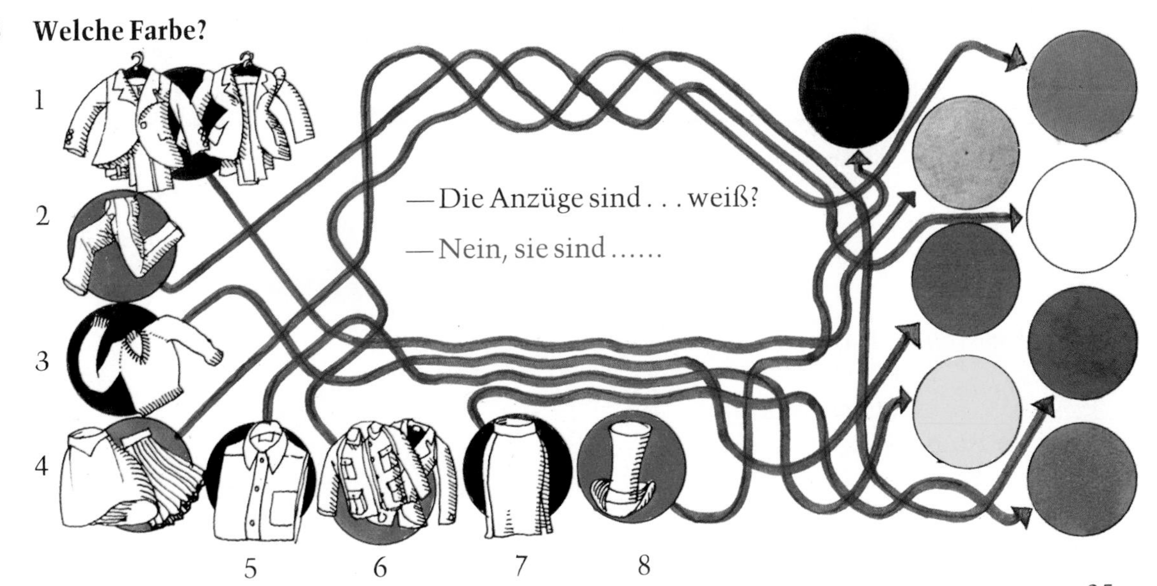

4 Here is the basic text of the customer/shopkeeper exchange at the dry cleaner's. Act it out in pairs, substituting other items of clothing, ticket numbers, colours, and sums of money in the boxes.

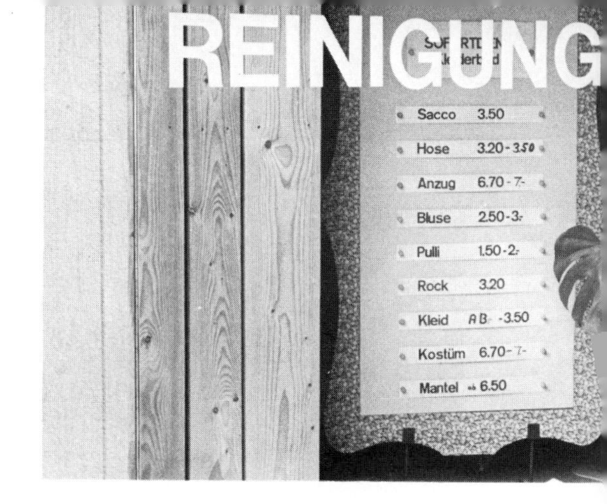

— [Ein Anzug]. Nummer [siebzehn].

— [Ein Anzug]. Ich habe so viele [Anzüge]. { Welche Farbe? / Ist [er] [grün]? }

— { [Braun]. / Nein, [braun]. }

— Ach ja, hier ist [er]. Nummer [siebzehn]. [Dreizehn Mark zehn], bitte.

— Bitte schön.

— Danke schön.

5 **That new assistant can't find anything**

Customer Eine Bluse, bitte.

Assistant Tja, wo sind die Blusen?

Customer { Dort hinten. / Hier vorne. } Und auch ein ......

Assistant Tja, wo sind die ......?

Customer ......

......

UNIT 12 REVISION

Grammar

1 The pattern of regular verbs (usually called 'weak' verbs in German) in the present tense is:

sagen	*to say*
ich sage	wir sagen
du sagst	ihr sagt
	Sie sagen
er, sie, es sagt	sie sagen

Most German verbs follow this pattern.

Haben (*to have*) loses its *b* in the **du** and **er** forms:

du hast   er hat

and **sein** (*to be*) is quite irregular:

ich bin	wir sind
du bist	ihr seid
	Sie sind
er ist	sie sind

Verbs ending in **-ten** and **-den** add **-est** and **-et** in the **du** and **er** forms, instead of **-st** and **-t**, to ease pronunciation: **kosten** — **es kostet**.

With all verbs the **wir, Sie**, and **sie** (*they*) forms are identical. **Ihr** is used to address more than one person with whom you are on familiar (**du**) terms. **Sie** is the polite form for *you* in both singular and plural.

The infinitive form of the verb (= English *'to . . .'*) always ends in **-n** or **-en** (usually **-en**).

2 Plural of nouns: ¨-e

der Anzug → die Anzüge
der Hut → die Hüte
der Rock → die Röcke

Many masculine nouns form their plural in this way.

Note that the plural form of **der, die, das** (*the*) is **die** for all three genders.

3 Trinkst du gern Cola? – *do you like . . . ?*
Ja, aber ich trinke lieber Rotwein. – *I prefer . . .*

To say you *like* or *prefer* doing something in German, use the adverbs **gern** (*gladly*) and **lieber** (*for preference, 'more gladly'*), as in the examples above.

der Pullover pullover
der Mantel coat
der Anzug (¨-e) suit
der Hut (¨-e) hat
der Name (-n) name
der Rock (¨-e) skirt

die Brille (-n) pair of spectacles
die Hose (-n) pair of trousers
die Jeans (*plural*) pair of jeans
die Farbe (-n) colour
die Nummer (-n) number
die Jacke (-n) jacket
die Bluse (-n) blouse

das Haus house
das Zettelchen ticket

kosten cost
sagen say
wissen know
stimmen be correct

grün green
braun brown
rot red
weiß white
blau blue
grau grey
gelb yellow
schwarz black

mit with (me)
vorne at the front
hinten at the back
rechts on the right
links on the left
teuer dear
ganz right
so like that
aber but
viel much
viele many
besser better
welcher which
gern gladly
sie they
wir we
ihr you (*fam. pl.*)
wie? what . . . like?
mein my
lieber rather; for preference
wieviel how much

4 der Mantel – welcher Mantel?
die Jacke – welche Jacke?
das Hemd – welches Hemd?

The endings on **welch-** are **-er** masculine, **-e** feminine, **-es** neuter. We shall meet other words like **welcher** that follow this pattern.

5 Sie sind nicht krank? – Doch, ich bin krank!

Yes in response to a negative question or statement is **doch** in German (often *oh yes* in English).

A Write out in full adding **kaufe, kaufst, kauft**, or **kaufen**:

1 Anneliese? Ja, sie ...... ein Geschenk.
2 Was ...... du?
3 Wo ...... ihr Blusen?
4 Michael und ich ...... Platten.
...... Sie auch Käse, Frau Schmidt?
5 Ich ...... Rotwein.
6 Herr und Frau Schäfer ...... ein Auto!

B Invent questions to these answers:

1 Der Mantel dort hinten!
2 Ja, ich gehe in die Stadt.
3 Doch, ich gehe in die Stadt.
4 Es ist hier vorne.
5 Nein, sie ist blau.
6 Er kostet DM 300.

C 1 Kaufst du gern Platten?
— Ja, aber ich kaufe lieber Kassetten.

2 Trinkst du gern Milch? — Ja, aber ......
3 Kauft Annegret gern Jeans?
4 Trinkt Mutter gern Rotwein?
5 Kommt Uwe gern vormittags?

D Agree, using pronouns:

1 Wir sind krank?
— Ja, ihr seid krank!

2 Die Jeans kosten zu viel?
— Ja, sie ......
3 Wir wissen es?
4 Herr und Frau Braun sagen „Auf Wiedersehen"?
5 Wir putzen die Wohnung?
6 Die Brillen sind teuer?
7 Wir kommen zu spät?
8 Die Schmidts machen zu viel?
9 Wir gehen zurück?

E 1 Stefan sagt viel. Und du? — Ich sage auch viel.
2 Der Mantel kostet DM 100. Und die Anzüge? — Sie ...... auch.
3 Wir kaufen Wurst. Und Sie? — Ich ......
4 Ich habe Seife. Und Günter? — Er ......
5 Jens geht in die Stadt. Und wir? — Ihr ......
6 Maria hat sechzig Mark. Und ich? — Sie ......
7 Ich weiß, wo es ist. Und Sie? — Wir ......
8 Vati ist nicht krank. Und ich? — Du ......
9 Ulrike ist sehr schön! Und wir? — Ihr ......
10 Mein Pullover ist hier. Und die Jacken? — Sie ......
11 Renate ist müde. Und du? — Ich ......

F Wie viele? Welche Farbe?

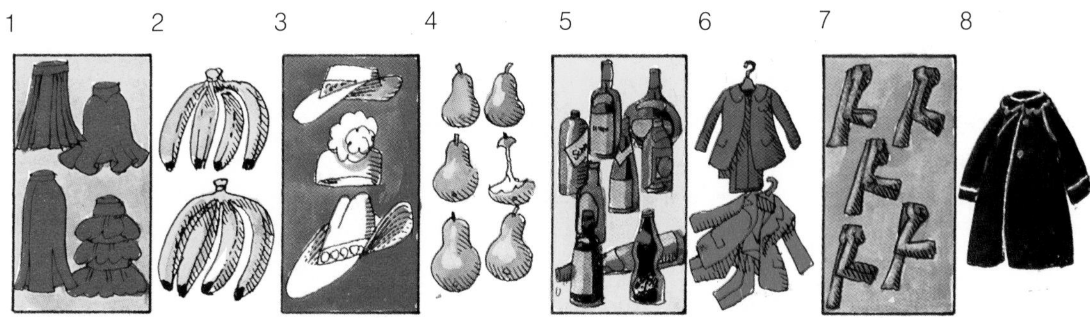

G Ask them what they're drinking:

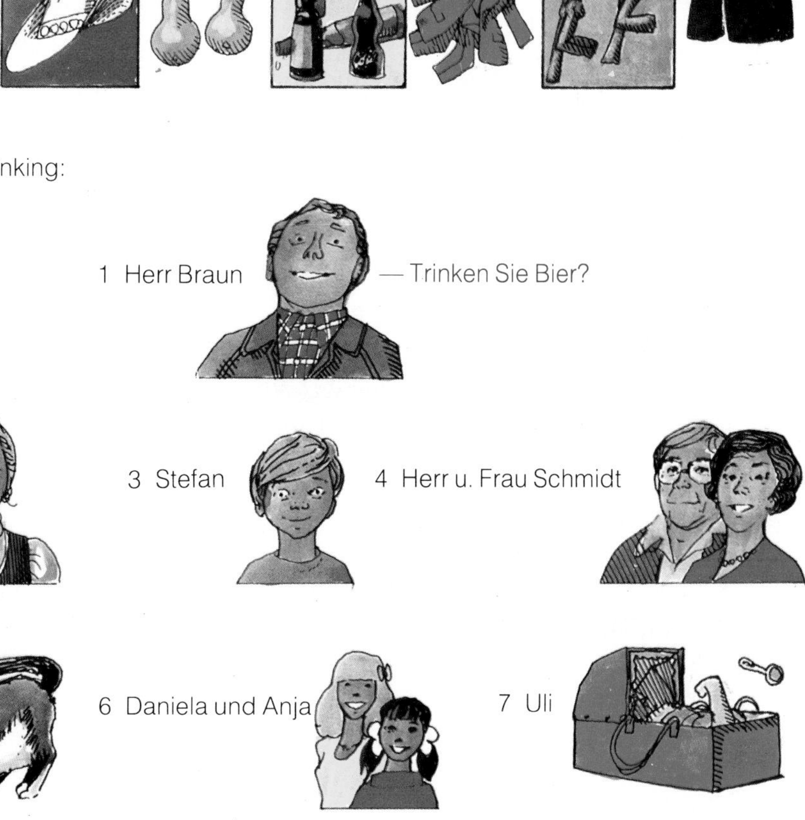

1 Herr Braun — Trinken Sie Bier?

2 Frau Braun

3 Stefan

4 Herr u. Frau Schmidt

5 Uschi

6 Daniela und Anja

7 Uli

H Rapidly draw an item of clothing in colour, and put a number in front of it (up to ten). Make sure you know the German for the colour, the piece of clothing and its plural. Don't let your pairwork partner see it. Your partner then has to guess a) the object, b) how many, c) what colour. Count the number of guesses needed to get the answer, then change round and see if you can get the details of your partner's drawing in fewer guesses. Follow this pattern:

— Ein Anzug? . . . Eine Bluse?
— Bluse ist richtig (*right*). Wie viele Blusen?
— Eine Bluse? . . . Drei Blusen?
— Drei Blusen ist richtig. Und welche Farbe?
— . . . Braun?
— Braun ist richtig.

UNIT 13

1

1 ein Kleid **2** kein Kleid **3** ein Rad **4** kein Rad **5** ein Kind **6** kein Kind

2 Aunt Ulrike's a bit of a problem

— Kinder, laßt die Räder dort und kommt schnell. Wir müssen doch ein Geschenk für Tante Ulrike kaufen. Was meint ihr? Was hat sie gern?
— Kleider!
— Sicher, aber wir können kein Kleid für sie kaufen.
— Bücher hat sie auch gern.
— Ja, aber was für Bücher liest sie?
— Ich weiß nicht – Krimis vielleicht?
— Krimis? Für Tante Ulrike? Besser keine Bücher!
— Sie trinkt gern Wein. Kaufen wir Weingläser!
— Gute Idee! D i e Weingläser da sind sehr schön.

lassen leave
schnell quickly
müssen must
meinen think

sicher certain(ly)
können can
das Buch book
lesen (sie liest) read
der Krimi thriller

die Idee idea

1 What do the three of them have to do?
2 Why don't they buy what is first suggested?
3 What sort of books does the boy think Aunt Ulrike might like?
4 Why don't they buy her any?
5 What are they sure she likes?
6 What do they decide to buy?

1 Was müssen die drei kaufen?
2 Was hat Tante Ulrike gern?
3 Was auch noch?
4 Was trinkt sie gern?
5 Was kaufen die drei?

3 — Können Sie die [children] sehen? — Nein, hier ist kein [child]

4 — Kaufen wir ein(e) [book]! — Ja, [book] hab' ich gern. / — Nein, [book] hab' ich nicht gern.

5 Just a little snack

Klaus Du, ich habe Hunger. Ich esse eine Wurst.
Jörg Ich auch. Was ißt du?
Klaus Eine Bratwurst. Und du?
Jörg Ich esse eine Currywurst. Mit Pommes frites. Und dann vielleicht ein Eis.
Klaus Du hast wirklich Hunger! Bezahlst du?
Jörg Nein, du . Hunger hab' ich zwar, aber kein Geld!

essen eat
die Bratwurst fried sausage
die Pommes frites chips
dann then
vielleicht perhaps
das Eis ice
wirklich really
bezahlen pay
zwar certainly
das Geld money

1 Was ißt Klaus?
2 Was ißt Jörg?
3 Was ißt er auch noch?
4 Wer hat Hunger?
5 Wer hat kein Geld?
6 Wer muß bezahlen?

6 Definitely not!

1 Ißt du eine Wurst? —Nein, ich esse keine Wurst.
2 Hast du Geld? —Nein, ich ......
3 Sie kauft ein Kleid?
4 Liest er Bücher?
5 Ißt du ein Eis?
6 Hast du eine Idee?

7 Lesen oder essen?

1 Was macht Peter?

2 Und Susi?

3 Und ich?

4 Und die Kinder?

5 Und Vati und ich?

6 Und Annette and Corinna?

7 Und du?

8 Do you really have to go?

—Du mußt doch nicht schon gehen, Bärbel?
—Doch, ich muß nach Hause, ich kann nicht länger bleiben.
—Bleib noch eine halbe Stunde. Es ist erst halb zwölf.
—Nein! Du weißt, wie mein Vater ist! Ich muß wirklich gehen.
—Du kannst doch noch ein paar Minuten bleiben! Zehn Minuten noch? Fünf Minuten?
—Nein! Sei doch nicht albern – ich muß gleich weg. Tschüs Dieter!
—Na, okay. Tschüs Bärbel. Bis morgen.

schon already
nach Hause home
länger longer
bleiben stay
noch ein another
die Stunde hour
erst only
noch more
albern silly
ich muß weg I must be off
gleich straight away
tschüs goodbye
bis morgen see you tomorrow

9 When you've got to go, you've got to go

— Bleib noch ein paar Minuten!
(Tell him you can't, you've really got to go home.)

— Es ist aber erst halb elf.
(Tell him no, it's half past eleven.)

— So spät? Mußt du wirklich gehen?
(Tell him you must, he knows what your father's like.)

— Und du mußt gleich gehen?
(Tell him yes, you must go straight away.)

— Also tschüs.
(Say goodbye, you'll see him tomorrow.)

10 Wann kannst du kommen?

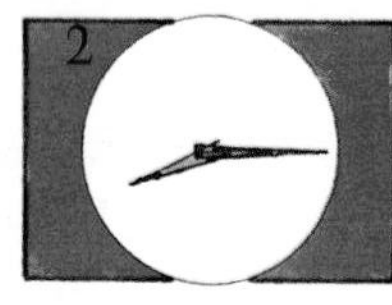

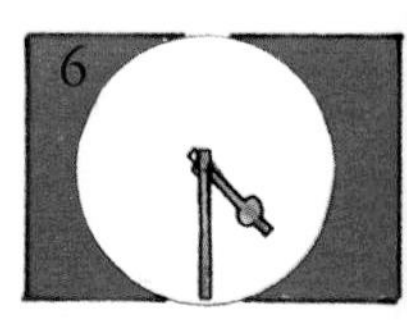

Und wann mußt du gehen?

Wie lange kannst du denn bleiben?

11 Right then, get on with it!

1 Wir gehen!
— Also geht!

2 Ich kaufe das Kleid!
— Also k...... das Kleid!

3 Wir kommen nachmittags!

4 Ich trinke ein Bier!

5 Wir lassen die Räder dort!

6 Ich komme schnell!

7 Wir bleiben hier!

8 Ich bin nicht so dumm!

12 Let's have a snack!

Hast du Hunger?
Was ißt du?
Was kostet das?
Was kann i c h essen?
Ist das teuer?
Was kostet alles zusammen?

die Semmel (*S. German*) bread roll

UNIT 14

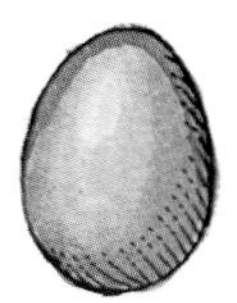

ein
Ei

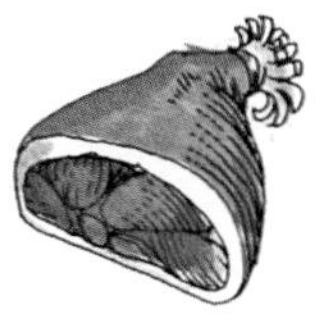

der
Schinken

die
Marmelade

ein
Brötchen

der
Tee

ein
Zwieback

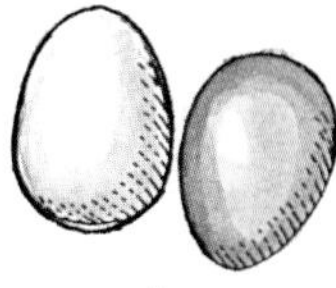

zwei
Eier

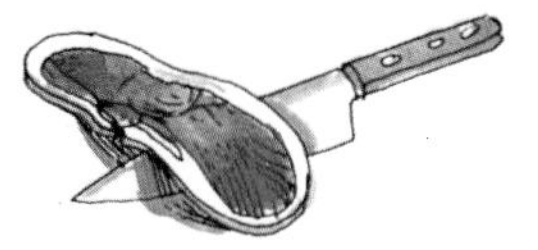

eine Scheibe
Schinken

drei
Brötchen

eine
Tasse Tee

Zwiebäcke

1 He takes no notice of anything I suggest!

Answer these questions when you've heard the text twice:

Du bist Peter:
1 Ißt du ein Ei?
2 Warum nicht?
3 Was ißt du denn?
4 Ißt du auch eine Scheibe Schinken?
5 Was trinkst du?
6 Mit Milch?
7 Was trinkt Ilse?

And these when you've heard it three times:

Du bist Ilse:
1 Ißt du Brötchen?
2 Was ißt du lieber?
3 Was trinkst du?
4 Ißt du auch Schinken?

 **1**

Ilse Peter, ißt du ein Ei?
Peter Nein, Eier ess' ich nie. Das weißt du doch, Ilse.
Ilse Was ißt du denn?
Peter Was? Ach ja . . . Ich esse Brötchen. Nur mit Butter und Marmelade. Wie immer.
Ilse Ich esse lieber Zwiebäcke. Es gibt auch noch Käse und Schinken. Ißt du eine Scheibe Schinken? Der ist wirklich gut, der Schinken.
Peter Nein! Nur Brötchen und Marmelade.

Das Fräulein kommt.

Fräulein Ja, bitte?
Ilse Was trinkst du, Peter?
Peter Mensch, das weißt du doch . . . oh, Entschuldigung, Fräulein. Ja, ich trinke Tee. Mit Milch, bitte.
Ilse Und ich trinke Kaffee, bitte. Ich hätte gern auch ein weichgekochtes Ei.
Fräulein Danke schön.

nie never
es gibt there is
das Fräulein girl
Mensch! good heavens!
ein weichgekochtes Ei a soft-boiled egg

2 What are you having?

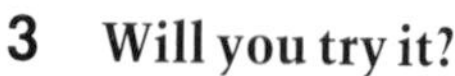

3 Will you try it?

1 Der Tee ist gut! Trinkst du den Tee?
2 Der Schinken ...... Ißt du ...... ?
3 Der Wein ......
4 Der Schnaps
5 Der Kaffee
6 Der Käse
7 Der Champagner

4 Men just can't make up their minds!

— Möchtest du einen Regenmantel?

— Nein, einen Regenmantel möchte ich nicht. Einen Schirm vielleicht.

— Also, du möchtest einen Schirm?
— Nein . . .

5 She takes no notice of anything I suggest!

— Dieser ...... ist prima!
— Welcher ...... ?
— Dieser hier!
— Der dort ist aber besser!
— Ja, richtig! Gut also, ich kaufe den ......
— Welchen? Den dort?
— Nein, diesen hier!

dieser Hut
dieser Käse
dieser Schinken

dieses Rad
dieses Kleid
dieses Hemd

diese Brille
diese Platte
diese Seife

6 I'd sooner have that one

In pairs, using the pictures, ask each other which you prefer.

Pattern: — Welche Platte hast du lieber, diese hier oder die dort?

— Ich habe | diese hier / die dort | lieber.

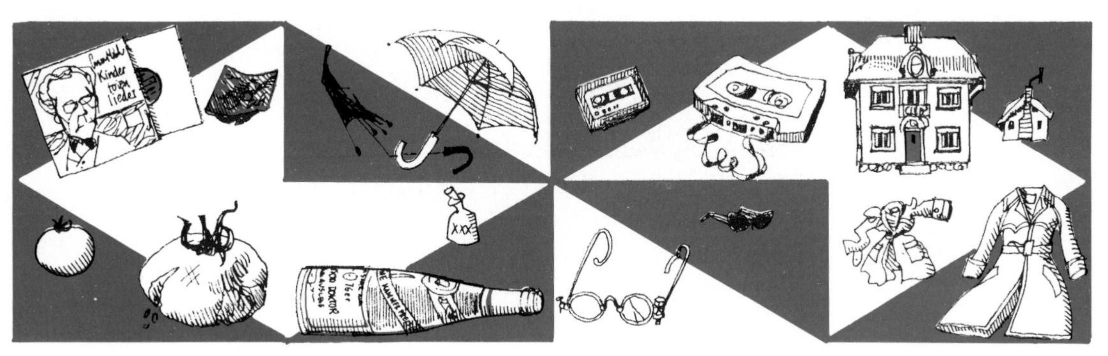

UNIT 15

1 He's bound to have forgotten something!

Jürgen!
Hast du die Sonnenbrillen?
die Räder
den Schirm
die Bücher
die Seife
das Geld
die Kinder
das Auto

Ja, ... hab' ich.
...... hab' ich auch.
......
Ach nein, das Auto hab' ich nicht!

2 What extraordinarily elegant people!

Was trägt er?
— Er trägt eine Jacke.
Die Jacke ist braun.

Was tragen sie?

3 Out of stock again

— Ich hätte gern	eine Flasche	Rotwein.	— Leider haben wir kein(e)(n) ......
	ein Pfund	Orangen	
	ein Kilo	......	
	zwei Stück		
	......		

4 Thinks . . . says . . .

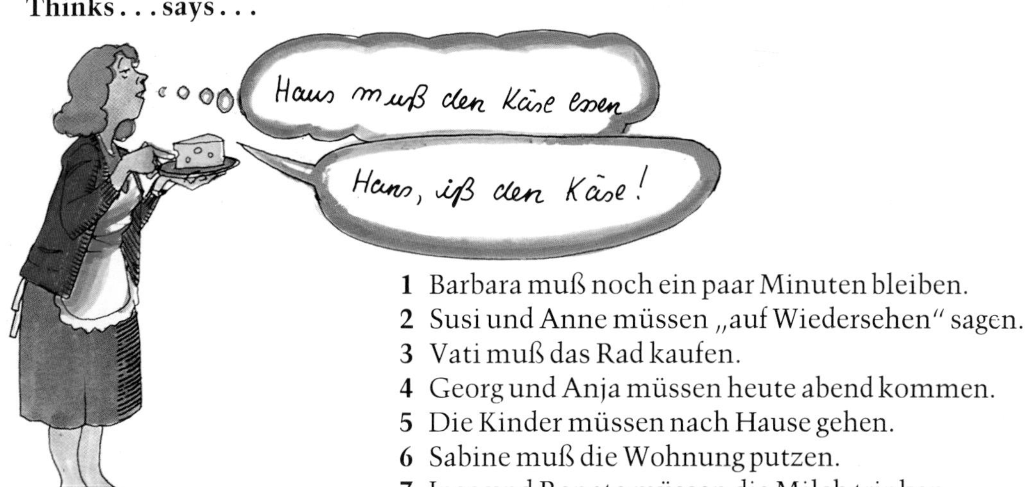

1 Barbara muß noch ein paar Minuten bleiben.
2 Susi und Anne müssen „auf Wiedersehen" sagen.
3 Vati muß das Rad kaufen.
4 Georg und Anja müssen heute abend kommen.
5 Die Kinder müssen nach Hause gehen.
6 Sabine muß die Wohnung putzen.
7 Inge und Renate müssen die Milch trinken.

5 Tell them politely!

— Wo können wir die Räder lassen?
(Tell them to leave the bikes there.)
— Lassen Sie die Räder dort.

— Aber was für Bücher liest Herr Braun?
(Tell her to buy a thriller.)

— Muß ich gleich bezahlen?
(Tell him yes please, tell him to pay straight away.)

— Was kann ich heute abend tun?
(Suggest he reads this book.)

— Ich kann nicht länger bleiben.
(Suggest she stays another half hour.)

— Wein kann ich nicht trinken.
(Tell him to drink a glass of milk.)

— Wann kommen wir?
(Tell them to come at half past seven.)

6 What shall we get granny for her birthday?

Brandy glasses? Sunglasses? A bike?
Make suggestions to your partner using this pattern:

— Kaufen wir ein Buch!
— Nein! Ein Buch hat sie schon!

UNIT 16 REVISION

Grammar

1 The accusative

Articles (words like **der, ein, kein** etc.) have a special form when the noun used with them is the object of the verb. In grammar this is called the *accusative*.

Hast du **den Schirm?** – *masculine object*
Ich kaufe **eine Sonnenbrille**. – *feminine object*
Ich habe **kein Geld**. – *neuter object*
Ißt du **die Zwiebäcke?** – *plural object*

Only masculine singulars show any difference from the subject form (called the *nominative*). Here is the whole pattern:

	singular *masculine*	*feminine*	*neuter*	*plural* *all genders*
nominative (subject)	der (k)ein	die (k)eine	das (k)ein	die keine
accusative (object)	den (k)einen	die (k)eine	das (k)ein	die keine

2 **Kein** (*not any, no*) is used rather than **nicht ein**. It follows the same pattern as **ein**.

3 Plural of nouns: **-er** or **¨er**

das Kind → die Kinder
das Rad → die Räder
das Buch → die Bücher

Many neuter nouns form their plural in this way. The vowel has an umlaut in the plural if this is possible (*i* and *e* cannot take umlaut). With a double vowel the umlaut goes on the first: **das Haus → die Häuser**.

We have now met the three basic plural forms:

masculine **¨e**, feminine **-n**, neuter **¨er**.

There are, however, other ways of forming the plural in German and we shall learn these gradually (the plural is dealt with in full in Unit 28). You may have noticed that **der Krimi** becomes **die Krimis** (most imported foreign nouns take **-s**) and that **das Brötchen** becomes **die Brötchen** (nouns ending in **-chen** (= *little*) remain unchanged in the plural).

der Krimi (-s) thriller
der Hunger hunger
der Schinken ham
der Tee tea
der Zwieback (¨e) rusk
der Regenmantel raincoat
der Schirm (-e) umbrella

die Tante (-n) aunt
die Idee (-n) idea
die Bratwurst fried sausage
die Pommes frites (*pl.*) chips
die Stunde (-n) hour
die Semmel (-n) (*S. German*) bread roll
die Marmelade jam
die Scheibe (-n) slice
die Sonnenbrille (-n) (pair of) sunglasses

das Kind (-er) child
das Rad (¨er) bicycle
das Kleid (-er) dress
das Buch (¨er) book
das Eis ice
das Geld (-er) money
das Ei (-er) egg
das Brötchen (-) bread roll
das Fräulein girl

lassen leave
müssen must
meinen think
können can
lesen read
essen eat
bezahlen pay
bleiben stay
sehen see
machen do
es gibt there is/are
tragen wear

schnell quickly
sicher certain(ly)
was für what sort of
dann then (*time*)
denn then (= *in that case*)

4 Wir müssen ein Geschenk kaufen.
Ich kann nicht länger bleiben.

Kaufen and **bleiben** are here infinitives dependent on **müssen** and **kann**, the main verbs of the sentences. In German the infinitive is put at the end of the sentence in such cases.

5 Bleib noch eine halbe Stunde! Trink ein Bier!
Laßt die Räder dort! Kommt, Kinder!
Bezahlen Sie gleich! Kommen Sie um halb acht!
Kaufen wir Weingläser! Gehen wir heute!

The command form of the verb (the *imperative*) is formed as follows:

du form: as the **du** form of the present without **-st**
gehen – du gehst → **geh!**

ihr form: as the **ihr** form of the present
gehen – ihr geht → **geht!**

Sie form: as the **Sie** form of the present plus **Sie**
gehen – Sie gehen → **gehen Sie!**

wir form: as the **wir** form of the present plus **wir**
gehen – wir gehen → **gehen wir!**

The **du** form is occasionally found with an extra **-e** (**gehe!**). Verbs like **tragen** that add an umlaut to the **du** form of the present do *not* add it to the imperative: **du trägst – trag!** The **wir** form of the imperative corresponds to the English *let's* . . .

Sein is irregular:

sei!, seid!, seien Sie!, seien wir!

Commands in German almost always have an exclamation mark.

6 dieser Mantel   diese Brille   dieses Zettelchen

Dieser follows the pattern of **welcher** and means *this*. It can be used either with a noun as above, or by itself (i.e. as a pronoun):

Dieser ist schön.

That in German is simply **der (die, das** etc.) spoken with emphasis:

D e r dort ist schön. (*that one there*)

7 Strong verbs

German irregular verbs are called *strong* verbs (as regular ones are called *weak* verbs). Most only show irregularity in the **du** and **er/sie/es** forms. Apart from **sein** (see Unit 12) we have so far met:

lesen: du liest, er liest
essen: du ißt, er ißt
tragen: du trägst, er trägt
lassen: du läßt, er läßt
können: ich, er kann, du kannst
müssen: ich, er muß, du mußt
sehen: du siehst, er sieht
haben: du hast, er hat

vielleicht perhaps
wirklich really
gleich right away
nach Hause home
lange long
länger longer
zwar certainly; admittedly
prima great; super
erst (+ *time*) only
noch more
noch ein another
tschüs (good)bye
albern silly
weg away
bis morgen see you tomorrow
warum why
nie never
ja (*intensifying*) perfectly well
weichgekocht soft-boiled
schon already
heute abend tonight
Mensch! good heavens!

A Add a number – any you like above one:

der Schirm —sieben Schirme

der Schirm	die Stunde	das Kind
der Rock	die Scheibe	das Buch
der Hut	die Minute	das Haus
der Anzug	die Brille	das Glas
der Wein	die Idee	das Rad

B Was siehst du hier?

— Ich sehe ......
......
......

C 1 Hast du einen Anzug?

— Nein, ich habe keinen Anzug
und auch kei ...... J ......

2 Hast du eine Birne?
3 Kaffee?
4 Pommes frites?
5 eine Brille?
6 Butter?
7 einen Regenmantel?
8 Rotwein?
9 Eier?

D 1 Wer macht Abendbrot? Du!

Mach Abendbrot!

2 Wer bleibt noch eine halbe Stunde? Sie! ...
3 Wer trinkt eine Tasse Kaffee? Ihr!
4 Wer ißt einen Zwieback? Du!
5 Wer kauft die Sonnenbrille? Sie!
6 Wer bezahlt die zehn Mark? Ihr!
7 Wer geht nach Hause? Du!

E Diese Frau ist schön! D i e Frau ist aber häßlich!

F 1 Bleib länger!

— Aber ich kann nicht länger bleiben!

3 Kauf eine Sonnenbrille!
5 Geh in die Stadt!
7 Iß eine Pflaume!

2 Trink kein Wasser!

— Aber ich muß ......

4 Lies nicht!
6 Laß das Rad nicht dort!
8 Mach nicht so viel!

G

1

Was kaufst du links vorne?
Was kannst du rechts hinten kaufen?

3

Was kann ich hier kaufen?

5

Was kaufst du hier?
Was auch?
Was mußt du bezahlen?

Was kannst du hier essen?

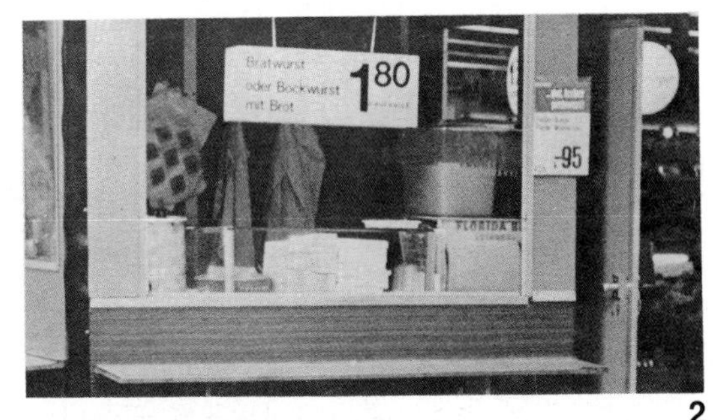

2

Was kannst du hier trinken?
Was trinkt Vater?

4

Was kaufst du hier?
Was kannst du auch kaufen?

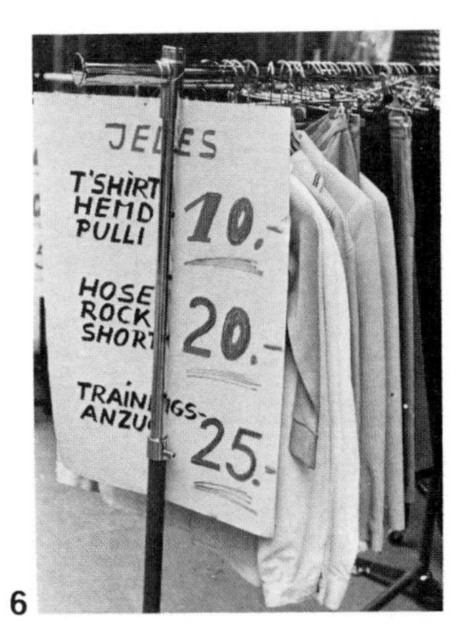

6

UNIT 17

1 Wie ist dein . . . Haar?

2 Portrait gallery

Listen to the descriptions of Stefan, Herr Kuffstein, the speaker himself and Helga, and after each description draw the individual's face on the basis of the information you're given.

Now look at each of your drawings. See if your art-work is good enough to answer these questions:

1 *Stefan*
Wie ist seine Nase?
— Seine Nase ist ......
Wie sind seine Augen?
Wie ist sein Mund?

2 *Herr Kuffstein*
Wie ist sein Mund?
— Sein ......
Wie ist seine Brille?
Wie ist sein Gesicht?

3 *'Ich'*
Wie ist mein Gesicht?
— Dein ......
Wie sind meine Augen?
Wie ist mein Haar?

4 *Helga*
Wie ist ihr Mund?
— Ihr ......
Wie ist ihr Haar?
Wie ist ihre Nase?

Turn to p. 54 to check the text.

3 More portraits

Now describe yourself . . .

Wie sind deine Augen?   Wie ist dein Haar?   . . . Trägst du eine Brille?

. . . and your teacher:

Sein/ihr Gesicht ist ......

4 You daren't put anything down here!

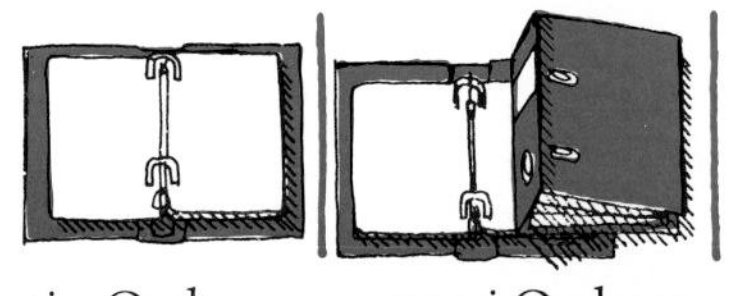

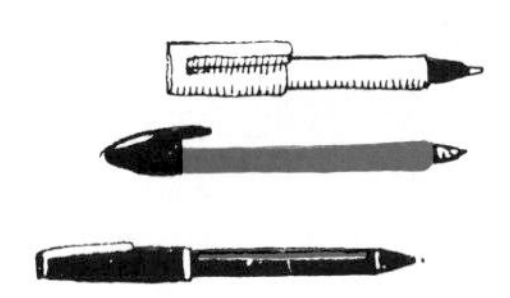

ein Ordner (der Ordner)   zwei Ordner   ein Kugelschreiber (der Kugelschreiber)   drei Kugelschreiber

Listen to the text as often as you need to to work out the correct answers to these questions. Make notes as you listen, if you want to.

1 Wer hat Annes Kugelschreiber?
— ...... hat i...... Kugelschreiber.
2 Wer hat Bertolds Kugelschreiber?
3 Wer hat Peters Kugelschreiber?
4 Wer hat Bertolds Ordner?
5 Wie viele Ordner hat Peter?
6 Wer hat Peters Ordner?

Now read through the text on p. 54 and see if your answers are correct.

5

In pairs: collect on the desk as many of your and your partner's pens, files, books, spectacles as you conveniently can. Share them out randomly between yourselves, then ask for them back, alternately, using this pattern:

— Entschuldigung, hast du meinen/meine/mein ...... ?
— { Ja, bitte, hier ist dein/deine ......
  { Nein, deinen/dein/deine ...... hab' ich nicht!

Don't hesitate to tell the occasional lie to retain the better quality items! (*Aber doch, du hast mein ...... da!* may be a useful phrase in reply to this ploy.)

2 Portrait Gallery

1 Ich beschreibe Stefan.

Sein Gesicht ist oval.
Seine Augen sind blau.
Sein Mund ist groß.
Seine Nase ist lang.
Und sein Haar ist sehr lang.

2 Ich beschreibe Herrn Kuffstein.

Sein Gesicht ist oval.
Seine Augen sind grün.
Seine Nase ist sehr lang.
Sein Haar ist kurz.
Sein Mund ist mittelgroß.
Und er trägt eine Brille: seine Brille ist braun.

3 Ich beschreibe mich.

Mein Gesicht ist rund.
Meine Nase ist lang.
Mein Mund ist mittelgroß.
Meine Augen sind grau.
Mein Haar ist kurz.

4 Ich beschreibe Helga.

Ihr Gesicht ist rund.
Ihre Augen sind braun.
Ihre Nase ist kurz.
Ihr Mund ist klein.
Ihr Haar ist halblang.

4 You daren't put anything down here!

Bertold Mensch, Peter! Du hast ja meinen Ordner!
Peter Nein, ich habe nur meinen Ordner! Aber du hast m e i n e n Kugelschreiber, Bertold.
Bertold D e i n e n Kugelschreiber? Nein, ich habe . . . ach, ich habe A n n e s Kugelschreiber! Wer hat meinen Kugelschreiber?
Anne Ich habe deinen Kugelschreiber – er ist rot, nicht?
Bertold Nein, mein Kugelschreiber ist grün.
Peter M e i n Kugelschreiber ist rot – du hast meinen Kugelschreiber, Anne!
Bertold Also wer hat meinen Kugelschreiber?
Peter Eh . . . i c h habe deinen Kugelschreiber, Bertold. Und ich habe auch zwei Ordner hier – ist das dein Ordner, Bertold?
Bertold Ja, sicher! Du hast doch meinen Ordner!

UNIT 18

1 Keeping up with the Schmidts!

— Wollt ihr unseren Wagen sehen? Das ist unser Polo!

— Euer Polo? Prima! Und wie findet ihr euren Polo?

— Wunderbar! Und was habt ihr jetzt für einen Wagen?

— Wir? Oh, wir haben einen Rekord.

wollen want
der Wagen car
sehen see
finden find
wunderbar wonderful
jetzt now

— Wollen Sie unseren Wagen sehen? Das ist unser Rekord!

— Ihr Rekord? S e h r schön. Und wie finden Sie Ihren Rekord?

— Toll! Und was haben Sie jetzt für einen Wagen?

— Wir? Oh, wir haben einen Porsche.

toll terrific

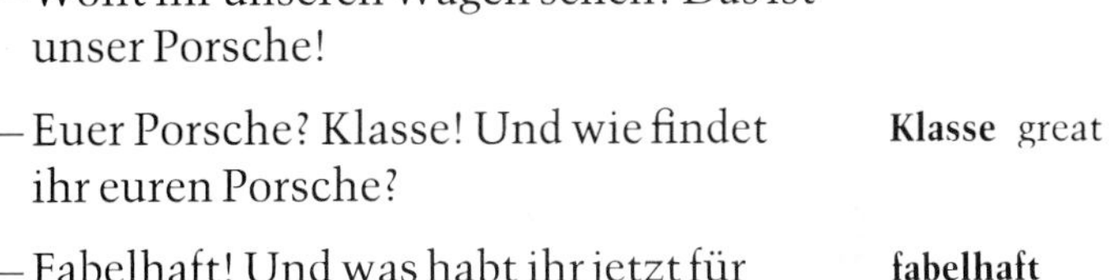

— Wollt ihr unseren Wagen sehen? Das ist unser Porsche!

— Euer Porsche? Klasse! Und wie findet ihr euren Porsche?

— Fabelhaft! Und was habt ihr jetzt für einen Wagen?

— Wir? Oh, wir haben einen Mercedes.

Klasse great
fabelhaft fabulous

— Das sind der Herr Baron von Mönchen-Gladbach und die Frau Baronin. Siehst du ihren Wagen?

— Welchen?

— Den dort rechts.

— Was? Den Rolls? D a s ist ihr Wagen? Der ist ja fantastisch! Und wir haben nur unseren Mercedes!

— Der Rolls? Nein, das ist ihr Wagen ganz rechts. Der Polo!

Learn the first three scenes in pairs, then act them out in sixes.

2

In each of the first three scenes on p. 55 two people talk to two other people. Go through them now imagining that just one person is talking to just one other person, and make the necessary changes. So you'll begin:

Willst du meinen Wagen sehen? . . .

3

— Was für einen Wagen habt ihr?
— Unser Wagen ist ein [Metro] .
— Wie ist er?
— [Fabelhaft] !

Find out from your neighbour what sort of car his family have and what it's like, using the above pattern. Your neighbour then turns to his neighbour, and so on round the class. Each person must find a new word to describe their car – no repeats allowed!

4 Er, yes, it's the wife's as well . . .

— Und da siehst du meinen Wagen!

— Entschuldigung, Liebling. Da sieht er u n s e r e n Wagen!

— Und da siehst du ......

5 That Frau Grüber will try to borrow anything!

Tell her it's broken.

— Können Sie mir bitte Ihre leihen?

— Es tut mir leid, unsere ...... sind leider kaputt!

6

Schuhe (der Schuh)	eine Strumpfhose	Socken (die Socke)	der Schlips	eine Strickjacke

— Was für eine Farbe haben eure Socken ?

— Unsere Socken sind schwarz und grau

— Ihre Socken sind schwarz und grau.

First member of each pair: ask the first member of the pair next to you about the colour of their clothes (you'll have to answer questions about your clothes too, of course). Then report back to the second member of your pair, who writes the answer down. This is a competition for the pair that ends up with the fullest and most accurate written report on the clothes of the pair next to them.

UNIT 19

1 Helmut has offered to cook supper for Monika for once

But shopping seems to be a problem.

Täglich geöffnet
9^{00} - 18^{30}
Mittagspause
13^{00} - 15^{00}

Cover p. 59 and listen to the tape once only. See how many of these questions you can answer. Then uncover p. 59 and listen to the tape again, following the text. See if you can now answer the questions you couldn't answer before.

1 Who has to shop for supper, Helmut or Monika?
2 When is Helmut's lunch break?
3 Why can't he shop then?
4 Why can't he shop when the shop opens at nine?
5 At what time does the shop close in the evening?
6 Why can't Helmut shop on the way home from work?
7 What does he eventually suggest?

die Sache thing
zwischen between
die Mittagspause lunch break
da then
nichts nothing
zu haben be shut
morgens in the morning
im Büro in the office
auf haben be open
immer noch still

2 How can you find anything in a bedroom as untidy as this?

1

Helmut	Sag mal, muß i c h die Sachen für das Abendbrot kaufen?
Monika	Na sicher, du hast doch zwischen eins und drei Mittagspause. Da kannst du gehen.
Helmut	Zwischen eins und drei kann ich aber nichts kaufen, da hat der Laden zu.
Monika	Und morgens? Willst du nicht gleich um neun gehen?
Helmut	Da muß ich schon im Büro sein.
Monika	Kannst du die Sachen nicht abends kaufen, der Laden hat bis halb sieben auf.
Helmut	Aber Monika, um halb sieben bin ich immer noch im Büro.
Monika	Wann willst du die Sachen denn kaufen?
Helmut	Das weiß ich nicht. Essen wir doch lieber im Restaurant!

3 Useless sending *him* shopping!

— Willst du … kaufen?

— Nein, … kann ich nicht kaufen!

— Aber du mußt unbedingt … kaufen!

Willst du auch … kaufen?

— ……

— ……

— Willst du auch … kaufen?

— Ja, … kann ich kaufen!

— D a s ist ja typisch!

UNIT 20 REVISION

Grammar

1 Possessive adjectives (*my, your*, etc.)

mein dein	unser euer (eur-)
Ihr	
sein (*his, its*) ihr (*her*)	ihr

All the possessive adjectives follow the pattern of **ein**. *Our bike, your bike* is **unser Rad, euer Rad (das Rad)** with *no* ending. This is the pattern they all follow:

	masculine	*feminine*	*neuter*	*plural*
nom.	unser Wagen	unsere Idee	unser Haus	unsere Socken
acc.	unseren Wagen	unsere Idee	unser Haus	unsere Socken

When **euer** has an ending it loses its second **-e-**: **euren Wagen, eure Idee**. In speech this also happens to **unser** and you will sometimes find it printed without the **-e-** too: **unsre Idee, unsre Socken, unsren Wagen** (also **unsern Wagen**).

Only the context makes clear which of the several possible meanings of **ihr** is intended.

2 Strong verbs

Notice these irregularities:

wollen: ich will, du willst, er will
finden: du findest, er findet, ihr findet
(the extra **-e-** is added to make the ending pronounceable)

3 Plural of nouns: no change from singular

der Kugelschreiber → die Kugelschreiber
der Ordner → die Ordner

Masculine and neuter nouns ending **-er** remain unchanged in the plural (feminines, as we already know, add **-n**).

The same applies to nouns ending **-en**:

der Wagen → die Wagen

A Say how many there are:

der Kugelschreiber (6)	die Nummer (100)	das Gesicht (5)
der Wagen (13)	die Tante (4)	das Restaurant (11)
der Krimi (10)	die Hose (7)	das Zettelchen (30)
der Schlips (15)	die Nase (2)	das Auge (3)
der Name (3)	die Sache (22)	das Brötchen (17)

der Mund mouth
der Ordner (-) file
der Kugelschreiber (-) ball point
der Wagen (-) car
der Baron (-e) baron
der Schuh (-e) shoe
der Schlips (-e) tie
der Liebling (-e) darling

die Nase (-n) nose
die Baronin baroness
die Strumpfhose (-n) (pair of) tights
die Socke (-n) sock
die Strickjacke (-n) cardigan
die Sache (-n) thing
die Mittagspause (-n) lunch break

das Auge (-n) eye
das Haar hair
das Gesicht (-er) face
das Büro (-s) office
das Restaurant (-s) restaurant

beschreiben describe
wollen want
finden find
leihen lend
auf, zu haben be open, closed (*shops*)
sag mal tell me

kurz short
lang long
halblang of medium length
rund round
oval oval
groß big
klein small
mittelgroß middle sized
nicht? isn't it?
wunderbar wonderful
jetzt now
toll terrific
Klasse! great
fabelhaft fabulous
fantastisch fantastic
von of
es tut mir leid I'm sorry
kaputt broken
immer noch still
zwischen between
mich me

B Complete:

1 Ich will m...... Kugelschreiber finden.
2 Du d...... Wagen ?
3 Sie (*you*) Restaurant ?
4 Er Büro .
5 Sie (*she*) Strickjacke .
6 Es Ei .
7 Wir Haus .
8 Ihr Mutter .
9 Sie (*they*) Schuhe .

nichts nothing
täglich daily
geöffnet open
unbedingt absolutely
typisch typical
na well
morgens in the morning
da then
ja (*intensifying*) definitely; really

C
1 Wer bekommt das Buch?
— Ich, es ist mein Buch!

2 Wer bekommt die Socken?
— Wir, ...

3 Wer bekommt den Ordner?
— Du, ...

4 Wer bekommt den Regenmantel?
— Er, ...

5 Wer bekommt den Schinken?
— Sie, ...

6 Wer bekommt die Pommes frites?
— Ihr, ...

D Add **müssen, können** or **wollen** and make any necessary changes:

1 Ich gehe heute. (müssen)
— Ich muß heute gehen.

2 Er leiht mir kein Geld. (können)
3 Schließen Sie das Büro? (müssen)
4 Er findet seine Sachen nicht. (können)
5 Sie beschreibt das Haus. (wollen)
6 Liest du das? (können)
7 Ihr eßt alles! (müssen)
8 Bezahlen Sie gleich? (wollen)

E Describe these people:

Fräulein Beck

Herr Kraus

Fräulein Dorff

...... ist rund
...... ist lang
...... groß
...... halblang

Siegfried

Frau von Hindenburg

UNIT 21

1

Der Golf parkt vor dem Rekord.
Der Rekord steht vor dem Porsche.
Der Porsche steht hinter dem Rekord.
Der Mercedes parkt zwischen dem Porsche und dem Rolls.

2

1 Wo ist das Postamt?
— Es ist links vom Supermarkt.

2 Wo ist der Supermarkt, rechts oder links vom Postamt?
3 Wo ist der Golf?
4 Wo ist der Rolls?
5 Ist das Postamt weit vom Supermarkt?
6 Wo kann ich parken?

3

Die Bank ist links von der Tankstelle.
Die Tankstelle ist rechts von der Bank.
Die Bäckerei ist links von der Apotheke.
Die Apotheke ist nicht weit von der Bank.

4 In der Karl-Marx-Straße

1 Wo ist die Bank?
2 Was ist vor dem Hotel?
3 Wo ist der Zeitungskiosk?
4 Wo ist das Postamt?
5 Wo ist die Apotheke?
6 Wo ist die Tankstelle?
7 Wo ist der Golf?
8 Wo ist der Mercedes?
9 Wo ist mein Rad?
10 Wo ist unser Hotel?
11 Ist das Postamt in der Nähe vom Hotel?

5 In der Konrad-Adenauer-Straße

— Entschuldigung, wo ist ......?

— Sehen Sie, dort ist

er sie es	rechts links nicht weit in der Nähe	vom von der	......

vor hinter	dem der	......

UNIT 22

1 Erika's diary

Montag 1. August mit Toni in der Stadt	Freitag 5. August ZAHNARZT!!!
Dienstag 2. August Peter hier	Sonnabend 6. August Diskothek m. Peter
Mittwoch 3. August mit Andreas Tennis spielen	Sonntag 7. August Nichts! (schlafen!)
Donnerstag 4. August Berlin, Tante Gertrude	

Vorgestern war Montag.
Am Montag war ich mit Toni in der Stadt.
Gestern war Dienstag.
Am Dienstag war Peter hier. Er war sehr, sehr nett.
Heute ist Mittwoch.
Andreas kommt heute. Wir wollen Tennis spielen.
Morgen ist Donnerstag.
Am Donnerstag fahre ich mit meiner Tante nach Berlin.
Übermorgen ist Freitag.
Am Freitag muß ich zum Zahnarzt! (Ich will aber nicht!)
Dann kommt Sonnabend.
Am Sonnabend gehe ich mit Peter tanzen, in der Diskothek in der Bismarckstraße.
Und dann Sonntag.
Am Sonntag schlafe ich sehr lange!

Answer Erika (that girl's always forgetting what she's supposed to be doing!)

1 Was mache ich am Sonntag?
— Du schläfst ......

2 Wo war ich am Montag?
— Du warst ......

3 Wer war am Dienstag hier? Wie war er?

4 Wer kommt am Mittwoch? Was wollen wir machen?

5 Wohin fahre ich am Donnerstag? Mit wem?

6 Wohin gehe ich am Sonnabend? Mit wem?

7 Wohin muß ich am Freitag?

2 1 When is the next collection from this post box?
2 How many collections are there from this box on weekdays?
3 This photo was taken in South Germany. The South German word for Saturday is not **Sonnabend**. What is it?
4 Where is the nearest postbox with special facilities?
5 What are these special facilities?

nächst nearest, next
die Leerung collection
der Briefkasten postbox

3 1 What sort of shop is this?
2 List as many things as you can that you can buy here.
3 What are the shop's opening times, on what days?
4 Is this shop in West or East Germany? How do you know?

1 Kann man hier Hosen kaufen?
2 Herrenhosen?
3 Kann ich hier um neun Uhr vormittags einen Rock kaufen?
4 Ist der Laden jeden Sonnabend geöffnet?
5 Was kann man am Montag abend um halb acht kaufen?
6 Es ist Mittwoch vormittag. Kann ich hier eine Strickjacke kaufen?

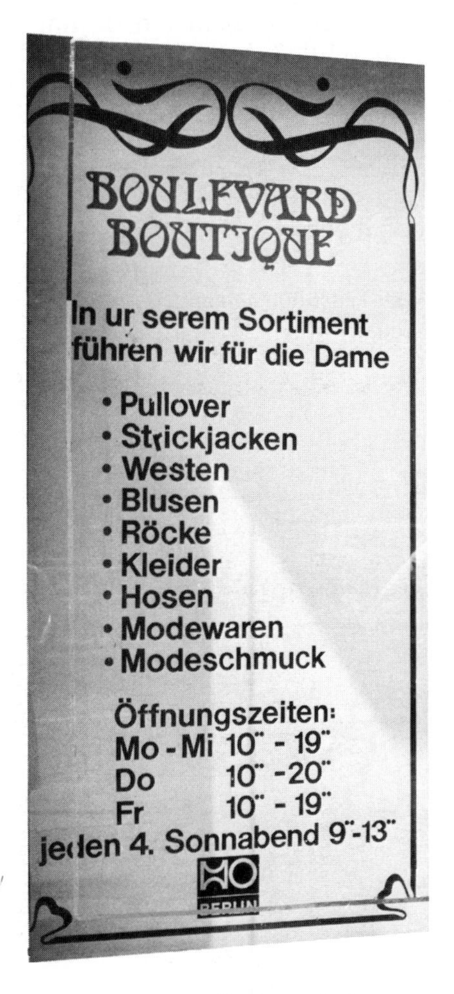

die Dame lady
die Mode fashion
der Schmuck jewellery
jeder every

Christian Damek
Zahnarzt
Sprechst. Mo.- Fr. 8 - 12 Uhr
15 - 18 Uhr
außer Mittwochnachmittag
4. ETAGE - FAHRSTUHL

4 1 Wann kann man nachmittags zum Zahnarzt gehen?
2 Kann man am Sonnabend zum Zahnarzt gehen?
3 Kann man am Dienstagnachmittag zum Zahnarzt gehen?
4 Und am Mittwochnachmittag?

die Sprechstunden surgery hours
außer except

5 1 Wann öffnet die Bank am Montag?
2 Wann schließt sie am Donnerstag?
3 Ist die Bank am Dienstag geöffnet?
4 Wann ist die Mittagspause?
5 Wann öffnet die Bank am Sonnabend?

die Kassenstunden banking hours

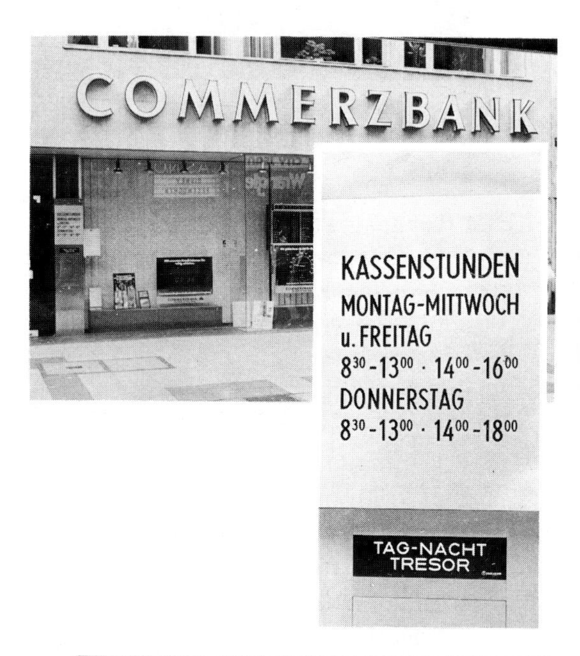

6 **What are you up to?**

1 Wohin fährst du?
—Ich fahre nach ...
2 Zu wem mußt du gehen?
3 Wo warst du gestern?
4 Wo ist das nächste Postamt?
5 Mit wem gehst du tanzen?
6 Ist der Laden jeden Tag geöffnet?
7 An welchem Tag siehst du Andreas?

UNIT 23

1

Der Hund sitzt auf dem Tisch.

Die Katze liegt unter dem Tisch.

Der Tisch steht unter einem Baum.

2 Detective

In each case listen to the available information and then solve the problem. Read the information afterwards on p. 68.

1 *The case of the sleeping man*
leer empty

2 *The case of the missing milk*
3 *The case of the vanishing cat*
nicht mehr no longer

4 *The case of the dirty suit*
schmutzig dirty
aus out of

5 *The case of the man without glasses*
ohne without
die Glasscherben broken bits of glass

6 *The case of the broken eggs*
die Tüte paper bag

Detective: the information

The case of the sleeping man

Die Bierflaschen stehen auf dem Tisch.
Sie sind leer.
Klaus liegt unter dem Tisch.
Er schläft.

Wo ist das Bier?

The case of the missing milk

Die Milchflasche liegt auf dem Tisch.
Die Katze liegt auch auf dem Tisch.
Die Flasche ist leer.

Wo ist die Milch?

The case of the vanishing cat

Der Hund ist unter einem Baum.
Die Katze war auch unter dem Baum.
Jetzt ist die Katze nicht mehr zu sehen.

Wo ist die Katze?

The case of the dirty suit

Der Anzug war schmutzig.
Der Anzug ist nicht mehr im Haus.
Frau Schäfer kommt aus einem Laden.
Sie hat ein Zettelchen.

Wo ist der Anzug?

The case of the man without glasses

Herr Schmidt kommt aus seinem Haus.
Er trägt immer eine Brille, aber heute trägt er keine.
Ohne Brille kann er nicht gut sehen.
Im Haus unter einem Tisch liegen Glasscherben.

Warum trägt Herr Schmidt heute keine Brille?

The case of the broken eggs

In meiner Tüte habe ich Orangen, Eier, Tomaten und Pflaumen.
Die Orangen liegen nicht unter den Tomaten.
Die Tomaten liegen nicht unter den Pflaumen.
Die Pflaumen liegen nicht unter den Eiern.

Wo sind die Eier?

3 Wo ist, wo sind?

der Golf?

Herr Braun?

der Hund?

Helmut?

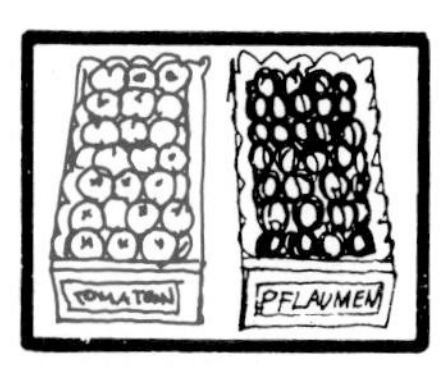

die Pflaumen?

die Katze?

die Socken?

Herr Clouzot?

die Mädchen?

der Hund?

4 Maybe she doesn't love you any more?

1 Sie sitzt in meinem Porsche!
— In deinem Porsche sitzt sie nicht, sie sitzt in seinem Porsche!

2 Sie parkt vor meinem Laden!
3 Sie spielt mit meinen Tennissachen!
4 Sie kauft in meiner Bäckerei!
5 Sie schläft in meinem Hotel!
6 Sie trinkt aus meiner Tasse!
7 Sie liest mit meiner Brille!
8 Sie bezahlt mit meinem Geld!
9 Sie tanzt in meinen Socken!!

5 Just this one

1 Unter welchem Tisch sind Bierflaschen? Unter jedem?
— Nein, nur unter diesem.

2 In welcher Jacke ist Geld? In . . . . . .
3 Auf welcher Straße kann ich parken?
4 An welchem Baum sind Orangen?
5 In welchem Hotel ist ein Restaurant?
6 Zu welchem Zahnarzt gehst du?
7 In welcher Diskothek willst du tanzen?

UNIT 24 REVISION

Grammar

1 The dative

The dative endings are always: masculine and neuter, **-em**; feminine, **-er**; plural, **-en**.

masculine	*feminine*	*neuter*	*plural*
dem Hund	der Dame	dem Hotel	den Bäume**n**
einem Hund	einer Dame	einem Hotel	keinen Bäume**n**
diesem Hund	dieser Dame	diesem Hotel	diesen Bäume**n**

We usually find the dative after prepositions:

hinter dem Hotel   mit meiner Tante

In the dative plural the noun adds an **-n** to its normal plural form, unless this already ends in **-n** or in **-s**:

die Schuhe – den Schuhen
but die Katzen – den Katzen
die Hotels – den Hotels

2 The dative forms **dem, der**, and **den** contract with certain prepositions:

von dem → **vom**   in dem → **im**
zu dem → **zum**   an dem → **am**
zu der → **zur**

These contracted forms are almost always used unless the article is stressed (meaning *that*):

in dem Briefkasten dort (*in* that *postbox*)

Hinterm (= hinter dem), **hintern** (= hinter den), **unterm** (= unter dem), **untern** (= unter den) are also very frequent in spoken German and quite often found in modern printed German.

3 The pronoun **man** (= *one, you, people, they*) always takes the **er** form of the verb:

Was kann man hier kaufen? *What can you (one) buy here?*

4 The days of the week are

Montag   Freitag
Dienstag   Samstag
Mittwoch   (Sonnabend)
Donnerstag   Sonntag

Sonnabend is used for Saturday in the North and the East of Germany, **Samstag** elsewhere. *On* with days is **am: am Freitag**.

der Supermarkt (¨-e) supermarket
der Zeitungskiosk (-e) newspaper kiosk
der Briefkasten postbox
der Schmuck jewellery
der Nachmittag afternoon
der Zahnarzt (¨-e) dentist
der Laden shop
der Hund dog
der Tisch (-e) table
der Baum (¨-e) tree

die Bank (-en) bank
die Tankstelle (-n) filling station
die Apotheke (-n) chemist's
die Bäckerei (-en) baker's
die Straße (-n) street
die Zeitung (-en) newspaper
die Diskothek (-en) disco
die Leerung (-en) (postal) collection
die Dame (-n) lady
die Mode (-n) fashion
die Sprechstunden (*f.pl.*) surgery hours
die Kassenstunden (*f.pl.*) banking hours
die Katze (-n) cat
die Scherbe (-n) fragment
die Tüte (-n) paper bag

das Postamt (¨-er) post office
das Hotel (-s) hotel
das Tennis tennis

öffnen open
schließen close
parken park
stehen stand
spielen play
fahren travel; go by vehicle
tanzen dance
schlafen sleep
sitzen sit
liegen lie

hinter behind
vor in front of
in in
an on
nett nice
nach to (+ *town name*)
zu to

5 Plural of nouns: **-en**

die Leerung – die Leerungen
die Bäckerei – die Bäckereien

Feminine nouns that don't end in **-e**, **-el**, or **-er** add **-en** rather than **-n** to form their plural (thus making their plurals pronounceable!).

6 New strong verbs are:

fahren: du fährst, er fährt
schlafen: du schläfst, er schläft
sitzen: du sitzt
schließen: du schließt

We have also met the past tense of **sein**:

ich war	wir waren
du warst	ihr wart
er war	sie waren

außer except
auf on (top of)
unter under
aus out of
ohne without
in der Nähe von near
weit far
wohin where . . . to
nächst nearest; next
jeder every
man one; you; they
leer empty
nicht mehr no longer
schmutzig dirty
vorgestern the day before yesterday
gestern yesterday
übermorgen the day after tomorrow

A
1 Heute ist Samstag. Was ist übermorgen?
2 Gestern war Donnerstag. Was war vorgestern?
3 Morgen ist Sonnabend. Was war gestern?
4 Vorgestern war Dienstag. Was ist morgen?
5 Übermorgen ist Sonntag. Was ist heute?

B
1 Wo ist der Hund?
2 Wo sitzt die Dame?
3 Wo steht der Baum?
4 Wo ist die Katze?
5 Wo ist der Wagen?
6 Wo ist der Mann?
7 Wo ist der Kiosk?

C Rewrite with the words underlined in the plural:

1 Tanzt du gern in einer Diskothek?
2 Bleib nicht unter diesem Baum!
3 Die Sachen sind dort auf dem Tisch.
4 Ich kaufe lieber in einem Supermarkt.
5 Die Orange ist doch nicht auf dem Ei!
6 Ist meine Socke in meinem Schuh?
7 Ich gehe nicht gern zu diesem Kiosk.
8 Ich kann nicht in einer Intertank-Tankstelle kaufen.
9 Er kommt mit seiner Zeitung.

D
1 Was macht Herr Braun?
2 Was macht Herr Schmidt?
3 Was macht Herr Brandt?
4 Was macht Herr Strauß?
5 Was macht Herr Fein?
6 Wo war die Katze?
7 Was macht Fräulein Hammel?

E Was macht man hier?

Man......

1

2

3

4

5

6

7

UNIT 25

Zimmerpreise

	DM
Einzelzimmer	28
m. Dusche	37
m. Bad	42
Doppelzimmer/ Zweibettzimmer (2 Personen)	40
m. Dusche	52
m. Bad	60
(1 Person)	35
m. Dusche	45
m. Bad	50

Preise einschließlich Frühstück

das Zimmer room
der Preis price
Einzel- single
die Dusche shower
das Bad bath
Doppel- double
Zweibett- twin bedded

einschließlich inclusive of
das Frühstück breakfast

1 Ein Doppelzimmer

When you've worked through this scene in class act it out in pairs.

— Haben Sie ein Zimmer frei, bitte? Für heute abend?
— Ein Einzelzimmer?
— Nein, ein Doppelzimmer. Meine Frau ist draußen im Wagen.
— Ja, ich habe ein Zweibettzimmer mit Dusche.
— Was kostet es?
— Achtzig Mark einschließlich Frühstück.
— Darf ich das Zimmer bitte sehen?
— Bitte schön. Hier rechts Zimmer zwei. Hier ist der Schlüssel.

frei free
die Frau wife
draußen outside
darf ich may I

2 Zwei Einzelzimmer

Listen to the scene and then answer these questions:

1 How many rooms does the man want?
2 For how many nights?
3 Which nights?
4 What is he offered?
5 At what total cost?
6 Does he take them?

Now listen to the tape again. You are the man. Answer these questions:

1 Wieviele Zimmer möchten Sie?
2 Für wieviele Nächte?
3 Möchten Sie Einzelzimmer oder Doppelzimmer?
4 Wir haben nur ein Einzelzimmer und ein Doppelzimmer – geht das?
5 Nehmen Sie die Zimmer?

Now turn to the text (p. 76) and first read it in pairs. One partner should then close his or her book and try to act the part from memory, prompted by the other partner where necessary. Then change over, with the other partner trying to produce the other role from memory.

3 Ein Einzelzimmer

Listen to the conversation, then repeat each line after the tape. Then try to supply the customer's enquiries and responses with the help of the text below.

Say hello, ask if it's the Hotel zur Post and if they've still got rooms free for tonight. ← **noch**

— Ich habe leider nur ein Einzelzimmer.
(It's just what you need, ask him what it costs.) ← **genau, brauchen**

— Das ist ein Zimmer mit Bad. Es kostet zweiundvierzig Mark mit Frühstück.
(Tell him you'll take it.)

— Wie ist Ihr Name, bitte?
(You're Mr Schilling.)

— Gut, Herr Schilling. Können Sie bitte bis neunzehn Uhr hier sein?
(You certainly can.)

— Danke schön. Bis später also. Auf Wiedersehen.
(Say goodbye.)

Now play the scene again in pairs. The partner playing the receptionist should turn over to p. 76 and work from the full text, prompting if necessary.

2 Zwei Einzelzimmer

— Ich möchte zwei Einzelzimmer für drei Nächte bitte.
— Bis Dienstag morgen also?
— Ja, bis Dienstag. Haben Sie zwei Einzelzimmer frei?
— Nein, es tut mir leid. Ich habe nur ein Einzelzimmer und ein Doppelzimmer frei.
— Das geht auch. Was kosten sie?
— Das Einzelzimmer kostet achtundzwanzig Mark die Nacht, das Doppelzimmer mit einer Person fünfunddreißig, einschließlich Frühstück.
— Danke schön, ich nehme sie.

3 Ein Einzelzimmer

— Hallo! Hotel zur Post? Haben Sie für heute abend noch Zimmer frei?
— Ich habe leider nur ein Einzelzimmer.
— Das ist genau das, was ich brauche. Was kostet es?
— Das ist ein Zimmer mit Bad. Es kostet zweiundvierzig Mark mit Frühstück.
— Gut, ich nehme es.
— Wie ist Ihr Name, bitte?
— Schilling.
— Gut, Herr Schilling. Können Sie bitte bis neunzehn Uhr hier sein?
— Ja, sicher.
— Danke schön. Bis später also. Auf Wiedersehen.
— Auf Wiedersehen.

4 Now book *your* rooms

a You want a double room (two beds will do) with a shower, for tonight. Not more than DM 80 including breakfast.

b You want two single rooms, one room with bath, one with shower, for three nights. Ask if you can see them.

c You are telephoning. You want a twin-bedded room with bath for tonight.

a You have a twin-bedded room at DM 78 with a bath.

b You have the rooms required, but only for two nights. They are just on the left, numbers 3 and 4.

c You have it, it's DM 80 with breakfast. Ask him/her to be here by 7 p.m.

1 Some people are so fussy!

Ilse has come to have lunch with Christiane, but Christiane is having trouble finding something for Ilse to drink. Listen to the tape twice, then answer these questions.

der Magen stomach
gesund healthy
wieso? what do you mean?
sonst alles everything else

1 Möchte Ilse Tee trinken?
2 Und Kaffee?
3 Möchte sie Bier trinken?
4 Was für Wein ist da?
5 Warum möchte Ilse keinen Wein trinken?
6 Möchte sie Cola?
7 Warum trinkt man Milch?
8 Möchte Ilse Milch trinken?
9 Warum kann sie aber keine Milch trinken?

1

Christiane Möchtest du eine Tasse Tee trinken?
Ilse Danke, nein, ich darf keinen Tee trinken.
Christiane Möchtest du Kaffee, Ilse?
Ilse Ach . . . tut mir leid, Kaffee darf ich auch nicht trinken.
Christiane Wir haben Bier da. Möchtest du ein Bier?
Ilse Nein, Bier möcht' ich nicht zum Mittagessen trinken.
Christiane Möchtest du vielleicht Wein? Weißwein ist auch da.
Ilse Ach, mit meinem Magen darf ich keinen Wein trinken!
Christiane Vielleicht möchtest du eine Cola?
Ilse Cola? Oh nein. Wie k a n n man Cola trinken?
Christiane Was denn? Du darfst keinen Tee und keinen Kaffee trinken, auch keinen Wein. Bier oder Cola möchtest du nicht. Was trinkst du denn?
Ilse Hast du Milch da?
Christiane Ach ja, Milch! Sehr gut, sehr gesund. Wo ist denn nur die Milch . . . ach!
Ilse Ja, Milch möcht' ich gern trinken.
Christiane Milch kannst du leider auch nicht trinken.
Ilse Wieso denn nicht?
Christiane Es ist sonst wirklich alles da, aber die Milch ist alle!

2 May I?

3 Collectors' corner

Pairs put objects whose German names are known on desks. Teacher then asks one member of each pair for objects:

— Darf ich diesen [Kugelschreiber] haben, bitte?

Pupil replies, according to whether the object is his or his partner's:

— Ja, das dürfen Sie! Das ist sein [Kugelschreiber] !

or — Nein, das dürfen Sie nicht! Das ist mein [Kugelschreiber] !

Once the teacher has completed his collection, owners may get their possessions back by asking for them in German:

— Darf ich meinen Kugelschreiber haben, bitte?

4 I'm choosy about what I eat and drink

Möchten Sie Wein trinken? — Nein danke, ich trinke keinen Wein.

Möchten Sie [ham] — Nein danke, ich . . .

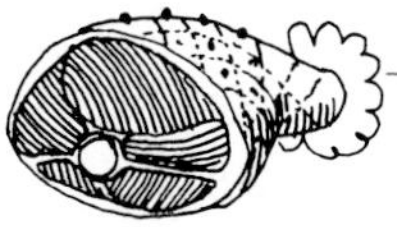

5 What would you like?

Everyone writes down on a piece of paper something that he or she would like to eat, thus:

— Ich möchte ein Eis (ein Brötchen, eine Bockwurst . . .)

One person is chosen to be 'on', the rest of the class suggest what he might like, thus:

— Möchtest du ein Ei essen?
— Nein danke, ein Ei möcht' ich nicht.

Whoever guesses correctly is 'on' next; the winner is the person whose food took the largest number of guesses to get.

UNIT 27

1 Welchen Monat haben wir? Und wie ist das Wetter?

Wir haben Januar.
Im Januar friert es.

Wir haben Februar.
Im Februar schneit es.

Wir haben März.
Im März ist es windig.

Wir haben April.
Im April regnet es.

Wir haben Mai.
Im Mai ist es schön.

Wir haben Juni.
Im Juni wird es warm.

Wir haben Juli.
Im Juli scheint die Sonne.

Wir haben August.
Im August ist es heiß.

Wir haben September.
Im September donnert es und blitzt.

Wir haben Oktober.
Im Oktober wird es kühl.

Wir haben November.
Im November ist es neblig.

Wir haben Dezember.
Im Dezember ist es kalt.

2 Wie ist das Wetter heute?

1 Karen trägt einen Bikini.

2 Georg trägt einen Schal.

3 Uwe trägt Gummistiefel.

4 Annamaria trägt ein Sommerkleid.

5 Pamela trägt einen Hut.

3 Nag, nag, nag!

Jetzt regnet es. Du solltest deinen Regenmantel finden!
...... einen Pullover
eine Sonnenbrille
deinen Schal
deine Gummistiefel

Heute wird's kühl. Und du hast keinen Schal!
...... keinen Schirm
keinen Bikini
keinen Mantel
kein Sommerkleid

4 Der Wievielte ist heute?

Heute ist der erste März.
zweite
dritte
vierte
...
sieb(en)te
achte
...
zwanzigste
einundzwanzigste
...
dreißigste
einunddreißigste

Und das Jahr?
— Neunzehnhundert ......

März

So		6	13	20	27
Mo		7	14	21	28
Di	1	8	15	22	29
Mi	2	9	16	23	30
Do	3	10	17	24	31
F	4	11	18	25	
S	5	12	19	26	

5 Was ist heute für ein Tag?

Der neunte? — Es ist Mittwoch.
Der zehnte?
Der zwölfte?
Der siebenundzwanzigste?
Der dritte?
Der siebente?
Der erste?
Der dreißigste?
Der achtzehnte?

6 In welcher Jahreszeit?

Brauchst du eine Sonnenbrille im Winter? Nein, im Sommer!
einen Schal im Herbst? Ja, ...
einen Hut im Frühling? ......
Gummistiefel im Sommer?
......

UNIT 28 REVISION

Grammar

1 Modal verbs

There are six German verbs which are normally used with the infinitive of other verbs to give meanings like *ought to do, will do, must do, can do*, etc. They are called modal verbs. We have met four of them in their present tense:

müssen – *must; have to*
(ich, er muß; du mußt)
können – *can; be able to*
(ich, er kann; du kannst)
wollen – *will; want to*
(ich, er will; du willst)
dürfen – *can; may; be allowed to*
(ich, er darf; du darfst)

The other two we have met in their more common conditional tense:

mögen		**sollen**	
ich möchte	—*I should like to*	ich sollte	—*I ought to*
du möchtest		du solltest	
er möchte		er sollte	
wir möchten		wir sollten	
ihr möchtet		ihr solltet	
sie möchten		sie sollten	

Notice the difference between **können** and **dürfen**:

Ich kann Tennis spielen – *I can play tennis, i.e. I know how to*
Ich darf Tennis spielen – *I can play tennis, i.e. I am allowed to*

Ich möchte is used with an object to mean *I want*:

Ein Ei möcht' ich nicht – *I don't want an egg*

It is more polite than **ich will**.

2 Noun plurals: the basic rules

The basic rules for forming the plurals of nouns are:

Nouns ending **-e** add **-n**, whatever their gender.
Most foreign nouns add **-s**.
Masculines and neuters ending **-el, -en, -er** don't change.
Neuters ending **-chen, -lein** don't change.
Feminines add **-(e)n** (and **-in** becomes **-innen**).
Masculines in general add **¨e** (**-e** if the vowel is **i** or **e** and so can't take umlaut).
Neuters in general add **¨er** (or **-er** if the vowel is **i** or **e**).

der Schlüssel (-) key
der Preis (-e) price
der Magen stomach
der Bikini (-s) bikini
der Gummistiefel (-) Wellington (boot)
der Schal (-e) scarf

die Frau (-en) wife
die Dusche (-n) shower
die Person (-en) person
die Sonne (-n) sun
die Jahreszeit (-en) season

das Zimmer (-) room
das Einzelzimmer (-) single room
das Doppelzimmer (-) double room
das Zweibettzimmer (-) twin-bedded room
das Frühstück (-e) breakfast
das Bad (¨er) bath
das Fenster (-) window
das Sommerkleid (-er) summer dress
das Jahr (-e) year

gehen be all right
dürfen be allowed to
mögen like
nehmen take
brauchen need
frieren freeze
schneien snow
regnen rain
donnern thunder
blitzen lighten
werden become
scheinen shine
draußen outside
einschließlich including
bis until; by
noch still
genau exact(ly)
hallo! hello!
wieso? what do you mean?
gesund healthy
sonst alles everything else
windig windy
warm warm
heiß hot
kühl cool
kalt cold
neblig foggy

There are a number of exceptions to these rules. Those we have met so far are:

Nouns in **-el, -en, -er** adding **¨** : der Mantel, der Briefkasten, der Laden, die Mutter.

Masculines and neuters adding **-e** : der Nachmittag, der Hund, der Schal, das Brot, das Geschenk, das Haar, das Jahr.

Feminines adding **¨e**: die Wurst, die Stadt.

Masculines adding **¨er**: der Mund, der Mann.

Nouns not ending **-e** adding **-(e)n**: der Herr, das Hemd.

There are, however, only a limited number of these exceptions. From now on these exceptional plurals will be printed in black in the vocabulary lists of the revision units.

3 Ordinal numbers (*first, second, third, etc.*)

These are formed by adding **-te** to the normal number up to and including 19th, and **-ste** from 20 on. *First, third,* and *eighth* are irregular:

erste	elfte	der 7. = der siebente
zweite	. . .	The ordinal is often indicated by putting a full stop after the figure.
dritte	zwanzigste	
vierte	einundzwanzigste	
fünfte	. . .	
sechste	dreißigste	
sieb(en)te	vierzigste	
achte	. . .	
neunte	hundertste	
zehnte	hunderterste	
	. . .	

4 Months and seasons

Januar	Mai	September	Frühling
Februar	Juni	Oktober	Sommer
März	Juli	November	Herbst
April	August	Dezember	Winter

All the above are masculine.

In January etc. is always **im: im Januar, im Frühling**.

5 Days, dates

Der Wievielte ist heute?
— Heute ist der erste/zweite/dritte . . . Januar
(neunzehnhundertdreiundachtzig).
Was ist heute für ein Tag?
— Heute ist Montag.

6 New strong verbs are:

dürfen: ich darf, du darfst, er darf
nehmen: du nimmst, er nimmt
werden: du wirst, er wird

Kosten and **regnen** add an extra **-e-** to make them pronounceable:
es kostet, es regnet.

A Say how many there are:

der Tisch (5)	die Straße (4)	die Dame (7)
die Mode (2)	das Hotel (5)	der Baum (20)
die Katze (10)	der Supermarkt (6)	die Tüte (100)
die Tante (12)	die Tankstelle (4)	das Fenster (8)
der Schlüssel (23)	das Bad (3)	das Kleid (14)

B Add a number – any you like above one:

der Herr	das Hemd	die Mutter
das Brot	der Mantel	die Wurst
die Stadt	das Geschenk	der Hund
der Laden	das Haar	der Nachmittag

C Die Woche:

1 Sonntag ist der erste Tag.
2 Und Montag?
3 Und Donnerstag?
4 Und Samstag?
5 Und Dienstag?
6 Und Mittwoch?
7 Und Freitag?

D 1 Wann ist es neblig?
— Im November.

2 Wann regnet es?
3 Wann wird es warm?
4 Wann ist es windig?
5 Wann schneit es?
6 Wann ist es heiß?
7 Wann scheint die Sonne?
8 Wann wird es kühl?
9 Wann ist es schön?

E Complete with modals:

„Nein, danke, ich m...... keinen Kuchen. Ich d...... nicht: ich w...... schlank werden. Du auch, du s...... nicht so viel Kuchen essen. Aber Mensch, es ist schon halb fünf! K...... es wirklich so spät sein? Ich m...... gehen! Ich s...... schon bei Bernd sein! Und ich k...... kein Taxi nehmen – ich habe kein Geld. D..... ich dein Rad leihen, bitte?"

der Kuchen cake
schlank slim
bei Bernd at Bernd's

F 1 Der wievielte ist heute?
2 Und gestern?
3 Was ist heute für ein Tag?
4 Und morgen?
5 Sind die Sommerferien im Januar?
(**die Ferien** holidays)
6 Ist Juni der fünfte Monat?
7 In welchem Monat hast du Geburtstag?
(**der Geburtstag** birthday)
8 Und deine Mutter?
9 Hast du den Winter gern?
10 Welche Jahreszeit hast du lieber?

G Write out these dates in full

H Pairwork

UNIT 29

Cölner Hofbräu P. Josef Früh
Brauerei für obergäriges Bier
Am Hof 12-14 · 5000 Köln 1 · Tel. Restaurant 21 26 21

Speisen- und Getränkekarte

früh am Dom *Abendkarte*

Tasse Hühnerbrühe mit Einlage und Brötchen	4,20
4/2 Russische Eier	6,60
Schweizer Käse mit Schwarzbrot und Butter	8,20
Geflügelsalat mit Toast und Butter	11,20
Kasseler, Sauerkraut und Püree	12,60
Schweineschnitzel mit Salzkartoffeln und gemischtem Salat	15,50
Filetsteak mit Champignons und Pommes frites	20,50
Wiener Schnitzel, Pommes frites und Salat	16,30
Huhn auf Reis mit Spargel	12,00

ENDPREISE

Warme Speisen bis 22,00 Uhr
Kalte Speisen bis 23,00 Uhr

die Speise(n)karte menu
die Getränkekarte wine list
die Hühnerbrühe chicken broth
die Einlage filling; garnish
russisch Russian
Schweizer Käse Swiss cheese
das Püree mashed potatoes
der Geflügelsalat chicken salad
Kasseler smoked (rib of) pork
das Schweineschnitzel escalope of pork
die Salzkartoffeln boiled potatoes
gemischt mixed
der Champignon mushroom
Wiener Viennese
das Huhn chicken
der Reis rice
der Spargel asparagus
der Endpreis price with service and VAT
die Speisen dishes

1 Listen to each of the scenes two or three times and then answer these questions.

Scene 1 *In the office. Andreas asks Eva to have a meal with him.*

1 What meal does he invite her to?
2 When?
3 Why?
4 Where does Andreas suggest they go?
5 Why?
6 At what time are they to meet?
7 Where?

Scene 2 *At the restaurant. The waiter takes their order.*

1 Are they going to eat something hot or something cold?
2 What does Eva choose?
3 What does Andreas choose?
4 Why does Eva not want a starter?
5 What does Andreas order to drink?
6 Why doesn't Eva order the same?
7 What does she order?

Scene 3 *Paying the bill.*

1 Do they both enjoy the meal?
2 Who pays the bill?
3 Why doesn't Andreas use his credit card to pay the bill?
4 What does the bill come to?
5 How much money has Eva?
6 When will she be repaid?
7 What does Andreas wish Eva?

Vocabulary

Scene 1
dich, dir you
das Abendessen dinner
einladen invite
es soll it's supposed to
vor allem especially
schön right
abholen call for
gegen towards

Scene 2
meine Herrschaften sir, madam
die Vorspeise starter
wünschen wish
das Kölsch *special Cologne beer*
der Apfelsaft apple juice

Scene 3
Herr Ober! waiter!
zahlen pay
jawohl yes indeed
mein Herr sir
die Rechnung bill
schmeckt es? are you enjoying it?
die Brieftasche wallet
zu Hause at home
warten wait
mal just
hoch high; big
die Handtasche handbag
Gott sei Dank thank goodness
(es) macht nichts it doesn't matter
das Essen food
übrigens by the way

1 In the office

Andreas Du hast morgen Geburtstag, nicht? Darf ich dich zum Abendessen einladen?
Eva Ja gerne, das ist nett von dir. Wo wollen wir denn essen?
Andreas Bei Früh soll es sehr gut sein. Vor allem abends.
Eva Schön. Wann willst du mich abholen?
Andreas Gegen sieben?
Eva Gut. Gegen sieben bei mir.

At the restaurant

Waiter Ja, meine Herrschaften. Was darf es sein?
Andreas Wir essen warm, ja, Eva? Du hast die Karte.
Eva Ja, bitte. Ich esse Huhn . . . Huhn auf Reis mit Spargel, bitte.
Andreas Huhn? Nein, Huhn ess' ich nicht. Ich esse lieber Kasseler.
Waiter Mit Sauerkraut und Püree?
Andreas Ja, bitte. Möchtest du auch eine Vorspeise, Eva?
Eva Nein, danke. So viel Hunger hab' ich nicht.
Waiter Und zu trinken wünschen Sie . . .?
Andreas Ein Glas Kölsch, bitte. Und du, Eva?
Eva Nein, Bier trinke ich nicht. Eine Flasche Apfelsaft, bitte.

Paying the bill

Andreas Herr Ober!
Waiter Schmeckt es, meine Herrschaften?
Andreas Ja, sehr gut danke. Dir auch, Eva?
Eva Ja, mir schmeckt es sehr gut!
Andreas Und jetzt möcht' ich bitte zahlen.
Waiter Jawohl, mein Herr. Bitte schön, die Rechnung . . .
Andreas Aber . . . du, Eva, ich . . . ich kann mein Geld nicht finden!
Eva Wo war es denn?
Andreas In meiner Brieftasche. Aber meine Brieftasche ist nicht hier – sie muß bei mir zu Hause sein!
Eva Hast du keine Kreditkarten mit?
Andreas Nein, sie sind auch in meiner Brieftasche. Was machen wir jetzt?
Eva Warte mal. In meiner Handtasche hab' ich Geld. Wie hoch ist die Rechnung?
Andreas Siebenundzwanzig Mark fünfundfünfzig.
Eva Gott sei Dank – ich habe genau dreißig Mark!
Andreas Recht vielen Dank, Eva. Ich gebe dir morgen das Geld, aber . . . es tut mir so leid!
Eva Macht nichts, Andreas. Das Essen war doch gut!
Andreas Ja, richtig. Übrigens, Eva, ich wünsche dir alles Gute zum Geburtstag!

2 It tastes fabulous! (or does it?)

— Schmeckt es dir?

— Ja, | mir schmeckt es . . .
Nein, |

fabelhaft | . Und dir?
fantastisch
sehr gut
gut
nicht sehr
nicht
wirklich nicht

— Mir schmeckt es ...... Und dir?
— ......

3 I'm sorry, but I really haven't got it!

Gib mir meinen Schlüssel!

— Es tut mir leid, ... kann ich dir nicht geben.

einen Apfelsaft
meine Brieftasche
ein Halstuch
meine Kreditkarte
die Gummistiefel
mein Geburtstagsgeschenk

4 When can I invite you for? And when am I to pick you up?

Darf ich dich für heute abend einladen?

— Ja, sicher. Du sollst mich um ? abholen.

Darf ich dich für morgen abend einladen?
heute nachmittag
heute morgen
Freitag abend
Sonntag morgen
morgen früh

5 Im Restaurant

Play waiter/waitress and diner ordering a meal, using the menu on p. 86 and following this pattern:

— Herr Ober!/Fräulein!
— Ja, mein Herr/meine Dame. Was darf es sein?
— Ich möchte ......
— Und als Vorspeise?
— Ich möchte ....../Danke, ich möchte keine Vorspeise.
— Was wünschen Sie zu trinken, bitte?
— Ein Glas Bier/Rotwein/Weißwein/Limonade/...... bitte.
— Also, ... (*waiter repeats order*) ......?
— Ja, bitte.
— Danke schön, mein Herr/meine Dame.

6 Die Rechnung, bitte!

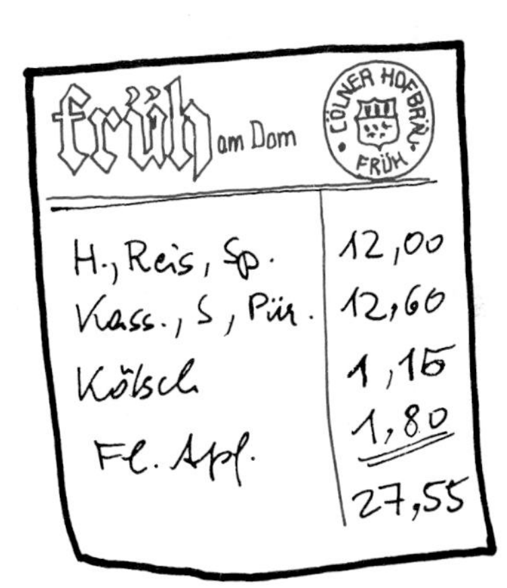

You are the waiter/waitress. Go through this bill with your customer, explaining each item, its price and the total:

— Die Rechnung, bitte!
— Bitte schön. Das war ......
Und das macht ...... insgesamt.

Now each member of the pair make out a different bill, using the menu on p. 86, and play the scene out twice more using these new bills.

UNIT 30

1 Listen to each scene *twice*, then decide on which of the three possible locations is the most likely one. Then turn to p. 92 and read through the texts to see if you were right.

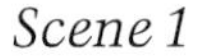

Scene 1
a In a bar.
b In a restaurant.
c In a kitchen.

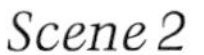

Scene 2
a In a restaurant.
b In a supermarket.
c In a kitchen.

Scene 3
a On the street.
b In a music shop.
c At the boy's home.

Scene 4
a At the cleaner's.
b At a disco.
c At home.

Scene 5
a In a restaurant.
b In the couple's garage.
c At a disco.

noch nicht not yet
zuerst first
das Fleisch meat
sehen look
neu new
hören hear
das Musikgeschäft music shop
bestimmt sure to be

2 Your teacher will play all the scenes again, giving you time to write at the end of each scene. Write down the *next* sentence in the scene after each of the following (do it without looking at p. 92!).

Scene 1 Willst du Apfelsaft trinken? ......

Scene 2 Der Edamer Käse dort ist so schön rot! ......

Scene 3 Hier, das ist meine Wings-Kassette. Sie ist ganz neu. ......

Scene 4 Wo ist mein Sommerkleid? ......

Scene 5 Hast du meine Handtasche, Peter? —Deine Handtasche? Ich? ......

Aber mein Geld hast du doch, oder? ......

Du hast aber meinen Schlüssel, Peter? ......

3 Answer these questions on each of the scenes in writing. Turn to p. 92 only if you are not sure of the spelling of a word.

Scene 1	Was will Dieter zum Mittagessen trinken? Warum will er keinen Apfelsaft?
Scene 2	Was kauft Ursel vielleicht zum Abendessen? Will sie den Käse kaufen?
Scene 3	Möchte das Mädchen die Wings-Kassette hören? Wo können sie das nicht machen?
Scene 4	Was macht die Mutter? Findet das Mädchen ihr Sommerkleid?
Scene 5	Hat Peter die Handtasche? Und das Geld? Und der Schlüssel? Wo sind sie?

4 Aber nein!

Answer 'no' to these questions:

1 Willst du mich abholen?
2 Hast du die Rechnung?
3 Darf ich dich einladen?
4 Braucht er den Wagen?
5 Siehst du dieses Mädchen?
6 Essen Sie Ihre Hühnerbrühe?
7 Soll ich sie bezahlen?
8 Hörst du meinen Vater?
9 Nimmt er das Doppelzimmer?
10 Trägt sie ihren Bikini?

5 Not appreciated

Write out in full using **nicht** and a pronoun in your answer. Try to vary the verb.

Das ist ein Schirm. Ich brauche ihn nicht.

Ich ...... nicht.

......

1 2 3 4 5 6 7 8

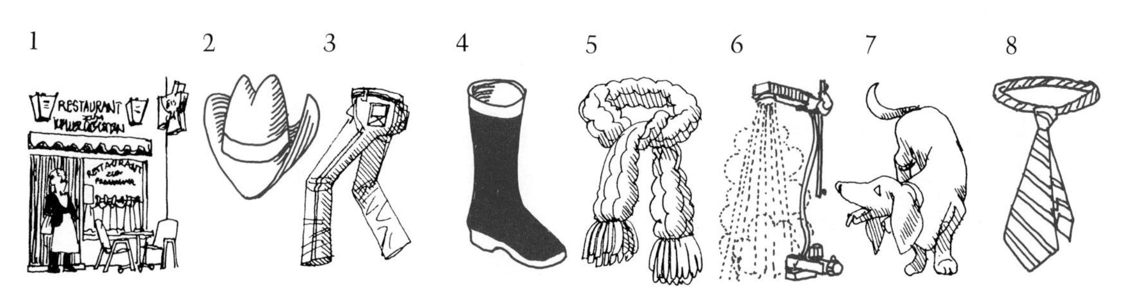

1

Scene 1

— Was trinkst du zum Mittagessen, Dieter?
— Limonade, bitte, Mutti.
— Tja, Limonade haben wir nicht. Willst du Apfelsaft trinken?
— **Ich trink' ihn nicht gern – das weißt du doch.**

Scene 2

— Was kaufst du zum Abendessen, Ursel?
— Das kann ich dir noch nicht sagen. Schweineschnitzel vielleicht.
— **Der Edamer Käse dort ist so schön rot! Willst du ihn nicht kaufen?**
— Warte nur. Ich muß zuerst das Fleisch kaufen.

Scene 3

— Hier, das ist meine Wings-Kassette. Sie ist ganz neu. Willst du sie mal hören?
— Ja gerne. Hier vor dem Musikgeschäft können wir das aber nicht!
— Bei mir zu Hause aber!
— Ja, schön! Gehen wir!

Scene 4

— Wo ist mein Sommerkleid? Ich kann es nicht finden.
— Ich weiß nicht – ich putze die Wohnung!
— Ich muß es aber haben.
— Es ist vielleicht in der Reinigung.
— Ach ja! Richtig! In der Reinigung. Aber was mache ich? Ich gehe heute abend in die Diskothek!

Scene 5

— Hast du meine Handtasche, Peter?
— Deine Handtasche? Ich? Nein, ich hab' sie nicht. Die ist bestimmt noch im Restaurant! Oder in der Diskothek.
— Aber mein Geld hast du doch, oder?
— Nein, *ich* hab' es nicht. Es muß in deiner Handtasche sein.
— Du hast aber meinen Schlüssel, Peter?
— **Nein, ich hab' ihn auch nicht – sieh mal, er ist dort im Wagen – und deine Handtasche auch!**

UNIT 31

1 Family tree

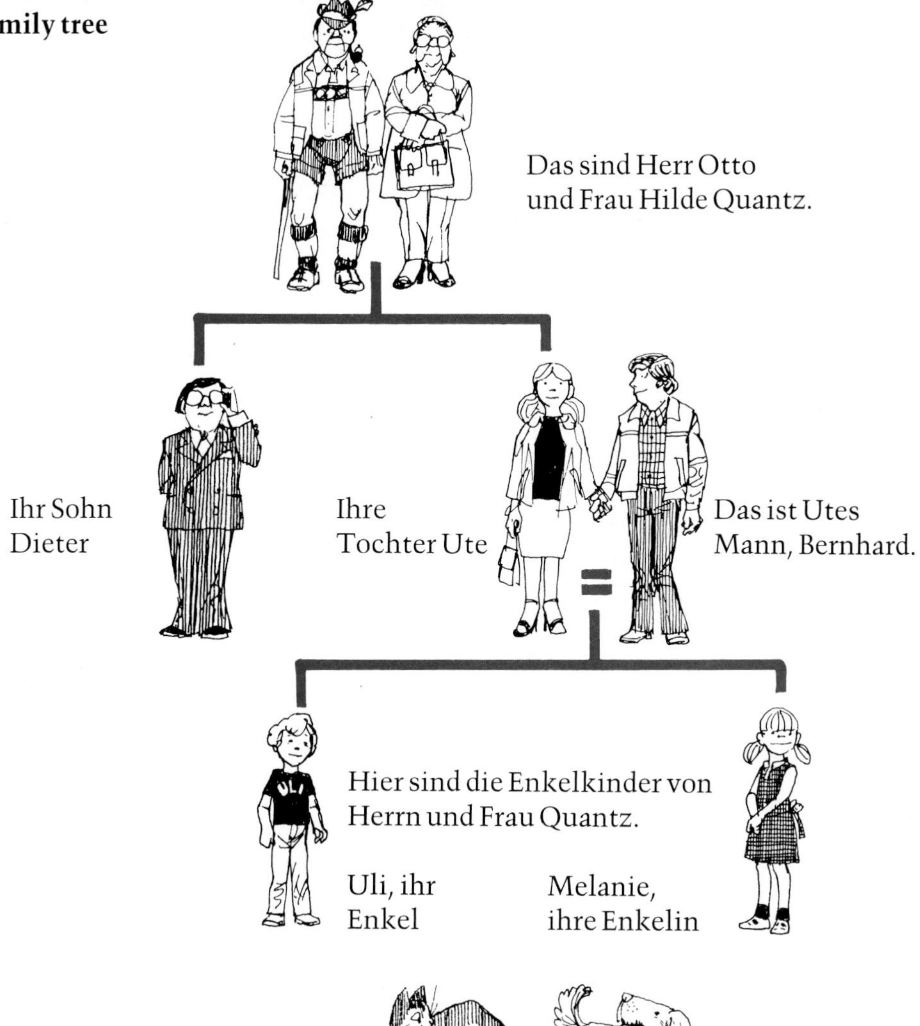

Sabrina, die Katze

Sam, der Hund

2

1 Wer ist der Onkel von Uli?
2 Hat Melanie eine Tante?
3 Wer ist die Mutter von Uli?
4 Wie heißt seine Großmutter?
5 Wer ist der Mann von Hilde?
6 Hat Dieter eine Frau?
7 Wer ist der Neffe von Dieter?
8 Und seine Nichte?
9 Wie heißt der Sohn von Bernhard?
10 Wer ist die Tochter von Otto?

3 **Du bist Melanie . . .**

1 Wer ist Bernhard?
—Mein ......

2 Wer ist Dieter?
3 Wer ist Hilde?
4 Wer ist Uli?
5 Wer ist Ute?
6 Wer ist Otto?

 4 **Gemeinsame Freunde**

Bernhard	Kennen Sie uns vielleicht? Wir heißen Lortzing. Ich heiße Bernhard mit Vornamen, und das ist meine Frau Ute.	**kennen** know **heißen** be called **der Vorname** first name
Franz	Sehr angenehm! Ich heiße Pfitzner, Franz Pfitzner . . . Nein, ich kenne Sie nicht. Wo wohnen Sie denn?	**sehr angenehm** pleased to meet you **wohnen** live
Bernhard	In der Frankfurter Straße, Nummer 17.	
Franz	In der Frankfurter Straße! Das ist gar nicht weit von uns. Wir wohnen in der Beckstraße. Die Seidels wohnen in der Frankfurter Straße. Kennen Sie sie?	
Bernhard	Nein, ich kenne sie nicht. Du, Ute?	
Ute	Nein, ich kenne sie auch nicht.	
Franz	Vielleicht kennen sie S i e . . .	
Ute	Wir kennen aber die Fischers! Sie wohnen in der Beckstraße!	
Franz	Fischers? In der Beckstraße? Ich kenne sie gar nicht. Wo in der Beckstraße?	
Ute	Nummer 70.	
Franz	Nummer 70! Dann müssen sie die Häckers kennen – die wohnen Beckstraße 72. Die Häckers sind Freunde von uns!	**der Freund** friend
Bernhard	Sicher kennen sie die Häckers, sie sind doch Nachbarn!	**der Nachbar** neighbour
Ute	Sicher kennen sie sie!	
Franz	Na, Herr Lortzing, Frau Lortzing, das ist aber schön: wir haben so viele gemeinsame Freunde!	**gemeinsam** mutual

Complete with the most appropriate pronouns:

1 Kennen Sie ...... ? Wir heißen Lortzing.
2 Nein, ich kenne ...... nicht. Wo wohnen Sie denn?
3 Wir kennen die Frankfurter Straße, die ist gar nicht weit von ......
4 Dort wohnen die Seidels – kennen Sie ...... ?
5 Fischers? Nein, ich kenne ...... gar nicht.
6 Die Häckers kennen wir sehr gut, sie sind Freunde von ......

5 Das Familienfoto

Großvater Otto

1 Wer steht hinter ihm?
—Hinter ihm stehen ......

2 Wer sitzt rechts von ihm?
3 Wer liegt vor ihm?
4 Wer sitzt links von ihm?

Großmutter Hilde

1 Wer liegt vor ihr?
2 Wer steht hinter ihr?
3 Wer sitzt links von ihr?
4 Wer sitzt rechts von ihr?

Die Großeltern

1 Wer steht hinter ihnen?
2 Wer liegt vor ihnen?
3 Wer sitzt links von ihnen?
4 Wer sitzt rechts von ihnen?

6 Humour them!

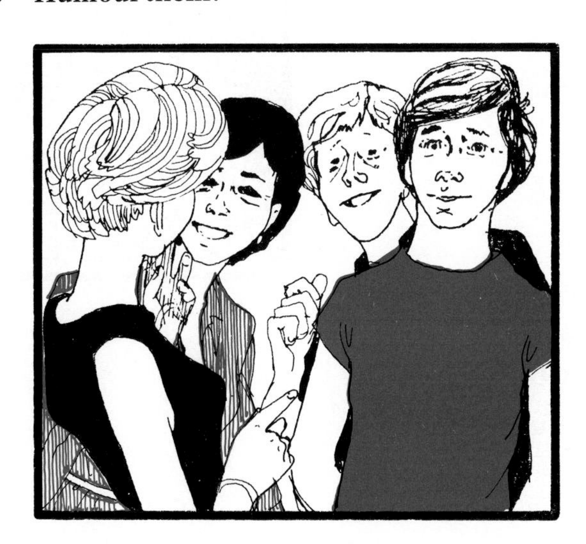

1 Kennt ihr uns?
—Ja ja, wir kennen euch!

2 Braucht ihr uns?
3 Wollt ihr mit uns essen?
4 Findet ihr uns nett?
5 Geht ihr mit uns ins Kino?
6 Wollt ihr mit uns tanzen?
7 Fahrt ihr uns nach Hause?

7 Um Himmels willen!

1 Gib mir den Schlüssel! — Gib ihm den Schlüssel!

2 Putz mir die Wohnung! — ...... ihr ......

3 Leih uns Geld! — ...... ihnen ......

4 Kauf mir Champagner! — ......

5 Beschreib mir den Wagen!

6 Mach uns Frühstück!

7 Bezahl mir das Essen!

8 Sag mir, wo du wohnst!

8 Teacher is a kleptomaniac!

Teacher approaches pairs and asks for object from one member of pair:

— Gib mir deinen ......!

Other member encourages the transaction with:

— Gib ihm (ihr) deinen ......!

or prevents it with:

— Nein, gib ihm (ihr) deinen ...... nicht!

When teacher has a really large collection of other people's property, owners may collect them back by asking

— Geben Sie mir meinen ...... zurück, bitte!

The other member of the pair must encourage the return with

— Ja, geben Sie ihm (ihr) seinen (ihren) ...... zurück!

UNIT 32 REVISION

Grammar

1 Object pronouns

		accusative	dative
ich	→	mich	mir
du	→	dich	dir
er	→	ihn	ihm
sie	→	sie	ihr
es	→	es	ihm
wir	→	uns	uns
ihr	→	euch	euch
Sie	→	Sie	Ihnen
sie	→	sie	ihnen

The accusative pronouns are used as direct objects:

Du sollst mich um sieben Uhr abholen.

The dative pronouns are used as indirect objects:

Er gibt mir das Geld

and after prepositions:

Er fährt mit uns nach Hause.

The dative pronoun is often used with the sense of *for*.

Putz mir die Wohnung! – *Clean the flat for me.*
Kauf mir Champagner! – *Buy me champagne.*

When used as objects, pronouns usually come immediately after the main verb in the sentence, or after the subject in inverted order:

Sicher kennen Sie uns!

2 Kennen Sie die Häckers?

Ich weiß nicht.

There are two verbs meaning *to know* in German. **Kennen** is to know a person or a place, to be acquainted with. **Wissen** is to know a fact. *Connaître* and *savoir* in French are exactly the same.

3 Wer ist der Onkel von Uli?

With names one can equally well say:

Wer ist Ulis Onkel?

There is no apostrophe before the **s** in German.

4 Notice the two most frequent meanings of **sollen** in the present:

Soll ich dich abholen? *Am I to pick you up?*
Bei Früh soll es gut sein. *It's supposed to be good at Früh's.*

der **Toast** toast
der **Geflügelsalat** chicken salad
der **Salat** (-e) salad
der **Champignon** (-s) mushroom
der **Reis** rice
der **Spargel** (-) asparagus
der **Endpreis** (-e) inclusive price
der **Apfelsaft** apple juice
der **Onkel** (-) uncle
der **Großvater** (¨) grandfather
die **Großeltern** (pl.) grandparents
der **Sohn** (¨e) son
der **Mann** (¨er) husband
der **Bruder** (¨) brother
der **Enkel** (-) grandson
der **Neffe** (-n) nephew
der **Vorname** (-n) first name
der **Freund** (-e) friend
der **Nachbar** (-n) neighbour

die **Speise(n)karte** (-n) menu
die **Getränkekarte** (-n) wine list
die **Hühnerbrühe** chicken broth
die **Einlage** (-n) garnish
die **Salzkartoffel** (-n) boiled potato
die **Speise** (-n) dish
die **Vorspeise** (-n) starter
die **Rechnung** (-en) bill
die **Brieftasche** (-n) wallet
die **Kreditkarte** (-n) credit card
die **Großmutter** (¨) grandmother
die **Tochter** (¨) daughter
die **Enkelin** (-nen) granddaughter
die **Nichte** (-n) niece

das **Schwarzbrot** black bread
das **Püree** mashed potatoes
das **Schweineschnitzel** (-) pork escalope
das **Huhn** (¨er) chicken
das **Abendessen** (-) dinner
das **Essen** food
das **Filetsteak** (-s) fillet steak
das **Mädchen** (-) girl
das **Fleisch** meat
das **Musikgeschäft** (-e) music shop
das **Enkelkind** (-er) grandchild
das **Kino** (-s) cinema

einladen invite
abholen call for

5 New strong verb is:

geben: du gibst, er gibt

and notice **heißen**: du heißt
and **warten**: du wartest, er wartet, ihr wartet.

A Answer yes or no, as you will, but use a pronoun instead of the words in italics in your answer:

1. Kennst du *meinen Freund Willi*?
2. Warst du mit *Willi* in Berlin?
3. Kennst du auch *seine Schwester Barbara*?
4. Warst du gestern bei *Barbara* zu Hause?
5. Fährst du morgen mit *Willi und mir* nach Köln?
6. Hast du *Barbara* gern?
7. Hast du *mich* gern?
8. Willst du mit *Willi und Barbara* ins Kino gehen?
9. Sollen sie *dich* gegen sieben abholen?
10. Oder willst du *Willi und Barbara* abholen?
11. Willst du auch mit *mir* ins Kino gehen?

B Complete using either **kennen** or **wissen** in each case:

„...... du Sabrina?"
„Ja, ich ...... sie sehr gut, aber ich ...... nicht, wo sie wohnt."
„Sie wohnt in der Beckstraße. Du ...... bestimmt das Haus."
„Ich ...... nicht."
„Aber sicher, es ist groß und blau."
„Blau? Das Haus? Dann ...... ich es nicht!"
„Aber doch, du ...... genau, wo es ist. Rechts vom Postamt."
„Ach ja, jetzt ...... ich!"

C Familie Finck

Construct their family tree, including ages, from the information on the next page:

wünschen wish
zahlen pay
schmecken taste (good)
warten wait
es macht nichts it doesn't matter
hören hear
wohnen live
geben give
kennen know
heißen be called
russisch Russian
gemischt mixed
Wiener Viennese
vor allem especially
schön! right!
gegen towards
mein Herr sir
meine Herrschaften ladies and gentlemen
Herr Ober! waiter!
Fräulein! waitress!
jawohl yes, certainly
zu Hause at home
hoch high; big
übrigens by the way
mal just
Gott sei Dank thank heavens
recht vielen Dank thank you very much
alles Gute all the best
morgen früh tomorrow morning
noch nicht not yet
zuerst first
neu new
bestimmt definitely
sehr angenehm pleased to meet you
gemeinsam mutual

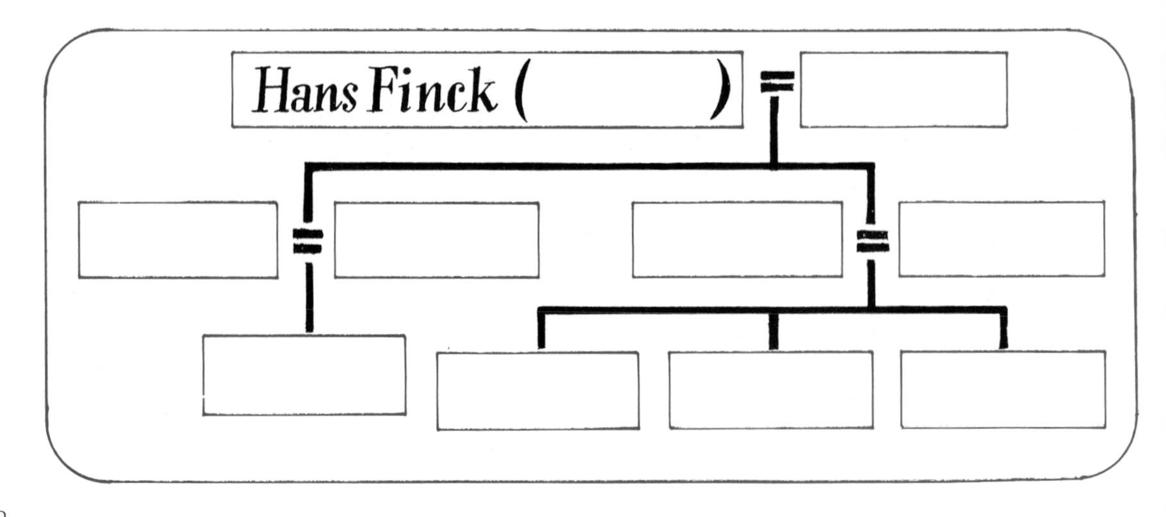

Ich bin Rudi Finck, ich bin achtunddreißig Jahre alt und habe drei Kinder.

Ich heiße Sebastian, ich habe zwei Schwestern und keinen Bruder.

Ich bin Susi, ich bin sechzig und habe zwei Enkelinnen und zwei Enkel.

Mein Name ist Hans, ich bin einundsechzig und habe zwei Söhne aber keinen Bruder; meine Söhne sind neununddreißig und achtunddreißig Jahre alt.

Ich heiße Trudi; mein Onkel heißt Viktor Finck.

Ich heiße Simone, ich bin zehn Jahre alt, meine Schwester ist neun und mein Bruder ist elf.

Mein Vorname ist Viktor. Ich habe einen Sohn, Dieter. Er ist dreizehn. Meine Frau heißt Sandra.

Ich heiße Dieter. Meine Tante heißt Annegret. Sie ist sechsunddreißig Jahre alt. Meine Mutter ist erst vierunddreißig.

D Now use your tree to answer these questions:

1 Wie heißt der Vater von Rudi?
2 Wie heißt der Onkel von Sebastian?
3 Wie heißt die Nichte von Annegret?
4 Wie heißt die Großmutter von Dieter?
5 Wie heißt die Schwester von Trudi?
6 Wie heißt die Frau von Viktor?

E Jetzt essen wir!

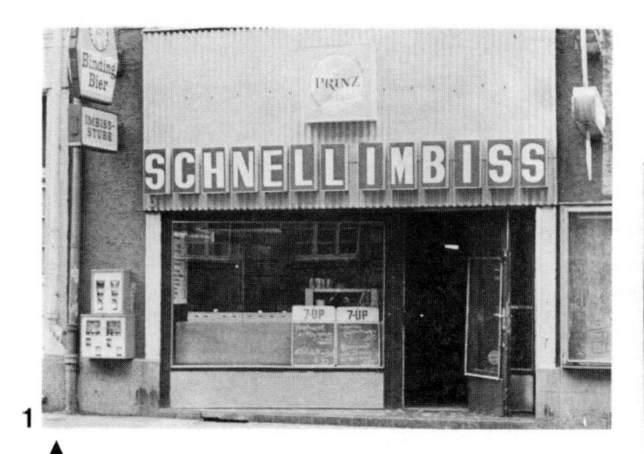

1
▲
What sort of eating place is this?

What do you think **die Zuckerwatte** is?
▼

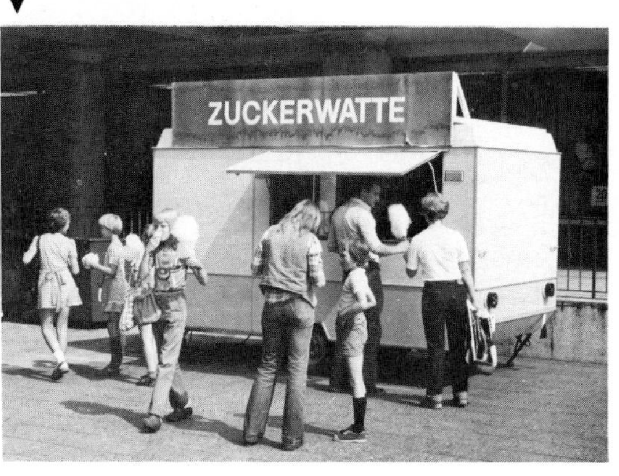

2

▶

What sort of restaurant is this? Can you find the German word for *fish cakes*? The German word for *cod* is **der Kabeljau** – can you get it here? Does the restaurant do take-aways? How do you know?

3

STEAKRESTAURANT

Wie hätten Sie denn gern Ihr Steak?

Rumpsteak vom Grill mit Salzkartoffeln	20,00
Rumpsteak mit Gemüse der Saison und Pommes frites	22,20
Filetsteak, Röstkartoffeln und Salat	25,00
Filetsteak mit Champignons und Pommes frites	24,50
Rumpsteak „London" mit Senf und Zwiebeln	20,00
Mexikanisches Pfeffersteak mit Paprika, Champignons und Pommes frites	27,00

Endpreise

▲

Das Gemüse is *vegetables*, **die Zwiebel** is *onion*, **der Senf** is *mustard*. What do you think **der Pfeffer** is? Now choose your steak and order it!

4

▲

Süd- means *south* – where do these peaches come from? What would a kilo and a half cost? How would you ask for a pound of peaches in German?

UNIT 33

1

Wo?

Er kauft in einem Supermarkt.

Sie liegt auf dem Tisch.

Er schläft unter einem Schirm.

Er steht zwischen den Mädchen.

Er bleibt hinter dem Baum.

Er wohnt über dem Laden.

Er sitzt neben meiner Tante.

Er parkt vor der Diskothek.

Er wartet an der Tür.

Wohin?

Er fährt in einen Supermarkt.

Sie steigt auf den Tisch.

Er läuft unter einen Schirm.

Er tanzt zwischen die Mädchen.

Er läuft hinter den Baum.

Er fliegt über den Laden.

Er läuft neben meine Tante.

Er fährt vor die Diskothek.

Er klopft an die Tür.

2 Das Riesenrad

1 „Du bist zum erstenmal hier in Wien, Carol. Also, du mußt unbedingt aufs Riesenrad!"
Carol ist siebzehn und blond und kommt aus Südengland. Sie ist eine Freundin von Rainers Schwester, sie ist hier in Wien auf Urlaub und Rainer kennt sie erst seit zwei Tagen.

zum erstenmal for the first time
Wien Vienna
das Riesenrad big wheel
auf Urlaub on holiday
seit for

2 Heute sind sie im Prater, ▲
essen Zuckerwatte und
sprechen vom Riesenrad.

sprechen talk

3 ◀ „Es ist eigentlich das
Symbol von Wien wie der
Eiffelturm von Paris. Der
Ingenieur vom Riesenrad
war aber ein Engländer.
Weißt du das? Sieh mal!"
„Ja, schön, aber können
wir nicht gleich Riesenrad
fahren? Komm, ich möchte
Wien von oben sehen!"

eigentlich in fact
der Ingenieur engineer
von oben from above

4 Da warten aber viele
Leute, und bald wird Carol
sehr ungeduldig.
„Du, ich will oben im
Riesenrad sein, nicht hier
unten in der Schlange."
„Warte nur! Sei nur ein
bißchen geduldig!"
Rainer kauft die Karten,
und bald dürfen sie in die
Gondel steigen.

die Leute people
bald soon
ungeduldig impatient
unten down here
die Schlange queue
ein bißchen a bit
die Karte ticket
die Gondel gondola; car

5 Langsam dreht sich das
Rad, und bald sind sie
oben. Das Rad bleibt stehen.
„Schön, die Aussicht,"
sagt Carol. „Man sieht
ganz Wien. Aber warum
stehen wir denn so lange
hier? Warum fahren wir
nicht weiter?"

langsam slowly
dreht sich turns (itself)
bleibt stehen stops
die Aussicht view
ganz all of
weiter further

6 Da hört man von unten über den Lautsprecher: „. . . Entschuldigung, meine Damen und Herren . . . technische Fehler . . . nicht gefährlich . . . vielleicht eine halbe Stunde warten.“ „Ich glaube, du mußt wieder geduldig sein,“ sagt Rainer.

der Lautsprecher loudspeaker
der Fehler error
gefährlich dangerous
glauben think
wieder again

7 Eine Stunde später sind sie wieder auf der Erde. „Na, die Aussicht war zwar schön, aber unten in der Schlange warten, oben in der Gondel warten – das ist ja unmöglich!“ „Das ist Wien,“ sagt Rainer. „Nur keine Eile! Komm, jetzt essen wir Kuchen mit Schlagobers!“

die Erde ground
unmöglich impossible
die Eile hurry
das Schlagobers whipped cream

1 Why hasn't Carol been on the big wheel before?
Where does she come from?
How does Rainer know her?
How long has he known her?

Ist Carol zum zweitenmal in Wien?
Wohin muß sie unbedingt?
Wie alt ist sie?
Was macht sie in Wien?

2 What are they doing here, apart from eating candyfloss?

Wo sind sie heute?
Wovon sprechen sie?

3 What does Rainer compare the wheel to?
Who was Walter Basset?
Why is Carol in such a hurry?

Was möchte Carol sehen?

4 What makes Carol impatient?
What does Rainer do before they get into the gondola?

Warum wird Carol ungeduldig?
Was kauft Rainer?

5 What happens when they get to the top?
What is Carol's opinion of the view?
Why does she become impatient again?

Wie dreht sich das Rad?
Was macht es oben?
Was kann man oben sehen?

6 What is the trouble?
How do they learn of it?
Is the situation dangerous?
How long are repairs expected to take?

Was hört man über den Lautsprecher?

7 How long does it take them to reach the ground?
What excuse does Rainer offer?
What does he suggest they do next next?

Was findet Carol unmöglich?
Was wollen sie jetzt essen?

3 How does he do it?

— Und wie lange kennst du Angela?

— Angela? Ich kenne sie seit drei Wochen.

— Und Karla?

— Karla? Ja, ich ......

— Und Gisela?
— Und Andrea?
— Und Karoline?
— Und Evita?
— Und Jill?
— Und Jenny?

4 Vor/vorn; hinter/hinten; über/oben; unter/unten

1 Er steht ganz ...... in der Schlange.

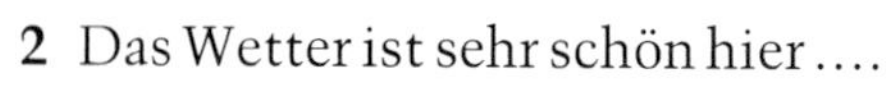

2 Das Wetter ist sehr schön hier ......

3 Er steht wie immer ...... seiner Frau.

4 Bist du ...... der Tür?

5 Prima, wir sind ......

6 Ist mein Schirm dort ...... ?

7 Ist die Katze ...... dem Wagen?

8 Die Schmidts wohnen ...... uns.

5 Recapitulation

Retell the story of **Das Riesenrad** using these pictures and this framework but without looking back to p. 101.

1 Zum erstenmal in Wien – unbedingt aufs Riesenrad – siebzehn, blond, aus England – auf Urlaub – erst seit zwei Tagen.

2 Im Prater – essen Zuckerwatte – sprechen vom Riesenrad.

DAS RIESENRAD WURDE 1896-97 VON DEM ENGLISCHEN ING. WALTER BASSET ERBAUT ES IST 64.75m HOCH SEIN GEWICHT BETRÄGT 430.05 t DIE ACHSENMITTE BEFINDET SICH 34.2m ÜBER DEM BODEN

3 Symbol von Wien – der Ingenieur ein Engländer – gleich Riesenrad fahren – Wien von oben sehen.

4 Viele Leute – bald sehr ungeduldig – warte nur – kauft die Karten – dürfen in die Gondel steigen.

5 Langsam – dreht sich – bleibt stehen – die Aussicht – sieht ganz Wien – stehen so lange – fahren nicht weiter.

6 Von unten – über den Lautsprecher – technische Fehler – nicht gefährlich – eine halbe Stunde – wieder geduldig sein.

7 Eine Stunde später – auf der Erde – unmöglich – nur keine Eile – Kuchen mit Schlagobers.

UNIT 34

1 Wo ist . . .?

Im Norden?
Im Süden?
Im Osten?
Im Westen?

Wo ist Bayern?
Dresden?
Helgoland?
Stuttgart?
das Rheinland?
Mainz?
Berlin?
München?
Hamburg?

2 Wohin von Mainz?

Wohin wollen Sie denn fahren?

......

Nach Österreich vielleicht? Nach Wien?

......

Nach Dresden vielleicht?

......

Helgoland vielleicht?

......

Bayern?

......

Ich weiß was – hier im Rheinland ist es wirklich sehr schön – bleiben Sie hier in Mainz!

Listen to the customer's answers and then see if you can produce them yourself. Then act the scene in pairs, with only the partner playing the travel agent having the full text (full text on p. 108).

3 He's decided to leave Mainz anyway!

Von Mainz Hbf

	ab	nach	an
	7.06	Düsseldorf-**Amsterdam**	12.46
Ⓐ	7.21	Düsseldorf-**Dortmund**	10.21
	7.43	München-**Berchtesgdn.**	15.14
●	7.46	Würzburg-**München**	12.22
	8.13	Hamburg-**Kopenhagen**	19.40
Ⓐ	8.20	Düsseldorf-**Dortmund**	11.22
TEE ⑤	8.32	Würzburg-**Nürnberg**	11.19
	8.43	Mannheim-**Basel SBB**	11.46
Ⓒ	9.13	Düsseldorf-**HamburgHbf**	15.19
TEE Ⓐ	9.33	Stuttgart-**München**	13.51
	9.43	München-**Innsbruck**	16.29
	10.13	Wuppertal-**Hamburg Hbf**	16.19
	10.43	Stuttgart-**München**	15.10
	11.13	Düsseldorf-**HamburgHbf**	17.21
⑤	11.13	Hamburg-**Westerl./Sylt**	20.21
	11.22	Düsseldorf-**Amsterdam**	16.56
Ⓒ	11.43	Mannheim-**Basel SBB**	14.46
Ⓒ	12.13	Düsseldorf-**HamburgHbf**	18.19
TEE	12.35	Mannheim-**Genf**	18.48
	12.43	München-**Gar.-Partenk.**	18.38
	13.13	Düsseldorf-**HamburgHbf**	19.19
Ⓒ	13.43	Stuttgart-**München**	18.10
Ⓐ	13.45	Düsseldorf-**HamburgHbf**	19.29
Ⓑ	14.13	Wuppertal-**HamburgHbf**	20.21

— Es ist neun Uhr zehn. Wann fährt der nächste Zug **nach Innsbruck?**

— In ...... Minuten.
  Um ......

— Und Ankunft in Innsbruck ist wann?

— Um ......

nach München
nach Stuttgart
nach Wuppertal
nach Hamburg

— Es ist elf Uhr einundzwanzig. Wann fährt der nächste Zug **nach Mannheim?**

— ......

— Und Ankunft in Mannheim ist wann?

— ......

nach Düsseldorf
nach Genf
nach Basel
nach Amsterdam
nach Garmisch-Partenkirchen

4 Awkward cuss, aren't you?

— Fährst du in den Norden?
nach Österreich?
......

— Nein.	Im Norden	ist es mir zu	windig
	Im Süden		kühl
	Im Osten		neblig
	Im Westen		warm
	In Österreich		heiß
	In England		schmutzig
	In Westdeutschland		kalt
	In Ostdeutschland		

5 Wohin? Nicht dahin!

1 Fliegst du 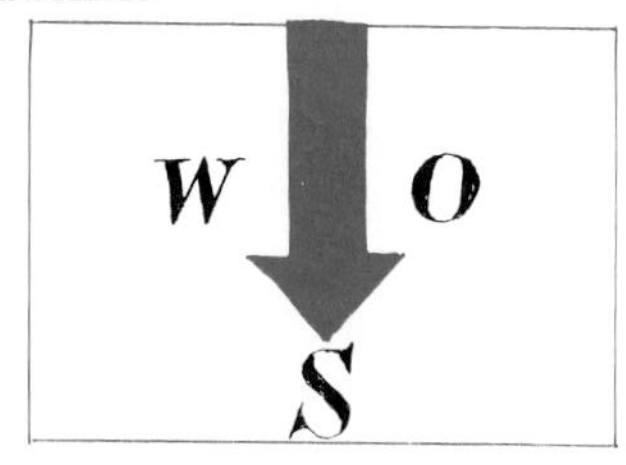

?

— Nein, in den Süden fliege ich nicht.

5 Steigst du 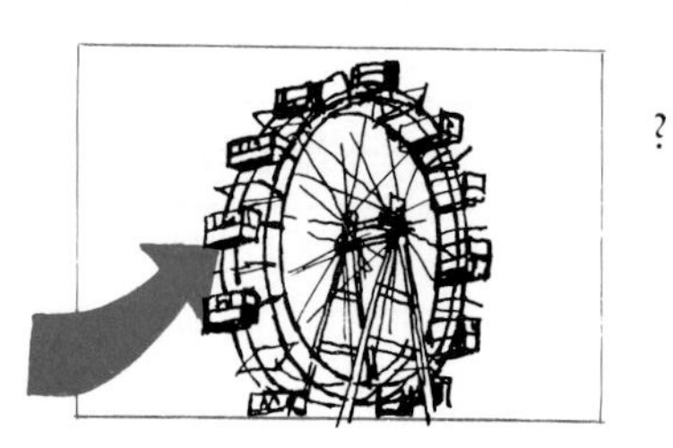 ?

2 Fährst du 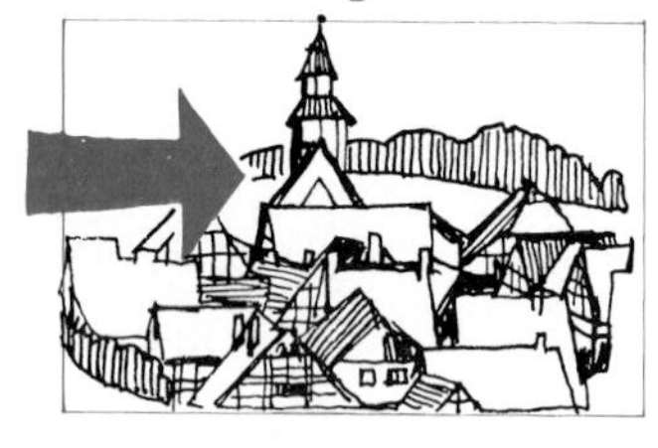 ?

— Nein, ...

6 Klopfst du 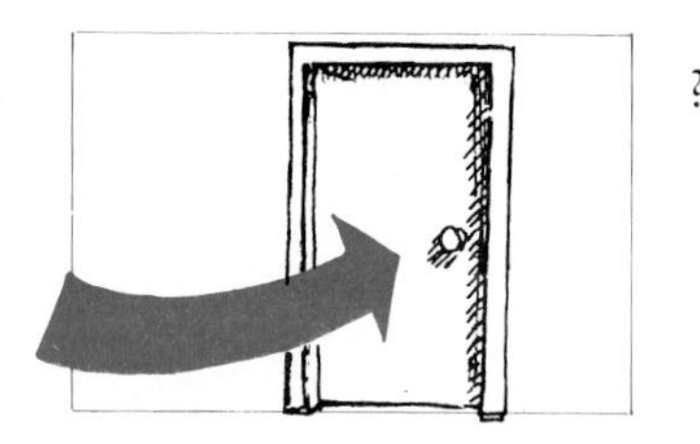 ?

3 Gehst du  ?

— ......

7 Läufst du 

?

4 Steigst du  ?

8 Fährst du 

?

2 Wohin von Mainz?

Verkäufer Wohin wollen Sie denn fahren?
Kunde Ich weiß nicht. Irgendwohin in den Süden.
Verkäufer Nach Österreich vielleicht? Nach Wien?
Kunde Nein, nicht nach Wien. Ich bleibe lieber in Deutschland.
Verkäufer Nach Dresden vielleicht?
Kunde Aber nein, nicht Ostdeutschland. Ich bleibe lieber hier in Westdeutschland.
Verkäufer Helgoland vielleicht?
Kunde Nein, im Norden ist es mir zu kalt.
Verkäufer Bayern?
Kunde Nein, im Süden ist es mir zu heiß.
Verkäufer Ich weiß was – hier im Rheinland ist es wirklich sehr schön – bleiben Sie hier in Mainz!

UNIT 35

1 Im Taxi

Taxifahrer Guten Abend! Schön heute, nicht?
Kunde Ja ja. Bitte zum Flughafen. Und so schnell wie möglich!
Taxifahrer Zum Flughafen? Wohin fliegen Sie denn?
Kunde Nach Amerika. Ich fliege um halb zehn.
Taxifahrer Halb zehn? Na, das schaff' ich spielend. Bis acht Uhr sind wir für Sie da. Sehen Sie, hier die Düsseldorfer Straße entlang – so brauchen wir nicht durch die Stadtmitte zu fahren.
Kunde Ja, aber ich muß gegen Viertel vor acht da sein.
Taxifahrer Viertel vor acht? Nein, so früh brauchen Sie noch nicht da zu sein. Bis acht sind wir bestimmt da, da haben Sie noch Zeit genug. Ihr Flugzeug fliegt nicht ohne Sie!
Kunde Sicher nicht! Ich bin der Pilot, und bis Viertel vor m u ß ich da sein!

der Flughafen airport
so . . . wie as . . . as
schaffen manage
spielend with no trouble
entlang along
durch through
die Stadtmitte town centre
früh early
die Zeit time
genug enough
das Flugzeug plane

Answer these questions, each time using a preposition:

1 Wann fliegt der Kunde?
2 Was sagt der Taxifahrer dazu?
3 Wie fahren sie zum Flughafen?
4 Warum?
5 Wann muß der Kunde am Flughafen sein?
6 Was sagt der Taxifahrer über das Flugzeug?

2 Taking a taxi

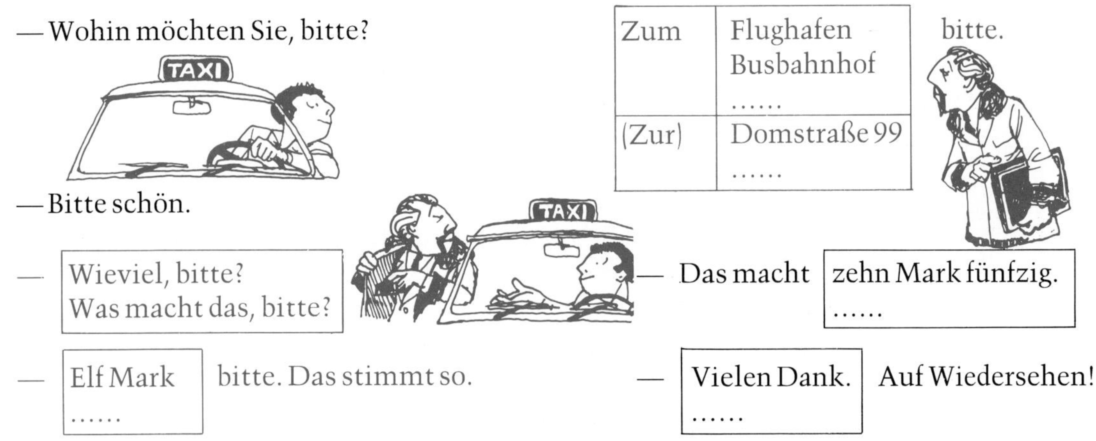

Use the above scheme to practise travel by taxi in pairs.

3 They're all turning down your invitations

Renate kommt nicht!
— Oh! Ohne sie gibt's keine Party!

Tristan ......
Die Wolfs ......
Deine Kusine ......
Werner ......
Ich ......

4 Better not to start from here?

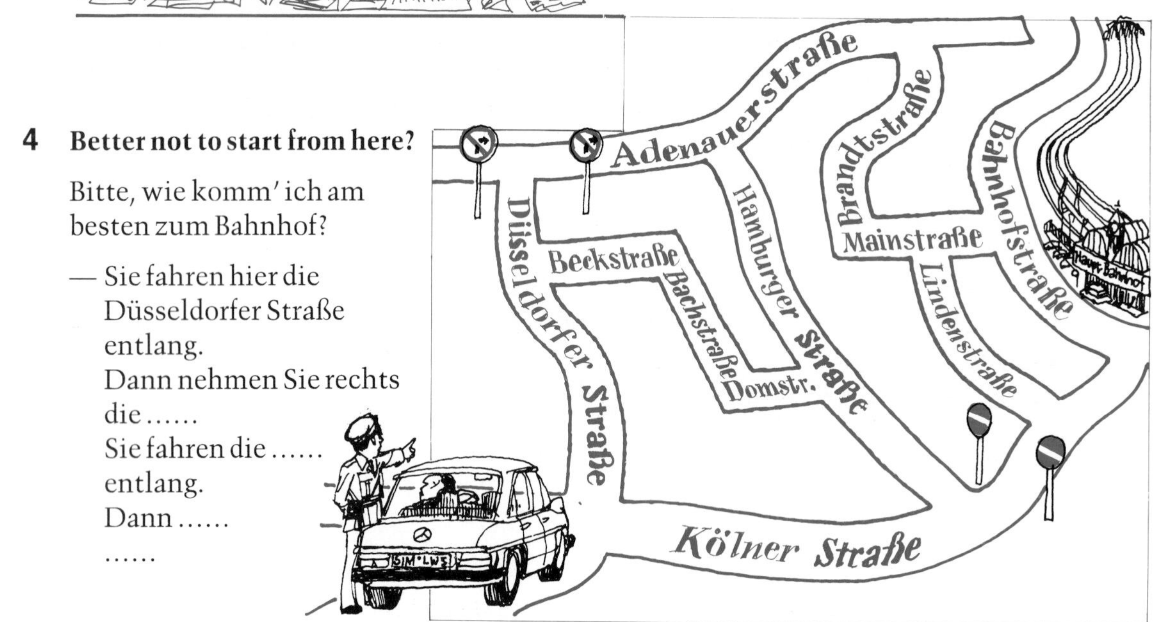

Bitte, wie komm' ich am besten zum Bahnhof?

— Sie fahren hier die Düsseldorfer Straße entlang.
Dann nehmen Sie rechts die ......
Sie fahren die ...... entlang.
Dann ......
......

5 Who gets what?

Pronoun in each answer please.

1 Ist das Bier für Karola?
— { Nein, es ist nicht für ......
  { Ja, es ist für ......

2 Ist der Rotwein für Lothar?
3 Ist die Milch für Roberta?
4 Ist der Weißwein für Manfred?
5 Sind die Colas für Magda und Pamela?
6 Ist der Champagner für Barbara?
7 Ist die Rechnung für mich?

UNIT 36 REVISION

Grammar

1 Prepositions + accusative/dative

Er geht zum Supermarkt.
Es liegt rechts von der Tankstelle.

Prepositions we met before unit 33 were followed by the dative case. This is by far the most common case after prepositions in German. However, a small group of prepositions can sometimes indicate *motion towards* and sometimes not. When they do indicate this, they take the accusative; when not, they take the dative. These prepositions are **in, an, auf, unter, über, vor, hinter, neben, zwischen**.

Er fährt in die Garage – motion *towards* (*into* the garage)
Er kauft im Supermarkt – may involve motion, but not *towards* (*in* the supermarket).

Note that **zu** and **nach**, in spite of the fact that they can indicate motion towards, are not members of this group of prepositions. **Zu** and **nach** always take the dative.

2 Prepositions + accusative

Er geht durch die Tür. Bis morgen. Die Straße entlang.

A further small group of prepositions *always* take the accusative case. With these prepositions the question of motion towards or not does not arise. They are **durch, für, um, ohne, entlang, gegen, bis**. The last two are most often met followed by expressions of time, in which the case is not usually evident. **Entlang** normally follows its noun.

3 The accusative forms **das, den** contract with certain prepositions (compare dative contractions, unit 24:2). The form **ins** (= **in das**) is almost always used in both spoken and written German unless the article is stressed; the neuter accusative forms **aufs, durchs, fürs, hinters, übers, ums, unters, vors** and the masculine accusative forms **hintern, übern, untern** are extremely common in spoken German and may also be found in modern printed German.

4 Wo bist du? Wohin gehst du?

In English we often use *where?* to mean *where to?* In German *where* with motion towards must always be **wohin**. The same applies with **da** (*there*) and **dahin** (*to there*).

der Urlaub holiday
der Turm (¨-e) tower
der Ingenieur (-e) engineer
der Engländer (-) Englishman
der Lautsprecher (-) loudspeaker
der Fehler (-) mistake
der Zug (¨-e) train
der Taxifahrer (-) taxi driver
der Abend (-e) evening
der Flughafen (¨) airport
der Pilot (-en) pilot
der Bahnhof (¨-e) station

die Tür (-en) door
die Schlange (-n) snake
die Karte (-n) ticket
die Gondel (-n) gondola; car
die Aussicht view
die Erde earth; ground
die Ankunft arrival
die Stadtmitte town centre
die Zeit (-en) time
die Kusine (-n) girl cousin
die Party (-s) party

das Riesenrad (¨-er) big wheel
Wien Vienna
England England
das Symbol (-e) symbol
München Munich
Bayern Bavaria
das Rheinland Rhineland
Österreich Austria
Deutschland Germany
Basel Basle
Genf Geneva
Amerika America
das Flugzeug (-e) aircraft
das Taxi (-s) taxi

die Leute (*plural*) people

klopfen knock
fliegen fly
laufen run
sprechen speak
steigen climb; get
glauben think
schaffen manage
es dreht sich it turns
es bleibt stehen it stops

über over; about
neben near

5 Nach Deutschland, nach Bonn.
In Deutschland, in Bonn.

To with names of towns and countries is **nach**, *in* is **in**.

In die Schweiz, in der Schweiz (*to Switzerland, in Switzerland*)

Almost all country names are neuter; with the very few feminine names *to* is **in die**, *in* is **in der**.

6 The compass points are **der Norden, der Süden, der Osten, der Westen**. Used attributively they lose their **-en: Westdeutschland**; **im Nordwesten**. Notice: **ich fahre in den Norden** (*to the north*).

7 Ich kenne sie seit drei Wochen – *I've known her for three weeks*.

English has a past tense in this expression, whereas German keeps a simple present (the logic of the German is 'I've known her for three weeks *and I still know her at the moment*').

8 New strong verbs are:

laufen: du läufst, er läuft
sprechen: du sprichst, er spricht.

zum erstenmal for the first time
blond blonde; fair
seit for
eigentlich in fact
oben on top; up there
unten at the bottom; down there
bald soon
geduldig patient
ein bißchen a bit
langsam slowly
ganz all of
weiter further
technisch technical
gefährlich dangerous
wieder again
später later
möglich possible
irgendwo(hin) somewhere
so . . . wie as . . . as
spielend easily; with no trouble
durch through
entlang along
früh early
genug enough
am besten best

A Interpret the pictures to complete the text.

Udo geht durch 

und 

entlang, dann geht er vor 

hinter 

, zwischen zwei 

und steht endlich vor 

Dort wartet er bis  aber Kerstin kommt nicht. Um  geht er sehr langsam

über und steht eine Zeitlang unter  . Es beginnt zu regnen. „Was mache

ich ohne m . . . . . .  ?“ sagt Udo. „Soll ich in 

gehen, oder in 

,

oder trinke ich irgendwo ein Bier?“ Plötzlich sieht er Kerstin – sie steht neben 

!

B Wo oder wohin?

1 ...... bist du jetzt?
2 ...... liegt der Hund also?
3 ...... geht er heute?
4 ...... war deine Strickjacke?
5 ...... läuft er? Auf der Straße?
6 ...... fährt der Zug?
7 ...... spielt man Tennis?
8 ...... darf ich parken, bitte?
9 ...... läuft er? In die Bäckerei?
10 ...... fliegst du morgen?

C

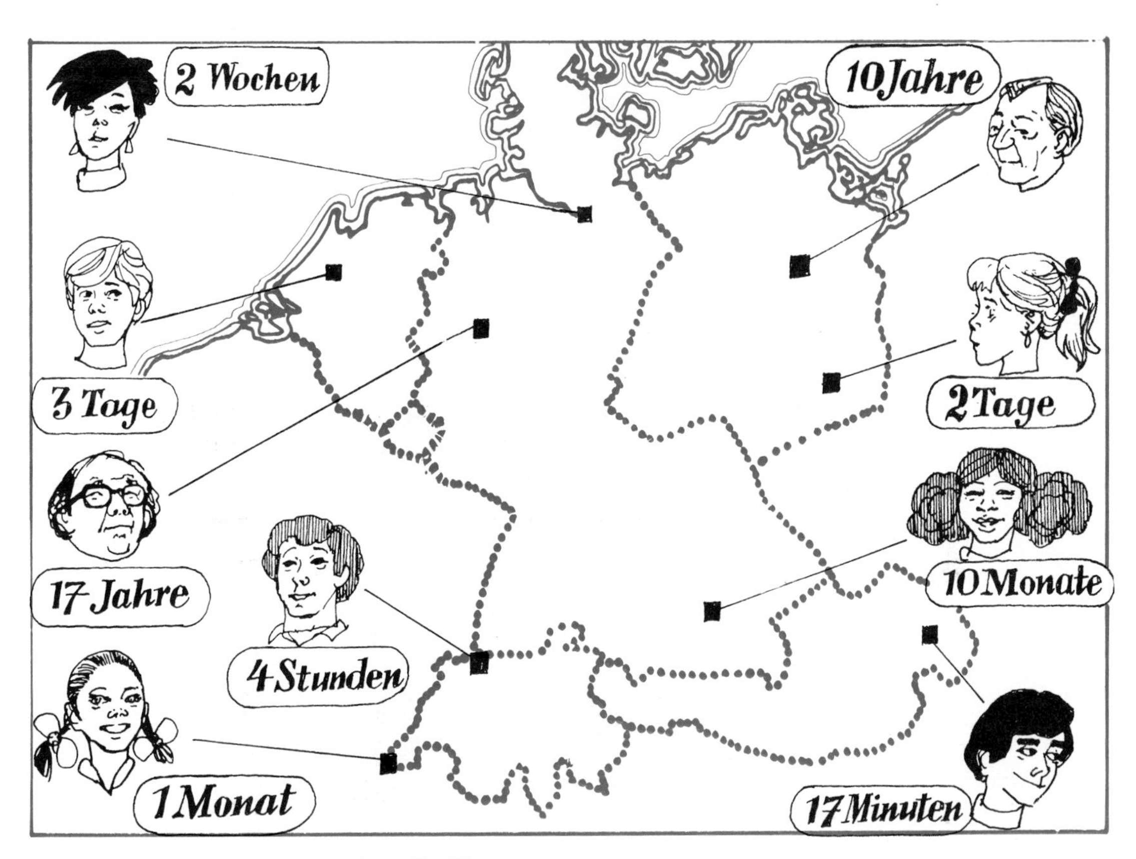

— Seit wann bist du in Amsterdam, Rudi?
— Ich bin seit drei Tagen in Amsterdam.

in Köln, Günter?
in München, Anneliese?
in Basel, Ueli?
in Genf, Heidi?
in Hamburg, Lili?
in Wien, Johann?
in Berlin, Peter?
in Dresden, Gisela?

D

Correct these statements:

1 Ostdeutschland liegt im Südwesten von Europa.
2 Frankreich liegt im Osten.
3 England liegt im Südosten.
4 Holland liegt im Süden.
5 Die Schweiz liegt im Norden.
6 Österreich liegt im Nordwesten.
7 Westdeutschland liegt im Süden.

E Wohin fährt Franz?

Zuerst fährt er ......
Und dann ......
Und dann ......

F Im Reisebüro

Verkäufer Wohin wollen Sie denn?
Kunde Ich weiß nicht. Irgendwohin in den Süden.
Verkäufer Vielleicht ......

Complete at least eight lines of this dialogue. Try to use as much of the material in the dialogue in unit 34 as you can remember, and make the rest up. Don't look back to unit 34, try to use only German that you know, and don't translate from English!

UNIT 37

1 **Good morning!**

1 Sie wacht auf (sie ist im Schlafzimmer).

2 Er steht auf.

3 Er zieht seinen Bademantel an.

4 Sie wäscht sich im Badezimmer.

5 Er rasiert sich vor einem Spiegel.

6 Er setzt seine Brille auf.

7 Er macht die Tür auf und geht hastig in die Küche.

2 Ein Kater!

Sieben Uhr! Herr Weber wacht auf, macht erst ein Auge auf, dann das andere, steht sehr langsam auf, zieht seinen Bademantel an und geht ins Badezimmer. Herr Weber ist weitsichtig: er sucht seine Brille im Bademantel und setzt sie auf. Dann sieht er sich im Spiegel. Hastig setzt er die Brille wieder ab. O weh! Gestern abend war er auf einer Party, und das kann man heute noch sehr deutlich sehen. Langsam wäscht er sich, sehr langsam rasiert er sich (das könnte heute gefährlich sein!). Dann setzt er seine Brille wieder auf. Hm. Nicht viel besser. Er geht ins Schlafzimmer zurück. Au, sein Kopf! Er sucht sich ein Hemd und eine Hose aus. Dunkel, schön dunkel. Und eine Jacke, auch dunkel. Er zieht sie an, geht in die Küche und trinkt eine Tasse Kaffee. Plötzlich sieht er seine Sonnenbrille auf dem Tisch. Er setzt die Brille wieder ab und die Sonnenbrille auf. Wunderbar! Alles wieder dunkel, schön dunkel wie im Schlaf!
„Jetzt kann der Tag beginnen," sagt Herr Weber.

andere other
weitsichtig long-sighted
suchen look for
absetzen take off
o weh oh dear
deutlich clearly
könnte could
der Kopf head
aussuchen choose
dunkel dark
der Schlaf sleep

1 Was macht Herr Weber um sieben Uhr?
2 Was macht er auf?
3 Wie steht er auf?
4 Was macht er mit der Brille?
5 Was macht er hastig?
6 Was setzt er wieder auf?
7 Wohin geht er?
8 Was sucht er sich aus?
9 Was macht er damit?
10 Was macht er mit der Brille und der Sonnenbrille?

3 It's the same every morning!

1 Sieben Uhr! Was muß man tun?
—...... aufwachen.

2 Und dann?
—Dann ...... die Augen aufmachen.

3 aufstehen
4 sich waschen
(5 sich rasieren)
6 Kleidung aussuchen
7 den Pyjama ausziehen
8 die Sachen anziehen

4 Do I have to?

1 Muß ich gleich aufstehen?
—Ja, steh gleich auf!

2 jetzt zurückgehen?
3 die Jacke ausziehen
4 die Tür aufmachen
5 den Mantel anziehen
6 früh aufwachen
7 eine Hose aussuchen

UNIT 38

1 In der Küche

Elke	Versuch du mal, dieses Gurkenglas zu öffnen. Ich kann's nicht.	**versuchen** try **das Gurkenglas** jar of pickled gherkins **leicht** easy
Carina	Du, es ist aber nicht leicht, dieses Glas zu öffnen. Mußt du wirklich das Glas aufmachen?	
Elke	Aber sicher! Ich brauche die Gurken unbedingt.	
Carina	Ich glaube, der Deckel beginnt locker zu werden. Versuch du nochmal, ihn abzumachen.	**der Deckel** lid **locker** loose **nochmal** again **abmachen** remove **völlig** completely
Elke	Ich kann nicht. Es ist völlig unmöglich, dieses Glas aufzumachen.	
Carina	Brauchst du die Gurken wirklich?	
Elke	Tja, ich weiß es nicht . . .	
Carina	Es ist bestimmt ungesund, zu viele Gurken zu essen.	
Elke	Ja, das stimmt.	
Carina	Und es ist eigentlich auch nicht richtig, Gurken mit Sauerkraut zu essen.	
Elke	Eben. Es ist viel besser, die Gurken im Glas zu lassen!	**eben** quite right
Carina	Das machen wir! Du brauchst das Glas nicht mehr aufzumachen – Gurken schmecken mir sowieso nicht!	

1 Was soll Carina versuchen?
2 Was ist nicht leicht?
3 Was glaubt Carina?
4 Was soll Elke nochmal versuchen?
5 Was ist völlig unmöglich?
6 Was soll ungesund sein?
7 Was ist nicht richtig?
8 Was ist viel besser?
9 Was braucht Elke nicht mehr zu tun?

2 Combine

1 (Er macht das Glas auf.)
Er versucht ......
Er versucht, das Glas a......

2 (Er ißt zu viele Gurken.)
Es ist möglich ......

3 (Er macht den Deckel ab.)
Er braucht nicht ......

4 (Er läßt alles im Glas.)
Es ist besser ......

5 (Er ißt Gurken mit Sauerkraut.)
Es ist nicht richtig ......

6 (Er trinkt zu viel Bier.)
Es ist ungesund ......

3 No chance!

1 Stehst du endlich auf?
—Nein, ich kann nicht ......

2 Klopfst du?
—Nein, ich brauche nicht ......

3 Fährst du heute?
—Nein, es ist nicht nötig ......

4 Steigst du aus?
—Nein, ich will nicht ......

5 Trinkst du Kaffee?
—Nein, ich darf keinen ......

6 Parkst du hier?
—Nein, es ist unmöglich ......

7 Holst du mich ab?
—Nein, ich soll dich nicht ......

4 Write the sentences in the correct order

so that they correspond to the order of the pictures.

Wo befindet sich die Küche, bitte?
Bitte, setzen Sie sich!
Ich möchte mich rasieren, bitte.
Interessierst du dich für Elefanten?
Sie fragt sich, was sie ißt.
Möchtest du dich waschen?
Wollen Sie bitte sich hinlegen?

UNIT 39

1 Who and where?

Listen to each dialogue twice and then decide who is speaking, or where they are.

1 Where are they?
- a on a battlefield
- b on the street
- c in the town centre

erst not before

2 Who are they?
- a two lovers
- b two children
- c two strangers

3 Where are they?
- a in a chemist's
- b at the doctor's
- c in a flat

es tut weh it hurts

4 Who are they?
- a husband and wife
- b baths attendant and lady swimmer
- c lady hairdresser and client

5 Where are they?
- a in an aircraft
- b in an airport
- c at a careers interview

überhaupt nicht not at all

6 Who are they?
- a young man and launderette attendant
- b mother and son
- c waitress and diner

sofort right away
fertig ready

7 Where are they?
- a on a fairground
- b in a slow-moving bus
- c on bicycles

natürlich naturally

8 Who are they?
- a garage mechanic and customer
- b young man and his aunt
- c lady and information kiosk assistant

nun (well) now

1

1 — Wo ist die nächste Tankstelle, bitte?
— Ach, die befindet sich erst in der Stadtmitte!

2 — Wollen Sie sich hier an den Tisch setzen?
— Danke, ich stehe lieber.

3 — Au, mein Kopf tut weh! Darf ich mich irgendwo hier in der Wohnung hinlegen?
— Aber bitte! Wollen Sie auch Aspirin nehmen?

4 — Liebling! Du bist seit einer Stunde im Badezimmer. Ich möchte mich rasieren!
— Ja, ja, Helmut, ich komme gleich!

5 — Möchtest du Pilot werden?
— Oh nein, ich interessiere mich überhaupt nicht für Flugzeuge.

6 — Ich brauche mich aber nicht zu waschen!
— Aber doch! Geh ins Badezimmer und wasch dich sofort! Das Abendessen ist fertig!

7 — Es dreht sich aber sehr langsam, nicht wahr?
— Ja, natürlich – ein Riesenrad dreht sich nie schnell.

8 — Der Wagen ist kaputt. Ich frage mich, was ich jetzt mache.
— Nun, Tante Trude, da mußt du eben mit dem Bus fahren.

2 Isn't it obvious?

1 Warum wartest du hier?
—Um ins Badezimmer zu gehen!
2 Und warum willst du ins Badezimmer gehen? —Um ...... zu ......
3 Und warum willst du dich rasieren?
—Um ...... zu ......
4 Und warum willst du in die Stadt gehen?
—Um ...... zu ......
5 Und warum willst du Hannelore treffen?
—Um ...... zu ......
6 Und warum willst du in die Diskothek gehen? —Um ...... zu ......
7 Und warum willst du mit Hannelore tanzen? —Sei nicht so albern – ich hab' sie gern!

3 Oh my head!

„Mein Kopf tut weh! Ich muß ein Aspirin nehmen!"
„Dann mußt du zur Apotheke gehen – Aspirin haben wir nicht im Haus."
„Ich bin aber viel zu krank, um zur Apotheke zu gehen. Ich sollte mich eigentlich hinlegen. Au, mein Kopf! Au! Au!"
„Du solltest versuchen, nicht so viel Lärm zu machen!"
„Aber mein Kopf tut so weh! Haben wir wirklich kein Aspirin da? Ist es wirklich nötig, zur Apotheke zu gehen?"
„Das kommt darauf an. Spalt-Tabletten haben wir, und Gelonida, und Melabon. Aber kein Aspirin. Um Aspirin zu bekommen, mußt du schon zur Apotheke gehen!"

1 Was muß der Junge haben?
2 Wohin muß er gehen?
3 Wozu ist er zu krank?
4 Was sollte er eigentlich tun?
5 Was sollte er machen?
6 Ist es wirklich nötig, zur Apotheke zu gehen?
7 Warum?

4 Not too ill for anything!

—Du bist nicht zu krank, um Tennis zu spielen!

—Nein, aber ich bin zu krank, um abzuwaschen!

Here, mixed together, are some possible suggestions and excuses. You can add more of your own.

Abendbrot machen; tanzen gehen; die Wohnung putzen; ins Kino gehen; aufstehen; Filetsteak essen; ein Bad nehmen; in die Stadt gehen; Bier trinken; die Hausarbeit machen; Platten spielen; auf die Party gehen.

UNIT 40 REVISION

Grammar

1 Separable verbs

aufstehen – ich stehe auf
anziehen – ich ziehe an

A large number of verbs in German are formed from a prefix – usually a preposition – and a verb. When used as an infinitive these stand together:

Ich muß meine Jacke **anziehen.**

When the infinitive is used with **zu** the **zu** goes between the prefix and the verb:

Du brauchst deine Jacke nicht **anzuziehen.**

But when the verb is used as a full main verb, the prefix separates and goes to the end of the clause:

Ich **stehe auf** und **ziehe** meine Sachen **an**.

The prefix takes the main pronunciation stress of the verb, wherever it stands.

Prefixes we have so far met are **auf-**, **aus-**, **an-**, **ein-** (= *in*), **zurück-** (= *back*), **ab-** (= *off*), **hin-** (= *down*).

Many (but not all) of these German separable verbs correspond to English 'prepositional' verbs: **aufwachen** – *wake up*; **aussteigen** – *get out*; **anziehen** – *put on*.

2 Reflexive verbs

Ich frage mich – *I ask myself*

Verbs with the same subject and object are called reflexive verbs. The reflexive object pronouns (= English *myself, yourself*, etc.) are the same, in the **ich, du, wir, ihr** forms of the verb, as the normal object pronouns; otherwise the reflexive pronoun is **sich**:

ich frage mich	wir fragen uns
du fragst dich	ihr fragt euch
Sie fragen sich	
er, sie, es fragt sich	sie fragen sich

Note that in the **Sie** (= *you*) form, **sich** has a small letter, not a capital.

der Bademantel (¨) dressing gown
der Spiegel (-) mirror
der Kopf (¨e) head
der Schlaf sleep
der Pyjama (-s) (pair of) pyjamas
der Deckel (-) lid
der Elefant (-en) elephant
der Lärm noise
der Junge (-n) boy
der Kater (-) tom-cat; hangover

die Küche (-n) kitchen
die Kleidung clothes
die Gurke (-n) gherkin
die Tablette (-n) tablet

das Badezimmer (-) bathroom
das Schlafzimmer (-) bedroom
das Glas (¨er) jar
das Aspirin aspirin

aufwachen wake up
aufmachen open
aufstehen get up
anziehen put on (*clothes*)
ausziehen take off (*clothes*)
aufsetzen put on (*glasses*)
absetzen take off (*glasses*)
suchen look for
sich waschen wash
sich rasieren shave
könnte could; might
zurückgehen go back
aussuchen choose
versuchen try
abmachen remove
aussteigen get out
sich befinden be (situated)
sich setzen sit down
sich interessieren für be interested in
sich fragen ask oneself; wonder
sich hinlegen lie down
ankommen auf (+ *acc.*) depend on
abwaschen wash up
weh tun hurt
treffen meet
gern haben like (*someone*)

andere other
weitsichtig long-sighted
hastig hastily
au! ouch!
deutlich clear

3 Infinitives

With the modal verbs the infinitive is used without **zu**:

Ich muß gehen . . . Ich möchte sagen . . .

With other verbs it is used with **zu**:

Ich versuche zu gehen . . . Es ist nötig zu sagen . . .

Where the meaning is *in order to*, **um . . . zu** is used:

Ich rasiere mich, um in die Stadt zu gehen.

Notice the word order in this expression: **um** is always at the very beginning after the obligatory comma, **zu** immediately in front of the infinitive.

Ich bin zu krank, um zur Apotheke zu gehen – *too ill to go* . . .

In this construction with **zu** meaning *too, to* is always **um . . . zu**.

dunkel dark
leicht easy
locker loose
völlig completely
sowieso in any case
eben exactly; quite right; just
o weh! oh dear!
nochmal again
nötig necessary
etwas something
wozu what for; for what
überhaupt . . . . . . at all
natürlich naturally
sofort right away
fertig ready
erst not before
nun (well) now

4 New strong verbs are:

treffen: du triffst, er trifft
tun: ich tue, du tust, er tut, wir tun, ihr tut, sie tun
waschen: du wäschst, er wäscht

and notice **setzen**: du setzt.

A

1 Du solltest Maria einladen.
— Gut, ich lade sie ein.

2 Du solltest das Fenster aufmachen.
3 Du solltest deinen Regenmantel anziehen.
4 Du solltest mein Geschenk aussuchen.
5 Du solltest Onkel Franz abholen.
6 Du solltest den Deckel abmachen.
7 Du solltest für mich abwaschen.
8 Du solltest dich eine Zeitlang hinlegen.
9 Du solltest am Bahnhof aussteigen.

B

1 Ich interessiere mich für Fußball. Und ihr i...... auch ......
2 Ihre Wagen befinden sich auf dem Parkplatz. Und mein Wagen ......
3 Du setzt dich nicht! Und wir ......
4 Fritz rasiert sich zweimal am Tag. Und ich ......
5 Sie legen sich hin. Und du ......
6 Ich frage mich, wo wir sind! Und Sie ...... !
7 Deine Tochter wäscht sich nicht! Und deine Söhne ......

C

1. Steig' ich hier aus? Ja, du mußt ......
2. Darf ich abwaschen? Nein, du brauchst nicht ......
3. Rasiere ich mich oder nicht? Ja, ...
4. Stehe ich morgen sehr früh auf? Nein, ...
5. Zieh' ich einen Pullover an? Ja, ...
6. Soll ich mich hinlegen? Nein, ...
7. Mach' ich die Flasche auf? Ja, ...
8. Soll ich den Deckel abmachen? Nein, ...
9. Wasch' ich mich vor dem Essen? Ja, ...

D Warum willst du in die Stadt gehen? Invent reasons based on these verbs and using **Um . . . zu**:

1. Brot kaufen
2. Tennis spielen
3. Peter treffen
4. ins Kino gehen
5. mit Susi auf eine Party gehen
6. im Restaurant essen
7. ein Geschenk für meine Großeltern kaufen
8. Friedel vom Bahnhof abholen

E Listen to Herr Weber getting up again (unit 37 section 2) and then write your version of it using this outline and getting as close to the original as you can.

Aufwachen – Augen aufmachen – langsam aufstehen – Bademantel anziehen – ins Badezimmer gehen – weitsichtig – Brille suchen, aufsetzen – wieder absetzen – gestern abend auf einer Party – sich langsam waschen – sich sehr langsam rasieren – Brille wieder aufsetzen – ins Schlafzimmer zurückgehen – Hemd und Hose aussuchen – anziehen – Kaffee trinken – Sonnenbrille sehen – Brille wieder absetzen – Sonnenbrille aufsetzen – schön dunkel – „der Tag kann beginnen".

F Some parking problems!

◀

1 Wann ist es unmöglich, hier zu parken?
Darf man hier mittwochs um halb neun parken?

▶

2 Wann darf man hier nicht parken?
Wann ist es am Mittwochnachmittag möglich, hier zu parken?

3 Du hast einen Lastkraftwagen – kannst du hier parken? ▼

4 Wie lange darf man hier parken? Muß man auch abends zahlen? ▼

5 Wie lange darf man freitags hier parken? Ist es erlaubt, sonntags hier zu parken? ▼

▲
6 Du hast einen Opel Ascona – ist es erlaubt, ihn hier zu parken?

▲
7 Ist es verboten, hier zu parken? Was muß man auch machen?

das Fahrzeug vehicle
höchst highest; greatest
die Dauer period
sauberhalten keep clean
werktags on weekdays
der Lastkraftwagen heavy goods vehicle
erlaubt allowed
verboten forbidden

UNIT 41

1 What's in a name?

„Schmidt und Söhne!"
„Hallo! Wer ist am Apparat, bitte?"
„Herr Schillinger."
„Ach so. Ich möchte Herrn Eibl-Eibesfeldt sprechen, bitte."
„Wen, bitte?"
„Herrn Eibl-Eibesfeldt. E – I – B – L – Bindestrich – E – I – B – E – S – F – E – L – D – T. Eibl-Eibesfeldt."
„Nein, es gibt niemand mit diesem Namen hier."
„Ist Frau Domagk da?"
„Wer, bitte?"
„Frau Ida Domagk. D – O – M – A – G – K. Kann ich sie sprechen, bitte?"
„Domagk? Nein, Frau Domagk kenn' ich nicht. Wir haben eine Frau Ida Lehnigk. L – E – H – N – I – G – K."
„Nein, das ist sie nicht. Also, ist Herr Quadflieg da? Kann ich i h n sprechen?"
„Herr . . . ?"
„Q wie Quelle, U wie Ulrich, A wie Anton, D wie . . . ach, lassen wir das! Verbinden Sie mich mit Herrn Schmidt, bitte, oder mit einem von seinen Söhnen!"

am Apparat 'speaking'
der Bindestrich hyphen
niemand nobody
verbinden connect

Read the dialogue aloud, first in chorus after the tape, then in pairs.

2 Here are the standard German equivalents for the letters of the alphabet when speaking over the telephone, etc. Learn to spell your own surname with its equivalents by heart.

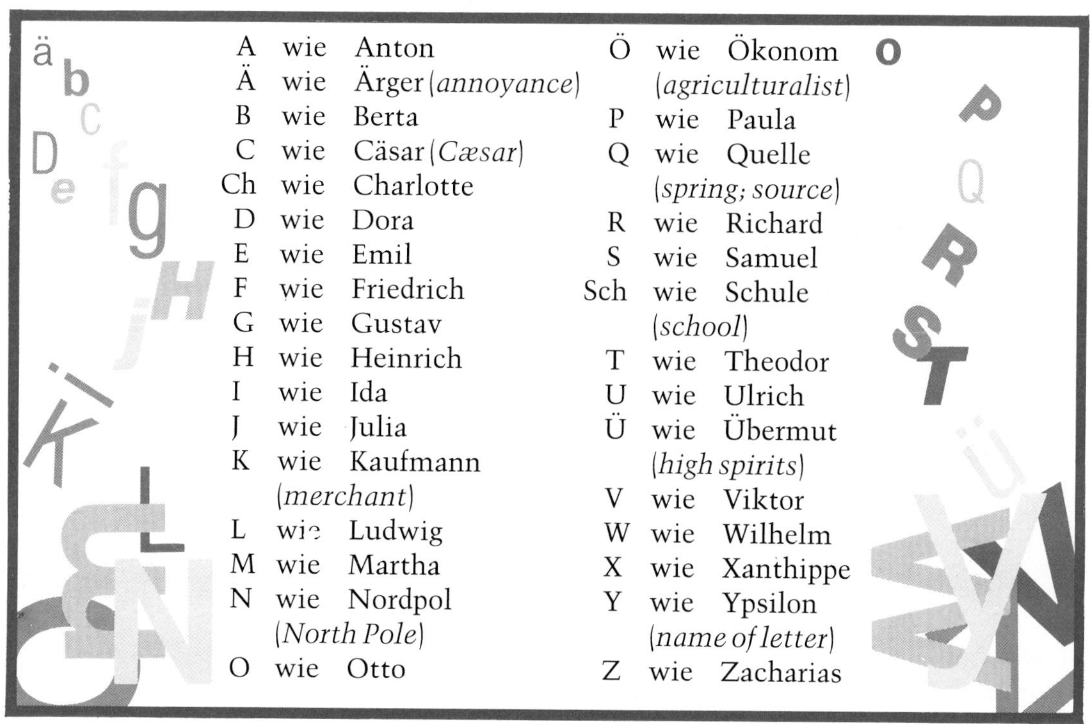

A	wie	Anton
Ä	wie	Ärger (*annoyance*)
B	wie	Berta
C	wie	Cäsar (*Cæsar*)
Ch	wie	Charlotte
D	wie	Dora
E	wie	Emil
F	wie	Friedrich
G	wie	Gustav
H	wie	Heinrich
I	wie	Ida
J	wie	Julia
K	wie	Kaufmann (*merchant*)
L	wie	Ludwig
M	wie	Martha
N	wie	Nordpol (*North Pole*)
O	wie	Otto
Ö	wie	Ökonom (*agriculturalist*)
P	wie	Paula
Q	wie	Quelle (*spring; source*)
R	wie	Richard
S	wie	Samuel
Sch	wie	Schule (*school*)
T	wie	Theodor
U	wie	Ulrich
Ü	wie	Übermut (*high spirits*)
V	wie	Viktor
W	wie	Wilhelm
X	wie	Xanthippe
Y	wie	Ypsilon (*name of letter*)
Z	wie	Zacharias

Beware of the difficult letters: E,I,J,V,W,Y.

3 Any excuse will do!

—Hallo! Kann ich Herrn Schmidt sprechen, bitte?

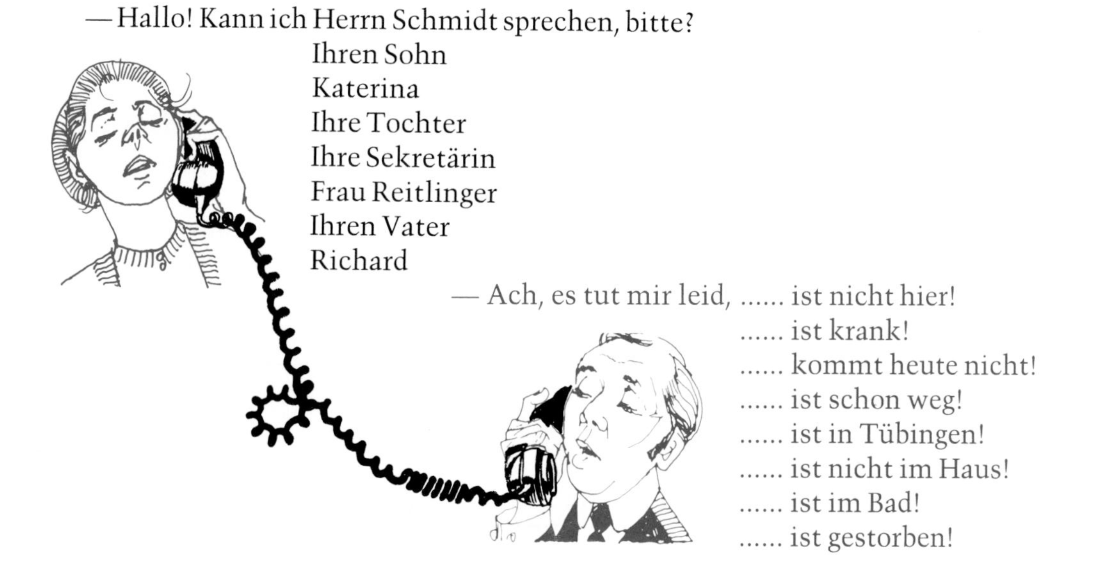

Ihren Sohn
Katerina
Ihre Tochter
Ihre Sekretärin
Frau Reitlinger
Ihren Vater
Richard

— Ach, es tut mir leid, ... ist nicht hier!
...... ist krank!
...... kommt heute nicht!
...... ist schon weg!
...... ist in Tübingen!
...... ist nicht im Haus!
...... ist im Bad!
...... ist gestorben!

4 Buchstabieren Sie diese deutschen Städte und Inseln!

5 Hold this phone conversation in pairs. Choose (or make up!) any names you like, but when you spell them give the equivalent for each letter.

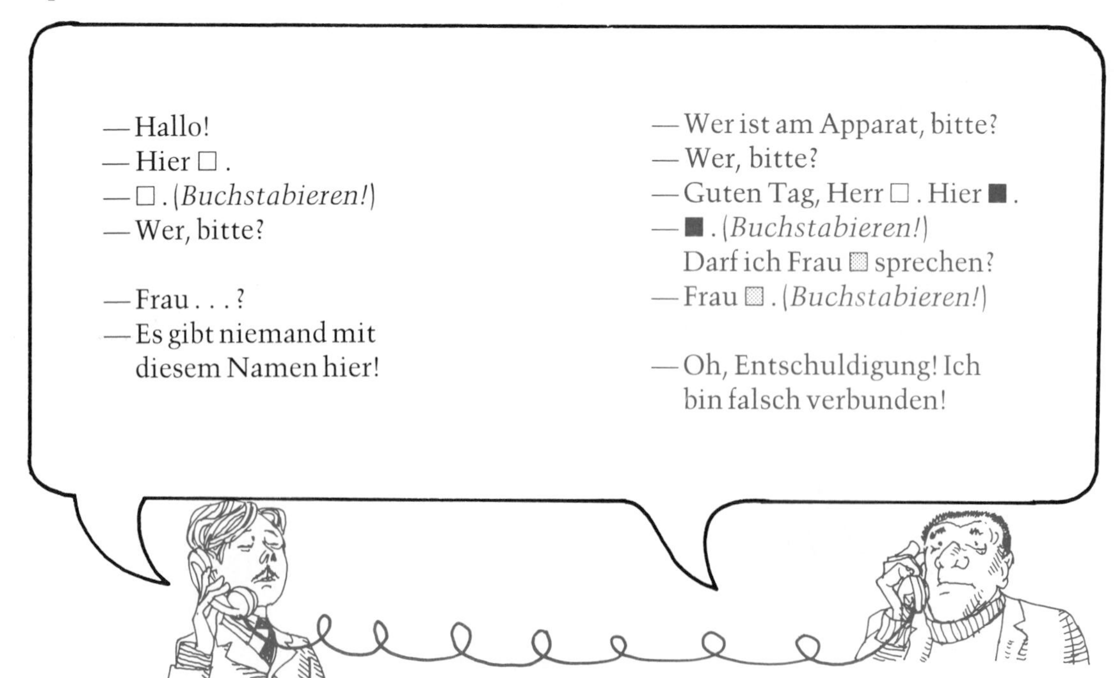

1

Die Möbel

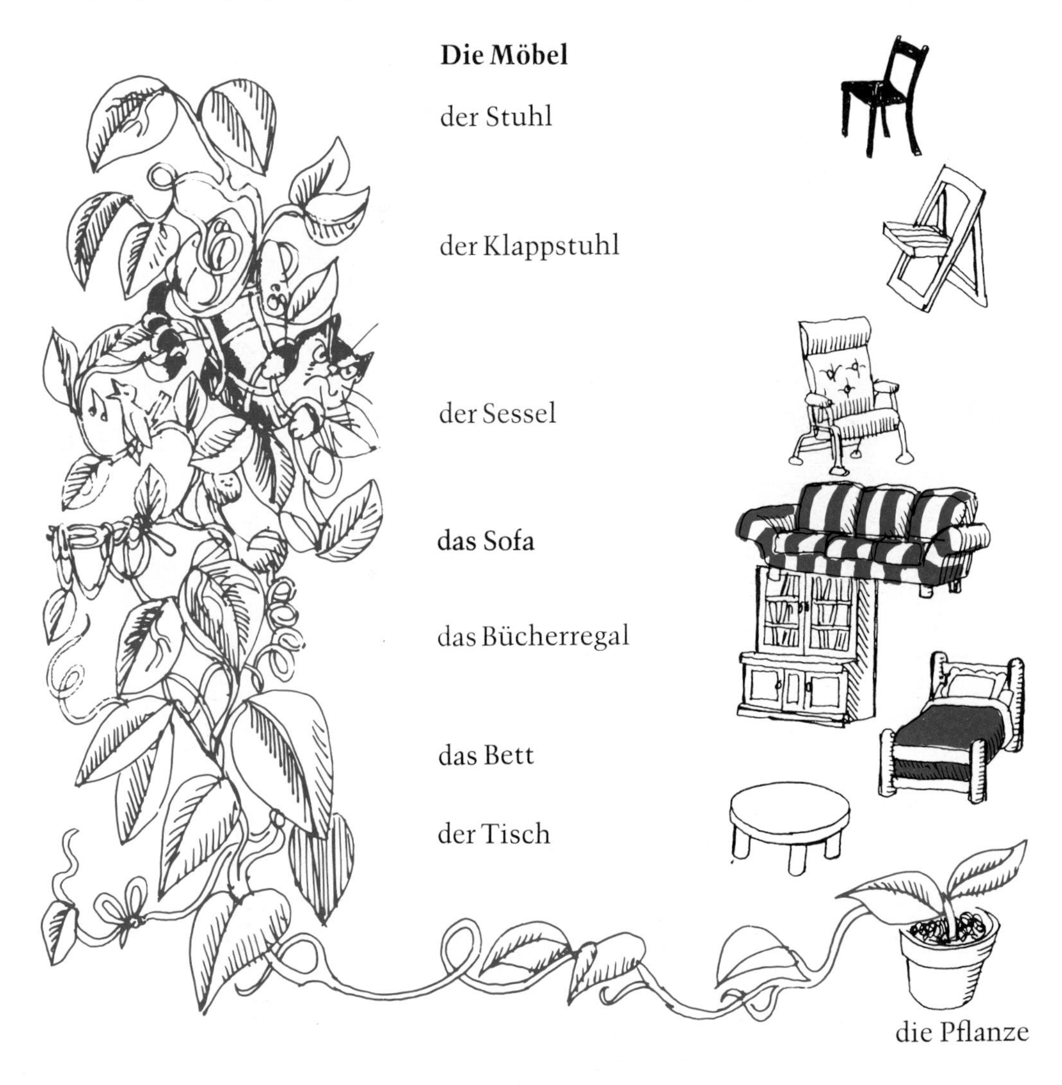

Adjective endings

A

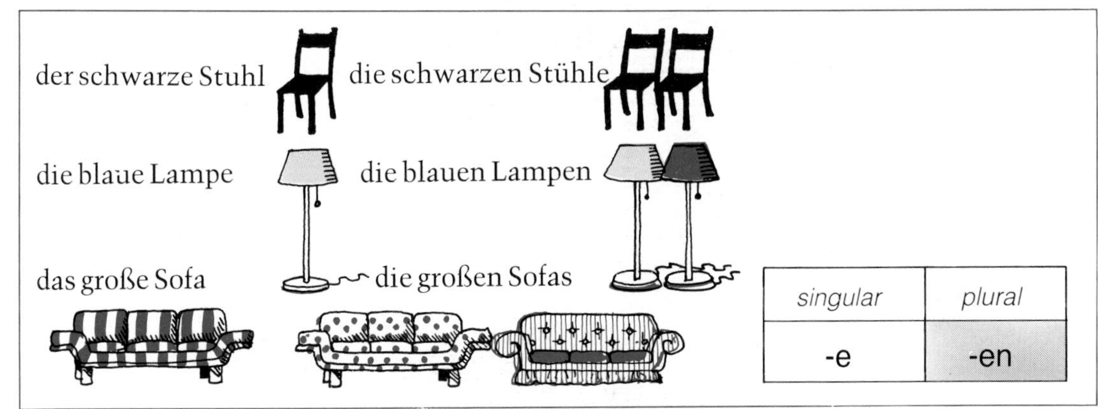

singular	*plural*
-e	-en

2 Die neue Wohnung

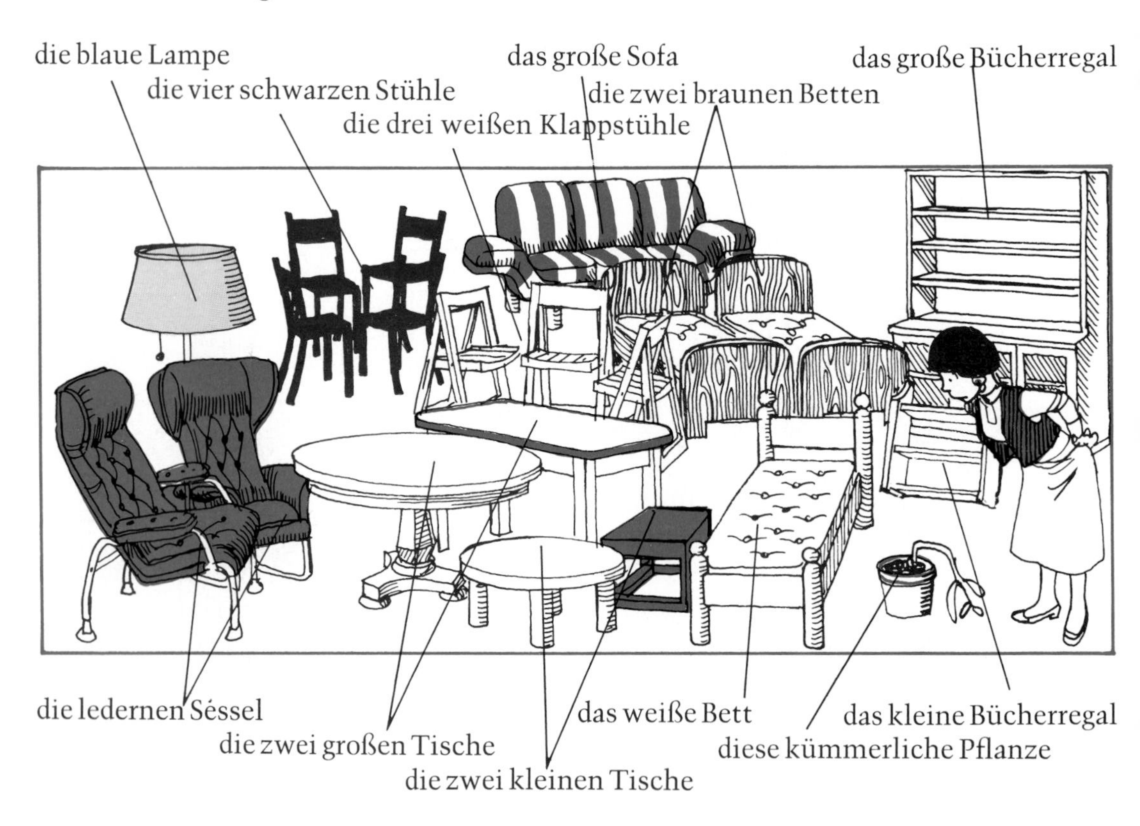

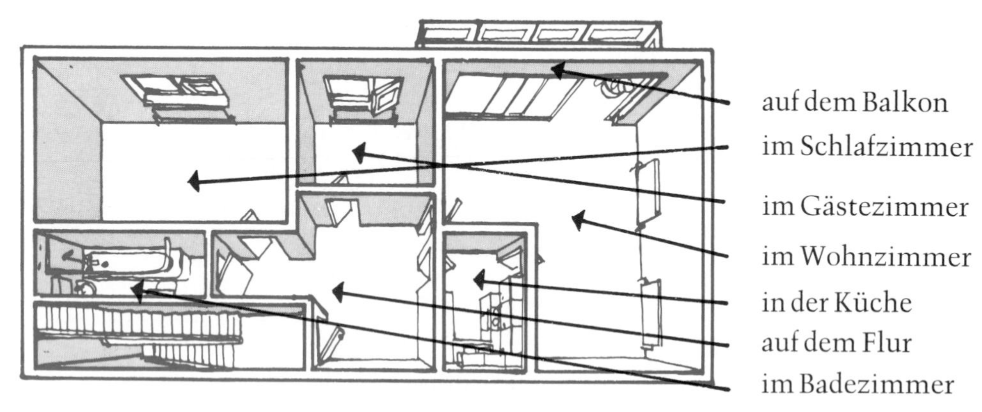

Decide where you want everything and make a note before the furniture men bring it all in, like this:

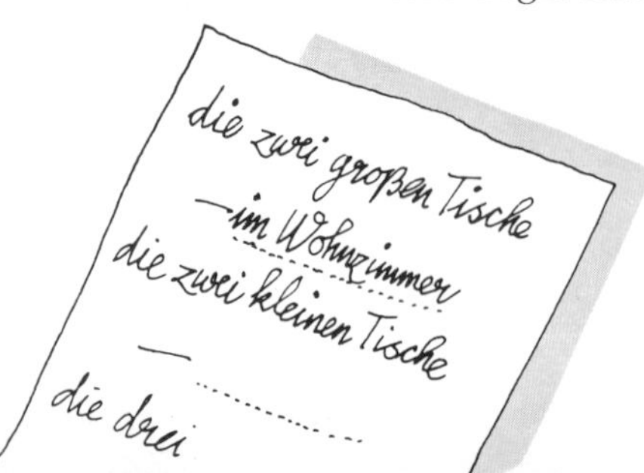

3 The furniture men arrive

In pairs: get the furniture distributed around the flat, the furniture man using the items of furniture in the picture opposite, the housewife using the list made in section 2.

4 That other man arrives!

In pairs: wife tell husband where everything has been put; husband tell wife where (you think!) it ought to be.

B

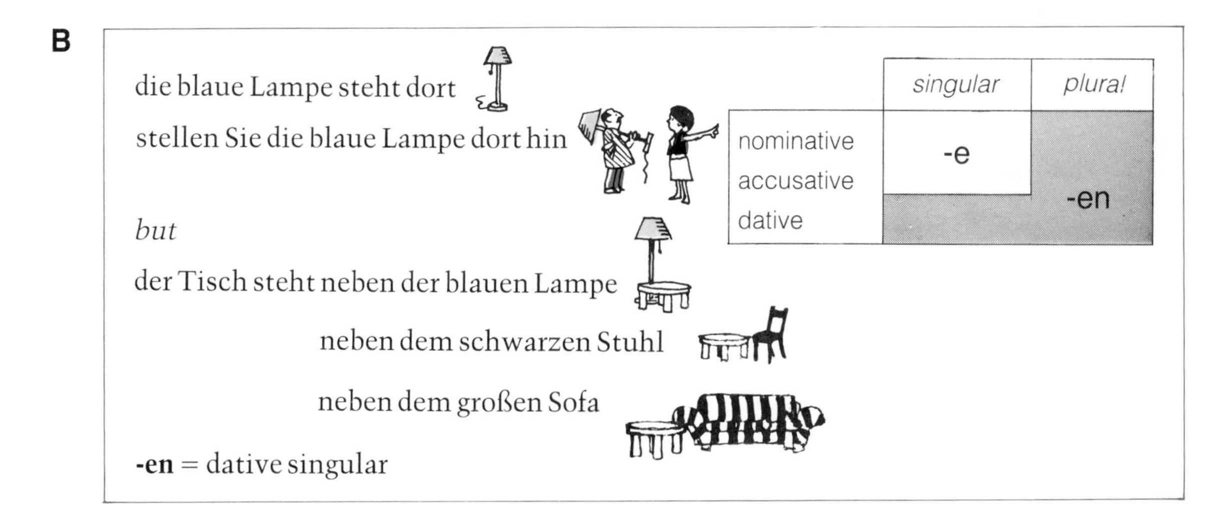

die blaue Lampe steht dort

stellen Sie die blaue Lampe dort hin

but

der Tisch steht neben der blauen Lampe

neben dem schwarzen Stuhl

neben dem großen Sofa

-en = dative singular

	singular	*plural*
nominative	-e	-en
accusative	-e	-en
dative	-en	-en

5 Where's everything now?

1 Die Sessel stehen unter der blauen Lampe.

2 Das Bücherregal steht ......

3 Das Bett steht ......

4 Der Stuhl steht ......

5 Der Tisch steht ......

6 Die Lampe steht ......

7 Diese kümmerliche Pflanze steht ......

C

der weiße Klappstuhl steht dort

but

stellen Sie den weißen Klappstuhl dort hin

-en = masculine accusative singular

	singular *m*	*f*	*n*	*plural*
nominative	-e	-e	-e	-en
accusative	-en	-e	-e	-en
dative	-en	-en	-en	-en

6 How they moved it!

—Wo ist der schwarze Stuhl?

der ....

der ....

der ....

der ....

—Mensch, hier, ich hab' den ....

7 How they packed it!

— Wo stell' ich denn die Pflanze hin?
den schwarzen Stuhl
die Lampe
das kleine Bücherregal

8 Actually, I hate all this stuff I have to move!

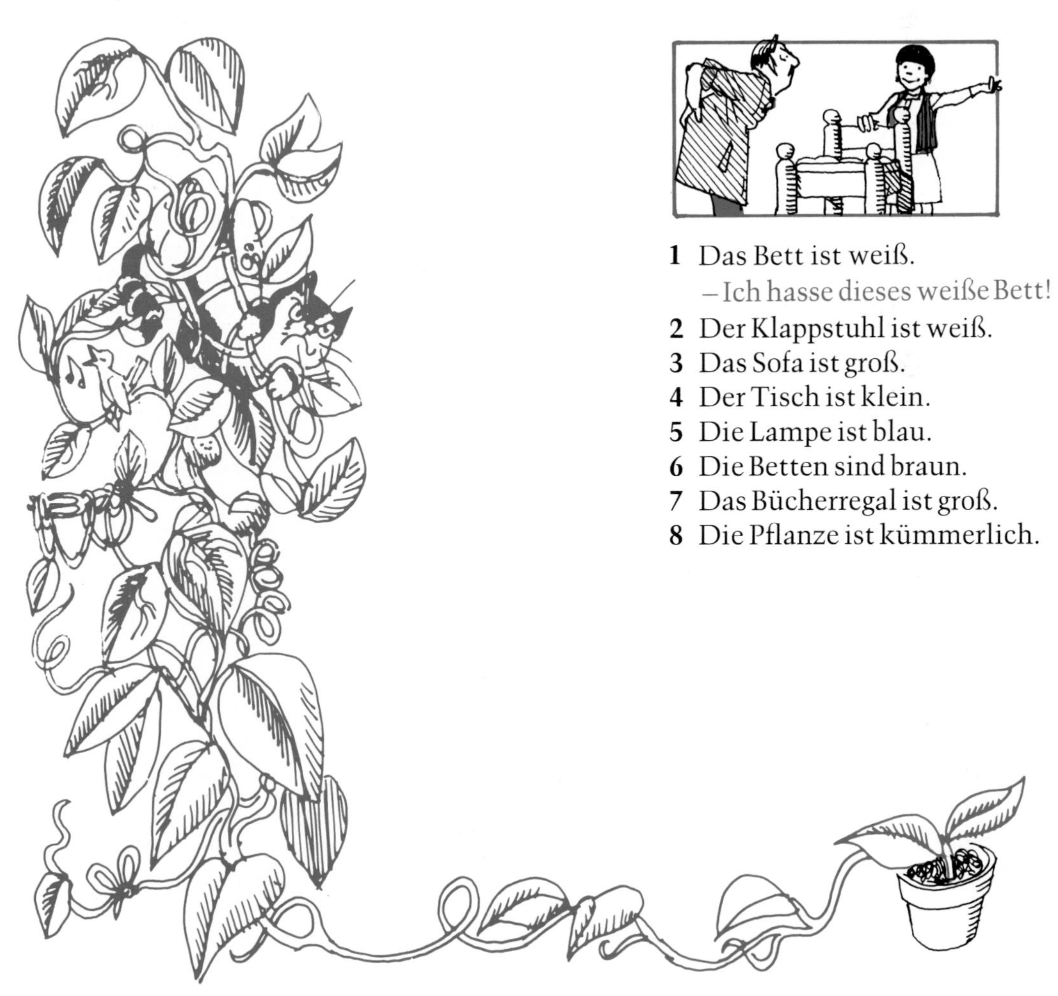

1 Das Bett ist weiß.
 – Ich hasse dieses weiße Bett!
2 Der Klappstuhl ist weiß.
3 Das Sofa ist groß.
4 Der Tisch ist klein.
5 Die Lampe ist blau.
6 Die Betten sind braun.
7 Das Bücherregal ist groß.
8 Die Pflanze ist kümmerlich.

UNIT 43

1 Verlorene Gegenstände

Listen twice to this story, following it in your books. Then answer the English questions that follow it.

In der Polizeiwache in der Kieler Straße steht der junge Wachtmeister Max Diels. Er langweilt sich. Nichts zu tun. Er sieht auf das Buch vor sich. Ein verlorener Hund. Eine verlorene Katze. Sogar ein verlorenes Meerschweinchen. Mensch!
Die Tür geht auf. Ein junger Mann kommt herein.
„Guten Morgen, Herr Wachtmeister."
„Guten Morgen. Kann ich Ihnen helfen?"
„Ach, Entschuldigung, ich möchte etwas melden. Einen verlorenen Wagen. Wahrscheinlich gestohlen. Einen roten VW Golf."
„So. Ihr Name, bitte . . . Vorname . . . Adresse . . . . . . Unterschrift, bitte!"
Einen verlorenen Wagen! Die Leute verlieren alles. Max schreibt es auf, der junge Mann unterschreibt und geht.
Dann geht die Tür wieder auf. Diesmal ist es eine alte Frau.
„Guten Morgen, gnädige Frau. Was haben Sie verloren?"
„Ich habe etwas verloren, aber . . . woher wissen Sie das?"
„Die Polizei weiß alles. Was war es denn?"
„Eine blaue Handtasche. Mit dreizehn Mark drin."
„So viel! Gut, ich schreibe das auf . . . wie heißen Sie, bitte? . . . Und mit Nachnamen? . . . Und Sie wohnen wo? . . ."
Er schreibt wieder alles auf, die alte Frau unterschreibt und geht. Dann geht die Tür zum dritten Mal auf. Diesmal ist es eine sehr hübsche junge Dame. Wachtmeister Diels wacht auf.
„Guten Morgen. Wie kann ich Ihnen helfen, bitte?"
„Ich möchte etwas melden," sagt die hübsche junge Dame. Ich habe meinen Mann verloren. Hier in der Stadt irgendwo."
So jung, so hübsch, und sie hat ihren Mann verloren! Prima, denkt Max.
„Das ist sehr bedauerlich," sagt Max. „Und auch wichtig. Das muß ich sofort aufschreiben."
Er sucht seinen Kugelschreiber, seinen schönen, neuen, silbernen Kugelschreiber. Er sucht ihn auf dem Tisch, unter dem Stuhl, auf dem Boden, überall.
„Mensch," sagt Max. „Ich muß auch etwas melden – ich habe meinen besten Kugelschreiber verloren!"

verloren lost
der Gegenstand object
die Polizeiwache police station
jung young
der Wachtmeister constable
sich langweilen be bored
tun do
sehen auf look at
sogar even
das Meerschweinchen guinea pig
aufgehen open
herein in
helfen (+ *dat.*) help
melden report
wahrscheinlich probably
gestohlen stolen
die Unterschrift signature
verlieren lose
aufschreiben write down
unterschreiben sign
diesmal this time
gnädige Frau Madam
woher how
die Polizei police
drin in it
zum dritten Mal for a third time
hübsch pretty
denken think
bedauerlich unfortunate
wichtig important
silbern silver
überall everywhere

1 What is Max's job?
2 Why is he bored?
3 What has he already got in the incident book?
4 What does the young man report?
5 What does he think has happened to it?
6 What details does Max take down?
7 What does the young man do then?
8 Why is the old lady surprised?
9 What does she ask Max?
10 What does he reply?
11 What has she lost?
12 What was in it?
13 What effect does the third person to arrive have on Max?
14 What has she lost?
15 What does Max think about this?
16 What does he say about this?
17 Describe Max's pen.

2 Answer, using at least one adjective each time!

1 Wer kommt zuerst herein?
2 Was möchte er melden?
3 Was für einen Wagen?
4 Wer kommt danach herein?
5 Was hat sie verloren?
6 Wer kommt dann herein?
7 Was sucht Max, um zu schreiben?
8 Was hat er verloren?
9 Wer, meinen Sie, hat den Kugelschreiber?

3 Adjective endings after *ein*

der verloren e Hund	die verloren e Katze	das verloren e Meerschweinchen
but	*and*	*but*
ein verloren er Hund	eine verloren e Katze	ein verloren es Meerschweinchen

-er, -e, -es after ein, eine, ein.

den rot en Wagen
and
einen rot en Wagen

-en = masculine singular accusative, and all dative, and all plural.

meine verloren e Katze
meine verloren en Katzen
für deinen verloren en Wagen

Adjectives after **mein, dein** etc., and after **kein**, follow the **ein** pattern.

	singular						*plural*
	after der *etc.*			*after* ein *etc.*			
	m	*f*	*n*	*m*	*f*	*n*	
nominative	-e			-er	-e	-es	-en
accusative							
dative							

4 The things people lose on the train!

Pairwork:

A You're the German Railways official. Ask the lady what she's lost. Write down a list of everything she says she's lost

B You're the absentminded lady. Follow the pattern below, adding adjectives to describe the things you've lost.

—Ja, gnädige Frau, was haben Sie verloren?
—Und was sonst?
—......

—Ich habe einen ...... Regenmantel verloren.
auch meinen ...... Kugelschreiber
meine ...... Handtasche
eine ...... Katze
ein ...... Buch
einen ...... Hund
ein ...... Meerschweinchen
meinen ...... Mann

5 How can you expect me to find anything in a bedroom as untidy as this?

—Kannst du meine	roten	Schuhe	sehen?
m	blau . . .	Hemd	
	grün . . .	Hose	
	......	Socken	
		Pullover	
		Schlips	
		......	

—Nein, ich kann keine roten Schuhe sehen!
......

6 Both members of each pair copy the form into your exercise books. Then, alternately playing the constable (East German this time, incidentally – how do you know?), ask your partner, who has lost something, for all the necessary information to complete the form. Then get him to sign (mind he doesn't keep your pen!). ▶

Volkspolizei der Hauptstadt Berlin

Verlorene Gegenstände

Meldezettel

Name ....
Vorname ....
Adresse ....
....
Was haben Sie verloren?
....
....
....
Wo? ....
....
Wann? ....
....
Unterschrift ....

UNIT 44 REVISION

Grammar

1 Adjective endings

a Du fährst langsam. Das Auto ist groß.

Adjectives used as adverbs, or otherwise standing alone (i.e. without a following noun) have no endings.

b das große Auto; vor dem großen Auto; die großen Autos

Adjectives following **der, die, das** (and words that take endings like **der, die, das: dieser, welcher, jeder**) have an **-e** in the nominative and accusative singular, **-en** in all other cases. Following masculine accusative **den**, adjectives have **-en**: den großen Wagen.

c *nom:* ein großer Wagen; eine große Lampe; ein großes Auto
acc: meinen großen Wagen; unsere große Lampe; euer großes Auto
dat.; plural: vor seinem großen Auto; keine großen Autos

Adjectives following **ein, eine, ein** (and words that take endings like **ein, eine, ein: kein, mein, dein, sein, ihr, unser, Ihr, euer**) have, in the nominative singular: **-er** in the masculine, **-e** in the feminine, **-es** in the neuter. In the accusative singular they have: **-en** in the masculine, **-e** in the feminine, **-es** in the neuter.

d verlorene Gegenstände; mit verlorenen Gegenständen

Plural adjectives used with a following noun but without an article have **-e** in the nominative and accusative, **-en** in the dative.

This can be schematized in the following diagram:

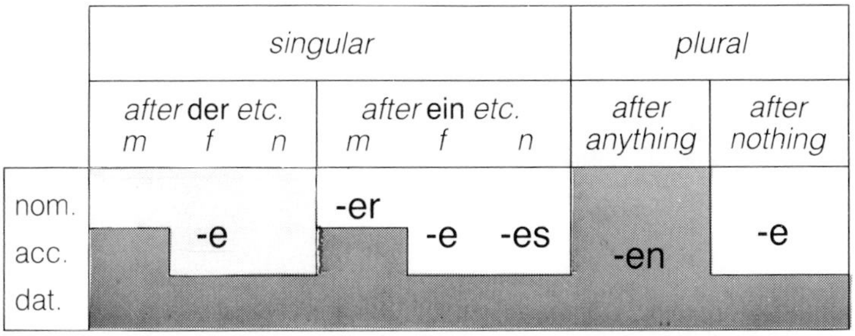

	singular						*plural*	
	after **der** *etc.*			*after* **ein** *etc.*			*after anything*	*after nothing*
	m	*f*	*n*	*m*	*f*	*n*		
nom.				-er				
acc.		-e			-e	-es	-en	-e
dat.								

Clearly it is not possible to check back against a diagram like this when *speaking* the language: it takes a lot of practice to get adjectives right all the time in the spoken language. As a quick rule-of-thumb the following will produce the right endings *nearly* always:

1 If you've already said **-en** (or **-em**) say **-en** again: dengroßen Wagen.

2 If you've said **-er, -e, -s** say **-e**: dieser alte Wagen.

3 If you've said **-ein** say { **-er** masculine / **-es** neuter } : { mein alter Wagen / kein altes Auto }

der Apparat (-e) machine
der Bindestrich (-e) hyphen
der Flur (-e) hall
der Balkon (-e) balcony
der Stuhl (¨-e) chair
der Klappstuhl (¨-e) folding chair
der Sessel (-) armchair
der Gegenstand (¨-e) object
der Meldezettel (-) report form
der Wachtmeister (-) constable

die Insel (-n) island
die Sekretärin (-nen) secretary
die Lampe (-n) lamp
die Pflanze (-n) plant
die Polizei police
die Hauptstadt (¨-e) capital
die Polizeiwache (-n) police station
die Adresse (-n) address
die Unterschrift (-en) signature
gnädige Frau Madam
die Möbel (*pl*) furniture

das Wohnzimmer (-) living room
das Gästezimmer (-) spare room
das Bücherregal (-e) bookcase
das Bett (-en) bed
das Sofa (-s) sofa
das Fundbüro lost property office
das Meerschweinchen (-) guinea pig
das Mal (-e) time (= *occasion*)

buchstabieren spell
verbinden connect
hassen hate
hinstellen put down
sich langweilen be bored
sehen auf (+ *acc.*) look at
verlieren lose
aufgehen open
hereinkommen come in
helfen (+ *dat.*) help
melden report
aufschreiben write down
unterschreiben sign
denken think

deutsch German
niemand no-one
gestorben dead
falsch wrong
kümmerlich miserable
ledern leather
silbern silver

2 Masculine nouns ending **-e** take **-n** in the accusative and dative *singular* as well as in the plural:

der Junge, den Jungen, dem Jungen
der Name, den Namen, dem Namen.

Notice the quite exceptional **Herr**. This takes **-n** in the singular, **-en** in the plural:

singular: der Herr, den Herrn, dem Herrn
plural: die Herren, die Herren, den Herren

3 The only new strong verb we have met is helfen: du hilfst, er hilft.

danach after that
jung young
verloren lost
sogar even
wahrscheinlich probably
gestohlen stolen
diesmal this time
drin in it
hübsch pretty
bedauerlich unfortunate
wichtig important
überall everywhere

A That was some party!

— Wie komm' ich nach Hause, Herr Wachtmeister?

— Sie nehmen die erste Straße links, Herr Braun, und dann ist es das dritte Haus links!

Now you tell Meyer, Schmidt, Gerstenberg, Quadflieg und Zwingli how to get home.

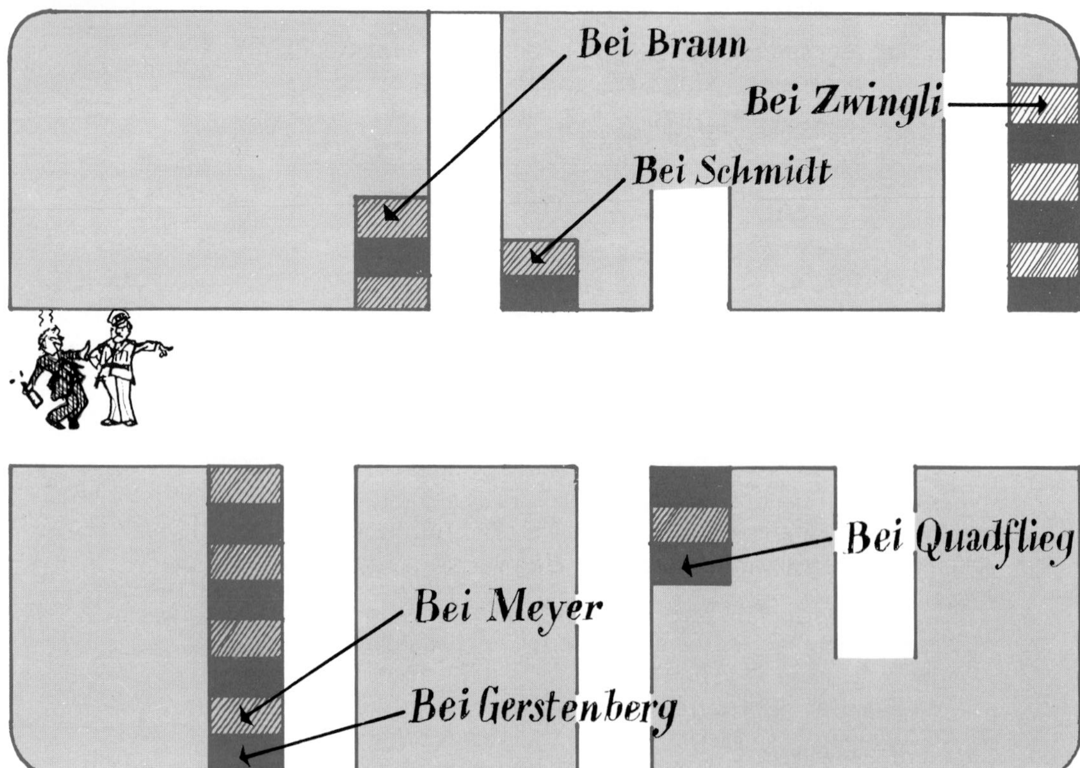

B 1 Welchen Stuhl möchten Sie hier? (schwarz)
— Den schwarzen Stuhl, bitte.

2 Und welche Lampe? (grün)
3 Und welches Bücherregal? (braun)
4 Und welchen Tisch? (groß)
5 Und welche Betten? (gelb)
6 Und welchen Sessel? (ledern)
7 Und welches Sofa? (lang)
8 Und welche Klappstühle? (klein)

C 1 Dieser rote Pullover ist schön.
— Nein danke, ich hab' schon einen roten Pullover.

2 Diese graue Hose ......
3 Dieser braune Mantel
4 Dieses weiße Hemd
5 Dieser blaue Schlips
6 Diese schwarze Jacke
7 Dieses gelbe Kleid

D

— Wo wohnen Sie denn?
— In ......

die nächste Stadt
die erste Straße links
das große Haus dort rechts
die dritte Wohnung links
der rote Wohnwagen
die westdeutsche Hauptstadt
die zwei kleinen Zimmer hier links

E Add the adjectives, with appropriate endings

Vor dem ...... Laden in der Friedrichstraße	erst
steht ein ......, ...	jung, hübsch
Mädchen in einem ......,	kurz
...... Regenmantel. Sie	rot
trägt eine ...... Jacke	ledern
mit einer ...... Kette.	silbern
Bald kommt ein	jung
Mann mit einem ......,	klein
...... Hund.	braun
„Haben Sie diesen Hund verloren?" fragt er.	
„Dieses ......, ...	häßlich, braun
Tier?" sagt das Mädchen. „Nein, das ist der	
...... Hund!"	falsch

F Listen to the scene in the police station from unit 43 again. Then write your own version of it following this outline:

Wachtmeister Max Diels – sich langweilen – Tür aufgehen – junger Mann – etwas melden – einen verlorenen Wagen – Name, Vorname, Adresse, Unterschrift – alte Frau – blaue Handtasche – DM 13 drin – unterschreiben – zum dritten Mal – hübsche junge Dame – meinen Mann verloren – ist bedauerlich – aufschreiben – Kugelschreiber suchen – auch etwas melden – meinen besten Kugelschreiber verloren.

1	12
2	13
3	14
4	15
5	16
6	17
7	18
8	19
9	20
10	21
11	22

You might meet any of these notices in Germany – some are self-explanatory, some are more difficult. Explain in each case what you can or can't do. There are some clues below to help with the trickier ones.

G

1 You'd find it on a unlocked door.
3 **Unberechtigt** = *unauthorized*.
7 We've just had **melden** = *report*. Where do you 'report' when you go into an office block or a hotel?
9 **Die Stufe** = *step*.
10 By a light switch.
11 By the hall doors of a block of flats?
14 By coat pegs in a restaurant. **Wird gehaftet** = *is liable*.
16 **Rauchen** = *smoke*.
17 By a doormat.
20, 21 On the two sides of a swing door. We've had **anziehen** for pulling on clothes . . .

UNIT 45

1

Die Humberbrücke ist sehr lang – länger als die Kennedybrücke.

Die Bundesrepublik ist groß – größer als die DDR.

Frau Schleiermacher ist stark – stärker als Frau Runge.

Herr Kleinholz ist alt – älter als Frau Kleinholz.

Der Berliner Fernsehturm ist sehr hoch – höher als der Eiffelturm.

Diese Pflanze ist sehr kümmerlich – noch kümmerlicher als deine Pflanze.

2

1 Die Kennedybrücke ist nicht kurz, aber kürzer als ......
2 Die DDR ist nicht klein, aber ......
3 Frau Runge ist nicht schwach, aber ......
4 Frau Kleinholz ist nicht jung, aber ......
5 Der Eiffelturm ist nicht niedrig, aber ......
6 Meine Pflanze ist nicht schön, aber ......

3 Now make up your own!

Dieser Kaffee ist warm, noch wärmer als ......
...... kalt ......
schwarz
krank
dumm
klug
arm
hoch

4 Which costs more?

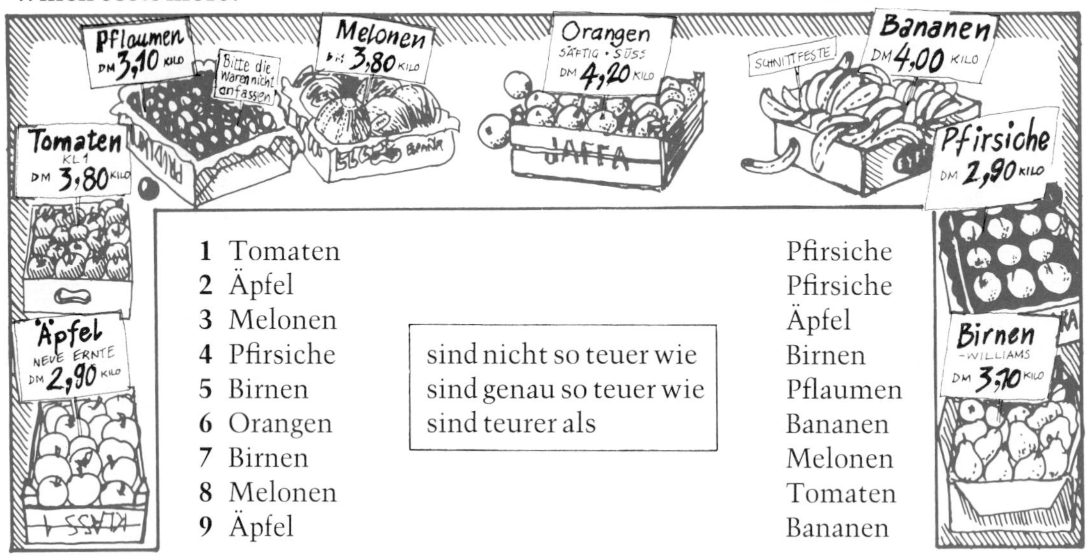

1 Tomaten	sind nicht so teuer wie	Pfirsiche
2 Äpfel	sind genau so teuer wie	Pfirsiche
3 Melonen	sind teurer als	Äpfel
4 Pfirsiche		Birnen
5 Birnen		Pflaumen
6 Orangen		Bananen
7 Birnen		Melonen
8 Melonen		Tomaten
9 Äpfel		Bananen

5 Who's the greatest?

1 Wer ist der klügste?
— Albert ist der klügste

2 Wer ist der ärmste?

3 Wer ist die kränkste?

4 Wer ist die jüngste?

5 Wer ist der dümmste?

6 Wer ist der größte?

7 Wer ist der kälteste?

UNIT 46

1 Beim Optiker

You're going to listen to a lady having her eyes tested by an optician; copy out the test sheet and fill it in as you listen. Put a tick against each item she gets right, a cross against those she gets wrong. If you get nine ticks she needs spectacles, if you get any other number *you* need a hearing aid!

Text of scene is on p. 145.

Optische Tests

Test 1 (Zeile 1) A Z Q B N P J ☐☐☐☐☐☐☐

Test 2 (Zeile 3) M Z W V O E Y ☐☐☐☐☐☐☐

Test 3
länger ☐
klarer ☐

Test 4
runder ☐
blasser ☐

Test 5
bunter ☐
grauer ☐

Vocabulary

ob whether
Platz nehmen take a seat
die Karte card
der Buchstabe letter
die Wand wall
die Zeile line (of type)
die Linie line
der Kreis circle
das Quadrat square
blaß pale
bunt brightly coloured

2 Beim Arzt

—Wo tut es denn weh?
—Hier am Kopf.
—Am besten nehmen Sie Aspirin dagegen.
—Auch hier im Magen.
—Da brauchen Sie Natron.
—Auch hier im Hals tut es weh.
—Da nehmen Sie am besten Hustenbonbons.
—Aber am schlimmsten ist es hier am Fuß.
—Da kaufen Sie lieber neue Schuhe!

1 Wo tut es weh?
2 Was kann die Patientin am besten dagegen tun?
3 Wo tut es auch weh?
4 Was braucht sie dafür?
5 Wie ist ihr Hals?
6 Was soll sie dafür nehmen?
7 Wo ist es am schlimmsten?
8 Was soll sie dagegen tun?

3 Beim Zahnarzt

—Mund aufmachen, bitte. Aha!
—Wie sieht es denn aus?
—Sehr braun, Ihre Zähne . . . Vorne sind sie braun, in der Mitte sind sie noch brauner, hinten sind sie am braunsten. Sehr schlimm ist das. Ich muß sie alle ziehen!
—Das brauchen Sie nicht, Herr Doktor! Setzen Sie bloß Ihre Sonnenbrille ab!

1 Was muß der Patient zuerst tun?
2 Wie sind anscheinend seine Zähne?
3 Wie sind sie vorne?
4 Wie sind sie in der Mitte?
5 Wie sind sie hinten?
6 Was will der Zahnarzt tun?
7 Was braucht er bloß zu tun?

4 Doctor, doctor . . .

— Wo ist es am schlimmsten?
— Hier, ...
Was mach' ich am besten?
— Nehmen Sie ......
Und wo ist es auch schlimm?
— ......

1 Beim Optiker

Optiker	Guten Tag, Frau Lensdorf.
Patientin	Guten Tag. Ich weiß nicht, ob ich eine Brille brauche, aber ich sehe nicht mehr so gut.
Optiker	Na, das wollen wir mal sehen . . . Nehmen Sie bitte hier Platz. Sie sehen die Karte mit den Buchstaben dort an der Wand? Wollen Sie bitte die erste Zeile lesen.
Patientin	A–Z–Q–P–M–B–J.
Optiker	Und die dritte Zeile.
Patientin	N–Z–V–W–O–I–Y.
Optiker	Danke. Jetzt sehen Sie bitte auf diese zwei Linien. Welche Linie ist länger?
Patientin	Die rechte.
Optiker	Und welche ist klarer?
Patientin	Die linke.
Optiker	Und jetzt die zwei Kreise. Welcher ist runder?
Patientin	Der rechte.
Optiker	Und welcher ist blasser?
Patientin	Der linke.
Optiker	Danke. Und jetzt die zwei Quadrate. Welches ist bunter?
Patientin	Das rechte.
Optiker	Und welches ist grauer?
Patientin	Das linke.
Optiker	Hm. Wissen Sie, Frau Lensdorf, sie brauchen ganz bestimmt eine Brille!

UNIT 47

1 Auf der Bank

A *Angestellte* Ja, bitte?
Kunde Ich möchte bitte Geld wechseln.
Angestellte Ja, bitte, wieviel?
Kunde Zwanzig englische Pfund. In Schillinge.
Angestellte Bitte schön, sechshundert Schilling. Wollen Sie bitte hier unterschreiben. Danke schön. Gehen Sie bitte mit dem Formular zur Kasse.
Kunde Danke schön.

wechseln change
die Kasse cashier's desk
das Formular form

B *Angestellte* Ja, bitte?
Kunde Ich möchte einen Reisescheck wechseln, bitte. Über fünfzig amerikanische Dollars.
Angestellte In D-Mark?
Kunde Ja, bitte.
Angestellte Bitte schön. Das macht hundert D-Mark. Haben Sie Ihren Paß, bitte?
Kunde Ja. Bitte schön.
Angestellte Danke. Wollen Sie den Scheck bitte unterschreiben und auch hier das Formular.
Kunde Bitte schön.
Angestellte Danke schön. Sie bekommen Ihr Geld nebenan an der Kasse.
Kunde Vielen Dank.

der Reisescheck traveller's cheque
der Paß passport
nebenan next door

In pairs, alternating roles, change:

$40 into Franken
DM 10 into Mark
A traveller's cheque for £20 into Schillinge
A traveller's cheque for $50 into D-Mark
A traveller's cheque for £25 into Franken
Sch 400 into pounds.

Work out the correct amount individually at the current exchange rates.

2 Money, money, money

Die Bundesrepublik

100 Pfennig = 1 Deutschmark

Die Deutsche Demokratische Republik

100 Pfennig = 1 Mark

Österreich

100 Groschen = 1 Schilling

Die Schweiz

100 Rappen = 1 Franken

Answer, using current currency exchange rates:

1. Ist ein amerikanischer Dollar mehr wert als ein englisches Pfund?
2. Ist ein Schilling mehr wert als eine westdeutsche Mark?
3. Ist ein Pfennig größer als eine Mark?
4. Ist ein schweizerischer Franken mehr wert als eine D-Mark?
5. Was ist am meisten wert: der Dollar, der Franken oder das Pfund?
6. Ist ein Franken kleiner als ein Rappen?
7. Was bekommst du am liebsten: zehn Pfund, zwanzig Dollars, fünfzig D-Mark?
8. Wer hat mehr Geld – ein Österreicher mit sechzig Schilling oder ein Deutscher mit zehn D-Mark?
9. Was ist besser – fünfundzwanzig Franken oder dreißig D-Mark?
10. Was hat den höchsten Wert: dreißig Schilling, zehn Franken oder fünfzehn Mark?

UNIT 48 REVISION

Grammar

1 Comparative of adjectives and adverbs

Das ist noch kümmerlicher. Welches ist bunter?

The comparative is formed by adding **-er** to the adjective, as in English. Unlike English this is also done with adjectives of more than one syllable (**kümmerlicher** = *more miserable*).

Er ist größer. Die Brücke ist länger.

The most common single-syllable adjectives also modify their vowel.

So groß wie ich. Größer als ich.

Though **wie** is used in the **so . . .** construction (= *as*), after comparatives **als** is used (= *than*).

All the above applies equally to adverbs.

Ein wertvolleres Buch – *a more valuable book*

Normal adjective endings are added to the comparative adjective when it is used before a noun.

2 Superlatives of adjectives and adverbs

Adjectives add **-st** to form the superlative, which has two forms:

der schönste **am schönsten**.

The **der** (**die, das** etc.) **-ste** form is used immediately in front of a noun or where the noun is clearly understood from earlier:

der schönste Wagen
Dieser Wagen ist der schönste (= der schönste Wagen).

Otherwise for adjectives, and always for adverbs, the **am -sten** form is used:

Sie sieht am schönsten aus.
Sie singt am schönsten.
Dieser Opel ist am schönsten. (. . . *is nicest*, i.e., *nicest car*, not *nicest Opel*)

die kürzeste Straße

-est rather than **-st** is used where **-st** would be difficult to pronounce (usually after **-s** sounds).

der ärmste Junge

Adjectives that modify in the comparative also modify in the superlative.

der Apfel (¨) apple
der Hustenbonbon (-s) cough sweet
der Fuß (¨e) foot
der Arzt (¨e) doctor
der Zahn (¨e) tooth
der Patient (-en) patient
der Arm (-e) arm
der Buchstabe (-n) letter
der Kreis (-e) circle
der Optiker (-) optician
der Hals (¨e) throat, neck
der Österreicher (-) Austrian
der Deutsche German
der Wert (-e) value
der Schilling (-e) (Austrian) schilling
der Franken (-) (Swiss) franc
der Reisescheck (-s) traveller's cheque
der Dollar (-s) dollar
der Paß (¨e) passport

die Brücke (-n) bridge
die Melone (-n) melon
die Mitte middle
die Hand (¨e) hand
die Karte (-n) card
die Wand (¨e) wall
die Zeile (-n) line (of type)
die Linie (-n) line
die Kasse (-n) cash desk

das Bein (-e) leg
das Penicillin penicillin
das Quadrat (-e) square
das Formular (-e) form

aussehen look (like)
abnehmen take off
Platz nehmen take a seat
wechseln change

dumm stupid
klug clever
arm poor
stark strong
schwach weak
niedrig low
schlimm bad
bloß simply
dafür for it
dagegen against it
anscheinend apparently

3 Irregular comparatives and superlatives

There are some irregularities in:

groß	größer	der größte; am größten
hoch	höher	der höchste; am höchsten
gern	lieber	am liebsten
viel	mehr	der meiste; am meisten
gut	besser	der beste; am besten

ob whether
blaß pale
bunt brightly coloured
schweizerisch Swiss
englisch English
amerikanisch American
meist most
nebenan next door
wert valuable

4 **Dafür** – *for it* **dagegen** – *against it*

Da + preposition = preposition + *it*.

Daraus; d(a)rin. If the preposition begins with a vowel, **-r-** is inserted. In this case the **-a-** often disappears in speech.

Wovon – *of what* **worin** – *in what*

Similarly **wo** + preposition = preposition + *what* in questions. Again the **-r-** appears between two vowels.

5 der Deutsche ein Deutscher die Deutschen

A very small number of nouns are formed directly from adjectives, taking a capital letter and normal adjective endings. **Der Deutsche** is the only noun of this kind we have met so far.

A 1 Franz, dumm?
— Ja, sicher! Franz ist viel dümmer als ich!

2 Hermann, stark?

3 Hugo, alt?

4 Wolfgang, groß?

5 Hannelore, jung?

6 Gitte, klug?

7 Wernher, arm?

8 Liese, schwach?

B Complete with comparatives:

1 Meine Kette ist zwar wertvoll, aber deine Kette ist noch w......
2 Unser Zimmer ist zwar bunt, aber euer Zimmer ......
3 Ihre Augen sind zwar blau, aber deine ......
4 Dieser Bus ist zwar voll, aber der Bus dort ......
5 Ihre Preise sind zwar niedrig, aber unsere ......
6 Die Äpfel sind zwar schön, aber die Pfirsiche ......

C Complete with a suitable superlative:

1 Der ...... Turm ist in Ostberlin.
2 Die ...... Brücke ist in Hull.
3 Der ...... Mann ist hundertzehn Jahre alt.
4 Das ...... Land ist die UdSSR.
5 Das ...... Kind hat überhaupt kein Geld.
6 Der ...... Fußballspieler bin ich!
7 Die ...... Schweizer sprechen Deutsch.

D Disagree:

1 Sie ist nicht so lang wie die Humberbrücke!
— Doch, sie ist viel länger!
2 Die Pflanze dort ist nicht so kümmerlich wie diese!
3 Sie ist nicht so blaß wie ich!
4 Ted ist nicht so alt wie deine Schwester!
5 Es ist nicht so kalt wie im Wohnzimmer!
6 Trudi ist nicht so krank wie Susi!
7 Es ist nicht so wichtig, wie du denkst!
8 Das Wetter ist nicht so klar wie gestern!
9 Der Rotwein ist nicht so teuer wie der Weißwein!

E Public telephones

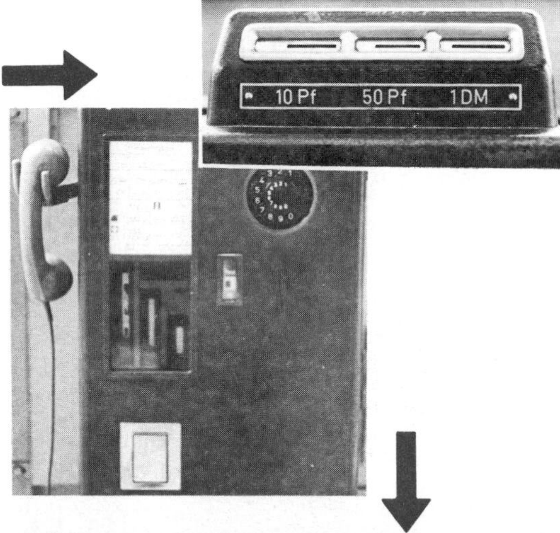

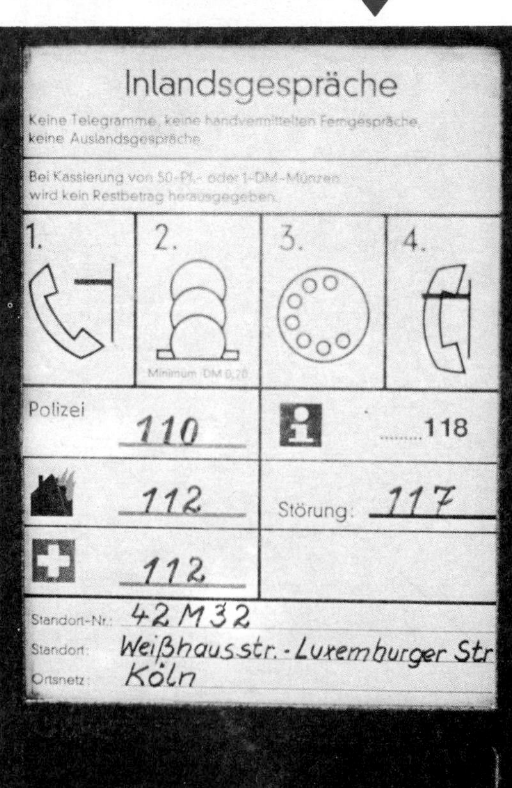

1 In what city is this phone box?
2 At the corner of which streets?
3 What types of calls *can't* you make from it? (There are three types. *Clue*: **handvermittelt** = *via manual exchanges.*)
4 What three coins (all illustrated in unit 46) does the machine take?
5 Does it give change if you use one of the two larger coins? (*Clue*: **Die Münze** is *coin*)
6 What's the minimum price of a call?
7 What number do you ring to get the police?
8 **Die Störung** means, literally, *disturbance*. What would you dial 117 for?

UNIT 49

1 Die Fensterputzer

Die Volkskammer der Deutschen Demokratischen Republik steht in Ostberlin in der Karl-Liebknecht-Straße dem Dom gegenüber. Es ist ein neues Gebäude mit sehr vielen Fenstern. Fenster brauchen Fensterputzer, vor allem die Fenster der Volkskammer. Eine Arbeitsgruppe von drei Männern macht das, und der neue Mann der Gruppe – seit heute morgen – ist Hans Ullmann. Es ist fast Mittag, und der Leiter dieser Gruppe, Kurt Roth, geht gleich essen.

. . . gegenüber opposite . . .
das Gebäude building
die Arbeitsgruppe working party
fast nearly
der Leiter leader

„Ich gehe jetzt essen. Ihr beide müßt erst noch die oberen Fenster an dieser Seite putzen, dann könnt ihr auch essen gehen."

ihr beide the two of you
ober upper
die Seite side

„Mensch, wir haben auch schon Hunger," sagt Franz, der dritte Mann der Arbeitsgruppe.

arbeiten work

„Dann müßt ihr eben schneller arbeiten," sagt Kurt, und er geht.

Hans und Franz steigen in die Gondel und beginnen, die Fenster an der Vorderseite des Gebäudes zu putzen. Sie machen es so schnell wie möglich, denn sie haben beide Hunger. Für Franz ist es leicht, aber für Hans, den neuen Mann, ist es schwerer.

Unten kommen einige Abgeordnete der Volkskammer aus dem Haupteingang. Für sie ist jetzt auch Mittagspause. Über ihnen in der Gondel lehnt sich Hans ein bißchen zu weit hinaus. Er beginnt, sein Gleichgewicht zu verlieren, tritt zurück, tritt gegen den Eimer voll Wasser, und . . .

die Vorderseite front
denn for
schwer difficult
einige some
der Abgeordnete member (of parliament)
der Haupteingang main entrance
sich hinauslehnen lean out
das Gleichgewicht balance
treten kick
der Eimer bucket

Der Eimer fällt dem Finanzminister vor die Füße. Das Wasser aus dem Eimer ergießt sich auf den Kopf des Ministers, auf die Schultern, die Arme, die Beine des Ministers, vor allem auf den schönen grauen Anzug des Ministers. Dem Minister gefällt das gar nicht.

„Herunter, Sie Esel, kommen Sie herunter . . .!"

Zwanzig Minuten später geht Hans essen. Mittagspause? Nein, Arbeitspause! Hans hat seine neue Stelle verloren. Morgen oder übermorgen aber bekommt er eine neue, weniger gefährliche Stelle: in der DDR gibt's glücklicherweise keine Arbeitslosigkeit.

fallen fall
der Finanzminister finance minister
vor die Füße at his feet
sich ergießen pour
die Schulter shoulder
gefallen (+ *dat.*) please
herunter down
der Esel ass

die Stelle job

weniger less
glücklicherweise luckily
die Arbeitslosigkeit unemployment

1. Where is the East German parliament building?
2. How many men are there in the window-cleaning team?
3. How long has Hans been working with them?
4. What is Kurt's job?
5. Why does he leave the others?
6. What do the others have to do before their lunch?
7. What people come out of the parliament building?
8. What causes Hans's accident?
9. What happens?
10. To whom?
11. What happens to Hans?
12. Why will the story probably have a reasonably happy ending?

2

1. Welches Gebäude steht in der Karl-Liebknecht-Straße?
2. Welche Arbeit hat Hans?
3. Seit wann?
4. Wer ist Kurt Roth?
5. Was tut er gegen Mittag?
6. Was müssen Hans und Franz vorm Mittagessen tun?
7. Für wen ist die Arbeit leicht, für wen schwer?
8. Wer kommt aus dem Haupteingang?
9. Was tut Hans in der Gondel?
10. Mit welchen Folgen?
11. Wie ist der Minister?

3 Say it more colloquially

1. Die Volkskammer der DDR.
   — Die Volkskammer von ......
2. Die Fenster der Volkskammer.
3. Der Leiter dieser Gruppe.
4. Die Fenster der Vorderseite.
5. Die Vorderseite des Gebäudes.
6. Einige Abgeordnete der Volkskammer.
7. Der Kopf des Ministers.

4

1	der Eimer	ein Fensterputzer	der Eimer eines F ......
2	der Eingang	ein Gebäude	......
3	die Beine	ein Mädchen	......
4	das Fenster	ein Musikgeschäft	......
5	die Tür	eine Wohnung	die Tür einer W ......
6	die Mitte	eine Stadt	......
7	der Fuß	eine Lampe	......
8	die Unterschrift	eine Patientin	......
9	die Vorderseite	der Turm	die Vorderseite des Turmes
10	der Boden	der Flur	......
11	das Bein	der Stuhl	......
12	der Deckel	das Glas	......

UNIT 50

1 Die Länder Europas

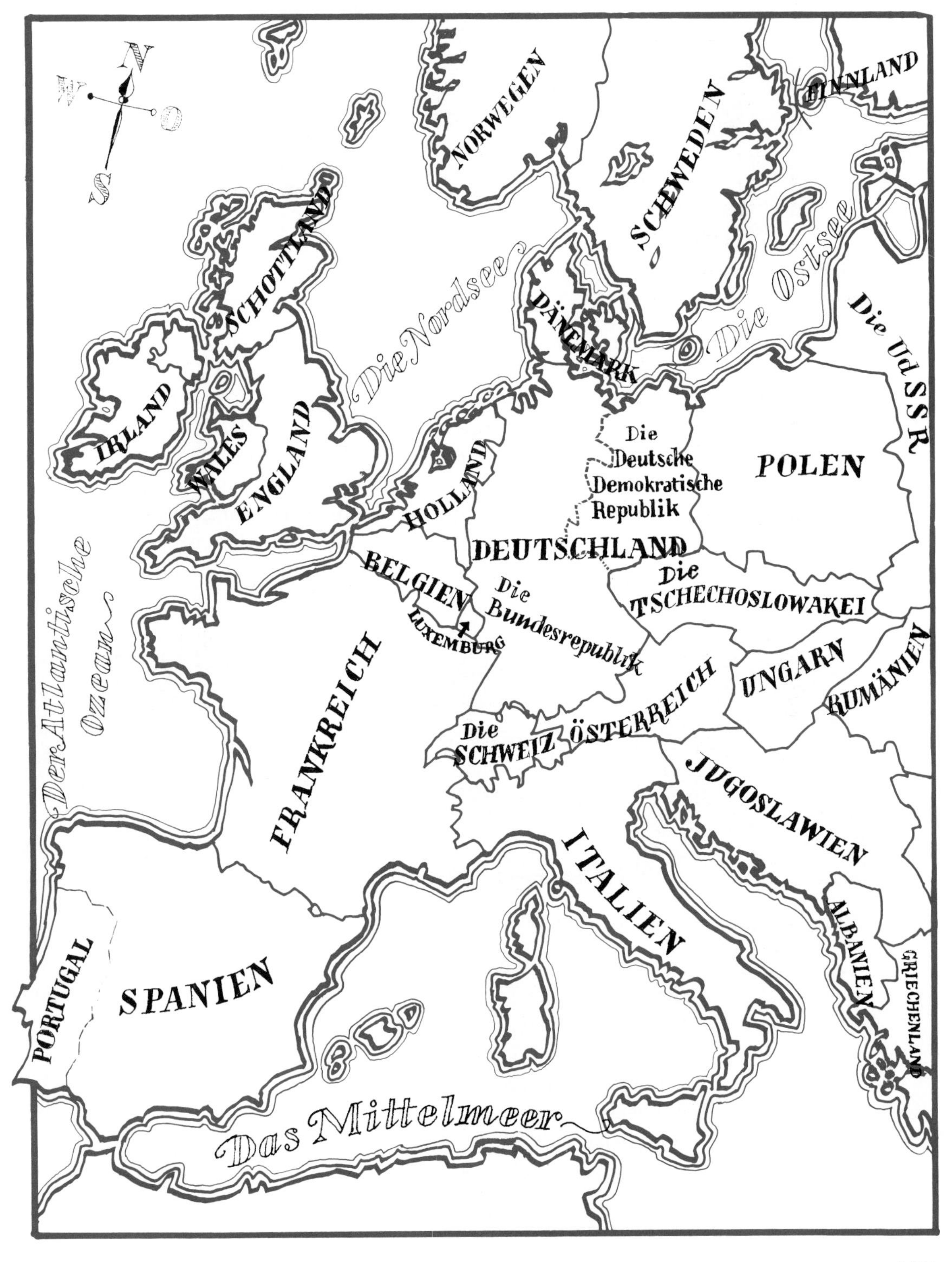

2 There's no pleasing some people

Wo verbringst du deine Ferien?

In Spanien?	—Nein, ich spreche kein Spanisch.
In Holland?	—Nein, Holland ist mir zu flach.
In Österreich?	—Nein, die Berge gefallen mir nicht.
In Belgien?	—Nein, Belgien ist mir auch zu flach.
In Polen?	—Nein, Polen ist mir zu gefährlich.
In Dänemark?	—Nein, Blonde gefallen mir nicht.
In Italien?	—Nein, Italien ist mir zu heiß.
In Frankreich?	—Nein, mein Französisch ist nicht gut genug.
In der Schweiz?	—Nein, wie gesagt, Berge gefallen mir nicht.
In Deutschland?	—Nein, ich war letztes Jahr in Deutschland.

Ach was! Bleib also zu Hause!

3 When in Rome . . . eat spaghetti?

Gefallen Gefällt	dir	italienische Spaghetti? österreichische Torten dänische Kuchen höllandischer Käse schottischer Lachs belgisches Bier französischer Wein norwegischer Schnaps ungarisches Gulasch irischer Whisky	—......	gefallen gefällt	mir	nicht nicht sehr gut noch besser am besten

QUIZ

Runde 1: Welches Land liegt ...

1 Nördlich von Österreich, südlich von Polen?
2 Nördlich von England?
3 Nördlich von Dänemark?
4 Östlich von Norwegen?
5 Südwestlich von Schottland?
6 Westlich von England, östlich von Irland?
7 Westlich von Spanien?
8 Östlich von Österreich?
9 Südöstlich von Österreich?
10 Östlich von Polen?

Runde 2: Nennen Sie bitte:

1 Den Namen der westdeutschen Hauptstadt.
2 Den Namen irgendeiner belgischen Stadt.
3 Den Namen einer großen Stadt am Rhein.
4 Die Hauptstadt irgendeines osteuropäischen Landes.
5 Die Hauptstadt Italiens.
6 Den Namen irgendeiner großen Stadt am Mittelmeer.
7 Den Namen der österreichischen Hauptstadt.

Runde 3: Welcher Staatsangehörigkeit war . . .

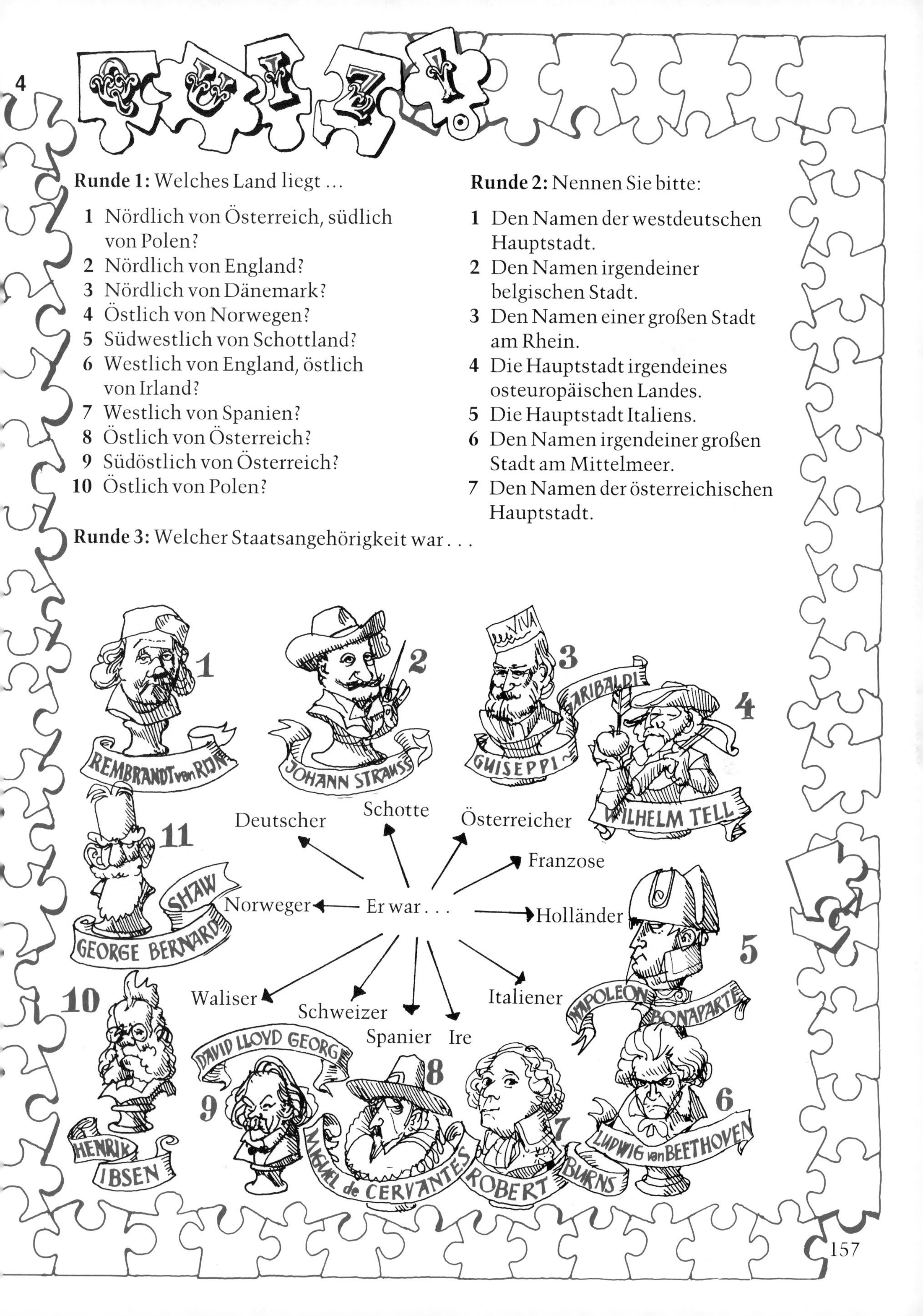

UNIT 51

1 Home sweet home?

Barbara and Daniela are discussing holidays (Barbara speaks first). Listen to their conversation twice, then write down whether each of the following statements is *true* or *false*.

1 Paris was fairly cheap for Daniela and Ludwig last year.

2 Barbara and Otto are not going to Venice this year because it's so expensive.

3 Ludwig finds holiday resorts expensive and noisy.

4 Barbara thinks that Daniela's bedroom needs repapering.

5 Ludwig wants to move the bath to the other side of the bathroom.

6 He also wants to build a shed and re-hang the sitting-room door.

7 Barbara thinks this won't cost very much.

Vocabulary

Venedig Venice
die Reisegruppe package tour
der Ferienort holiday resort
ruhig quiet
tapezieren wallpaper
umbauen rebuild
die Badewanne bath
der Gartenschuppen garden shed
andersrum the other way round
billig cheap

2
1. Wo waren Daniela und Ludwig letztes Jahr?
2. Wie war es?
3. Wohin fahren Barbara und Otto dieses Jahr?
4. Warum ist das nicht so teuer?
5. Was will Ludwig im Wohnzimmer machen?
6. Und im Badezimmer?
7. Und im Garten?
8. Was will er mit der Tür des Schlafzimmers machen?
9. Warum will er nicht in einen Ferienort fahren?

3 Family outing

Mir gefällt das Bild nicht.
Hier kommt dein Mann.
Meinem Mann gefällt es aber.
Hier kommt auch deine Schwester.
M ...... S ...... gefällt das Bild nicht.
Hier kommen deine Kinder.
......
Hier kommt deine Freundin Lu.
......
Hier kommt dein Vater.
......
Hier kommen deine Urgroßeltern.
......

4 Wer fährt wohin und wie?

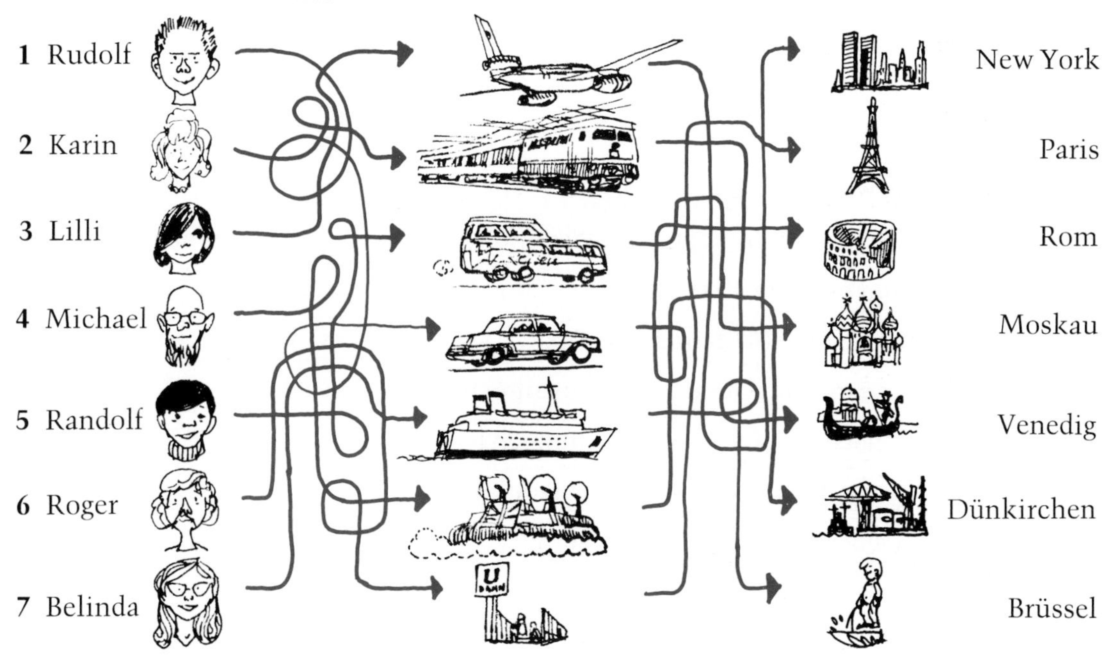

1 *Barbara* Wohin fahrt ihr dieses Jahr, Daniela? Nach Paris?
Daniela Nein, wir waren letztes Jahr in Paris. Es war sehr teuer. Weißt du, Barbara, die Pariser denken nur ans Geld.
Barbara Tja, das mag sein; aber Urlaub muß nicht immer teuer sein. Otto und ich fahren dieses Jahr nach Italien, nach Venedig.
Daniela Venedig muß aber affenteuer sein!
Barbara Nicht so sehr, wie man denkt. Wir fahren mit einer Reisegruppe dorthin. Was macht ihr denn?
Daniella Ach, wir bleiben zu Hause. Ludwig findet die Ferienorte zu teuer und nicht ruhig genug. Er will das Wohnzimmer tapezieren.
Barbara Das Wohnzimmer? Aber euer Wohnzimmer ist doch prima, es gefällt mir so, wie es ist.
Daniela Meinem Mann gefällt es aber nicht. Er will auch noch das Badezimmer umbauen.
Barbara Umbauen?!
Daniela Ja, er will die Badewanne an der anderen Seite haben.
Barbara Aber kann er denn das?
Daniela Das weiß ich noch nicht. Er auch nicht! Außerdem will er einen Schuppen im Garten bauen und die Tür vom Schlafzimmer andersrum hängen!
Barbara Das kostet aber eine Menge Geld, und ihr habt den ganzen Sommer Durcheinander! Es wäre besser und auch viel billiger, mit uns nach Venedig zu fahren.
Daniela Kann sein. Aber wie gesagt, mein Mann findet die Ferienorte zu teuer und vor allem nicht ruhig genug!

5 Wann, wie, wohin

Make new sentences by changing just one element of your last sentence each time.

1 Wir fahren mit dem Taxi dorthin. [dorthin] → [um drei Uhr]
2 Wir fahren um drei Uhr mit dem Taxi. [mit dem Taxi] → [nach Bremen]
3 Wir fahren um drei Uhr n...... [um drei Uhr] → [mit dem Bus]
4 ...... [nach Bremen] → [übermorgen]
5 ...... [mit dem Bus] → [in die Stadt]
6 ...... [übermorgen] → [ganz gern]
7 ...... [in die Stadt] → [jetzt]
8 ......

UNIT 52 REVISION

Grammar

1 Countries, nationalities, towns

Here are the names of the countries we have met, their adjectives, inhabitants and main differently spelled towns. Those printed in blue are new.

Amerika, amerikanisch, Amerikaner
Belgien, belgisch, Belgier; Brüssel
Dänemark, dänisch, Däne; Kopenhagen
Deutschland, deutsch, Deutscher; Hameln, Hannover, Koblenz, Köln, München, Nürnberg
England, englisch, Engländer
Europa, europäisch, Europäer
Frankreich, französisch, Franzose; Dünkirchen, Nizza
Holland, holländisch, Holländer
Irland, irisch, Ire
Italien, italienisch, Italiener; Mailand, Rom, Venedig
Jugoslawien, jugoslawisch, Jugoslawe
Norwegen, norwegisch, Norweger
Österreich, österreichisch, Österreicher; Wien
Polen, polnisch, Pole; Warschau
Portugal, portugiesisch, Portugiese; Lissabon
Schottland, schottisch, Schotte
Schweden, schwedisch, Schwede
Spanien, spanisch, Spanier
die Schweiz, schweizerisch, Schweizer; Basel, Genf
die Tschechoslowakei, tschechoslowakisch, Tscheche, Slowake; Prag
die UdSSR (Rußland), sowjetisch (russisch), Russe; Moskau
Ungarn, ungarisch, Ungar
Wales, walisisch, Waliser

2 Holländischer Käse, deutsche Butter und belgisches Bier gefallen mir.

Adjectives before nouns but without articles take the endings of **dieser**, e.g.

	singular	*plural*
nom.	holländischer Käse	italienische Spaghetti
acc.	holländischen Käse	italienische Spaghetti
dat.	holländischem Käse	italienischen Spaghetti

der Fensterputzer (-) window cleaner
der Leiter (-) leader
der Abgeordnete (*adj. as noun*) M.P.
der Eimer (-) bucket
der Minister (-) minister
der Esel (-) donkey
der Eingang (¨e) entrance
der Berg (-e) mountain
der Ozean (-e) ocean
der Lachs (-e) salmon
der Garten (¨) garden
der Ferienort (-e) holiday resort
der Schuppen (-) shed

die Arbeitsgruppe (-n) working party
die Seite (-n) side
die Vorderseite (-n) front
die Schulter (-n) shoulder
die Stelle (-n) job
die Arbeit work
die Arbeitslosigkeit unemployment
die Folge (-n) consequence
die Staatsangehörigkeit (-en) nationality
die Nordsee North Sea
die Ostsee Baltic
die Torte (-n) flan
die Schokolade chocolate
die Reisegruppe (-n) package tour
die Badewanne (-n) bath
eine Menge a lot
die Ferien (*pl.*) holidays
die Urgroßeltern (*pl.*) great-grandparents

das Gebäude (-) building
das Gleichgewicht balance
das Mittelmeer Mediterranean
das Gulasch goulash
das Luftkissenfahrzeug (-e) hovercraft
das Schiff (-e) ship

arbeiten work
sich hinauslehnen lean out
treten kick
fallen fall
herunterkommen come down
verbringen spend
nennen name
sich ergießen pour

3 Order of adverbs

Wir fahren um drei mit dem Taxi in die Stadt.

The normal order of adverbs in German is time, manner, place, i.e. telling us, in order, *when? how? where?*

4 The genitive case

As well as the three cases we have already met, nominative (subject case), accusative (object case), dative (case most frequent after prepositions, or = *to*. . .), there is a fourth case, the genitive, indicating possession. It is much less frequently met than the others, being usually avoided in spoken German, where it is thought rather pretentious. **Von** + dative is used instead. The genitive is normal in written German, however.

Endings of the genitive:

Masculine and neuter: **-es** on article, **-(e)s** on noun.
Feminine and plural: **-er** on article.
Adjective ending: **-en**
e.g.:
die Volkskammer der Deutschen Demokratischen Republik
die Länder des atlantischen Ozeans
die Freunde meiner Großeltern
(*in conversation*: die Freunde von meinen Großeltern)

The masculine or neuter noun in the genitive singular takes **-s** or **-es** according to these rules:

1 The noun ends in an **-s** sound already: add **-es**.
2 Stress is on the last syllable: add **-es**.
3 Otherwise: add **-s**. Foreign nouns normally add **-s**.

Obviously rule 2 includes single-syllable nouns.

Nouns that take **-n** in the accusative and dative singular also take **-n** in the genitive: **der Junge → des Jungen**.

Peters Buch; Annas Mutter

With proper nouns possession can be indicated as in English by adding **-s** to the name and putting it first. There is no apostrophe in German and this can only be done with names.

5 Für Hans, den neuen Mann, ist es schwer.

In this sentence **den neuen Mann** and **Hans** are identical (there is an invisible = sign before **den neuen Mann**). This is called apposition, and in German, nouns in apposition are always in the same case (here, accusative after **für**). Notice the commas round the second noun.

gefallen (+ *dat.*) please
tapezieren wallpaper
bauen build
umbauen rebuild
hängen hang

. . . gegenüber opposite . . .
fast nearly
beide both
ober upper
denn for
schwer difficult
einige some
weniger less
glücklicherweise luckily
flach flat
nördlich north
südlich south
östlich east
westlich west
atlantisch Atlantic
irgendein any
letzt last
affenteuer horribly dear
ruhig quiet
außerdem apart from that
anders(he)rum the other way round
billig cheap
voll full (of)

6 es gefällt mir; es gefällt meiner Mutter; die Berge gefallen mir nicht

Gefallen = *to like* literally means *to be pleasing*. So it is followed by a dative: **er gefällt mir** = *he is pleasing to me* = *I like him*.

7 New strong verbs we have met are:

fallen: du fällst, er fällt (*similarly*, gefallen)
mögen: ich mag, du magst, er mag
treten: du trittst, er tritt

A

1 Wer wohnt in London? —Engländer.
2 in München
3 in Moskau
4 in Genf
5 in Wien
6 in Venedig
7 in Dublin
8 in Nizza
9 in Madrid

B

1 Trinkst du Bier aus Portugal?
—Nein, p ...... B ...... gefällt mir nicht.

2 Ißt du Spaghetti aus Schweden?
3 Trinkst du Wein aus Schottland?
4 Ißt du Schokolade aus Rußland?
5 Trinkst du Whisky aus Wales?
6 Ißt du Gulasch aus Holland?

C

1 Wir fahren mit dem Taxi. – Wann, um drei?
—Ja, wir fahren um drei mit dem Taxi.

2 Vater arbeitet im Garten. – Wann, heute?
3 Mutti geht ins Wohnzimmer. – Wie, schnell?
4 Es schneit bald. – Wo, in der Schweiz?
5 Die Sonne scheint so schön. – Wann, den ganzen Tag?
6 Er zahlt mit seinem eigenen Geld! – Wann, jetzt?
7 Sie wohnt seit drei Jahren in Amerika. – Wie, glücklich?

D

1 Er kommt mit Klaus. Klaus ist ein alter Freund.
Er kommt mit Klaus, seinem a...... Freund.

2 Er bringt Rainer und Maria. Das sind seine Kinder.
3 Er hat nur einen Freund. Es ist sein Hund.
4 Er wohnt bei Ilke. Ilke ist eine Freundin seiner Schwester.
5 Er fährt immer in seinen eigenen Wagen. Er hat zwei blaue Mercedes.
6 Er steht auf der Zugspitze. Das ist der höchste Berg Deutschlands.

E Write as genitives:

1 Die Freunde von meinen Großeltern.
2 Die Tür vom Badezimmer.
3 Die letzte Seite vom Buch.
4 Der Leiter von einer Arbeitsgruppe.
5 Der erste Tag von deinem Urlaub.
6 Die Folgen von der Arbeitslosigkeit.
7 Die Eingänge von den Gebäuden.
8 Der Deckel vom Glas.

F Listen again to the tape of Die Fensterputzer, unit 49, and then write your own version of the story using this outline.

Arbeitsgruppe von Fensterputzern – die Fenster von der Volkskammer putzen – neuer Mann, Hans Ullmann – Leiter geht essen – Hans und Franz müssen die Vorderseite putzen – in die Gondel steigen – beginnen – Abgeordnete kommen aus dem Haupteingang – sich zu weit hinauslehnen – Gleichgewicht verlieren – gegen den Eimer voll Wasser treten – sich ergießen – auf den schönen grauen Anzug – gefällt ihm nicht – herunterkommen – zwanzig Minuten später – die Stelle verloren.

G It's a dog's life!

In pairs: discover exactly what you can't or should do with or for your dog in each case.

1

2

3

4

5

6

7

8

Vorsicht beware
bissig savage
ausnahmslos without exception
führen lead
werden erschossen will be shot
die Tollwut rabies
das Kurkonzert spa concert
das Mitbringen bringing
streng strictly
nicht gestattet not allowed
der Dienstraum office

UNIT 53

1 Briefkasten

The first letter box ▶
is in West Germany. Where are the others? How do you know?

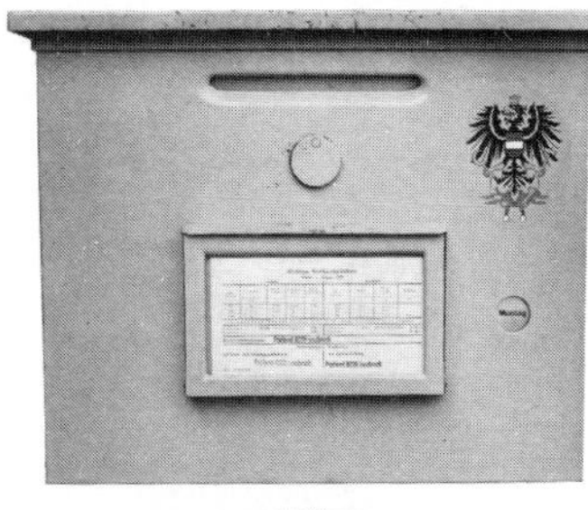

2

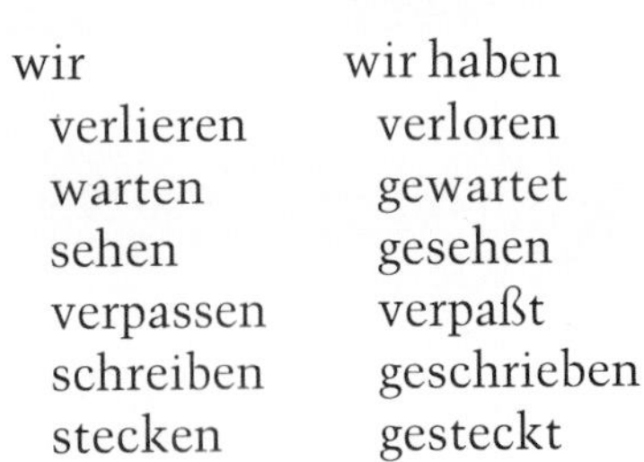

heute	**gestern**
wir	wir haben
verlieren	verloren
warten	gewartet
sehen	gesehen
verpassen	verpaßt
schreiben	geschrieben
stecken	gesteckt
vergessen	vergessen

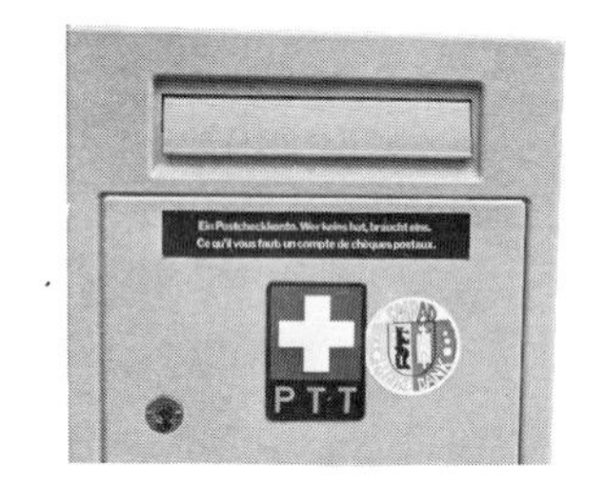

3 Auf der Post

Listen twice to the dialogue in the post office between Aldo and Daniel. Then explain in English in as much detail as you can what happens.

Listen to the tape again, and answer these questions orally. Then read the text on p. 168 and answer the questions in writing.

1. Szene

1 Was will Aldo kaufen?
2 Warum kauft er sie nicht am Automaten?
3 Warum kann Daniel hier nicht helfen?
4 Wen bittet Aldo, seine Briefmarke zu kaufen?
5 Was sagen die anderen Leute?
6 Wieviel Uhr ist es jetzt?
7 Wann ist die nächste Leerung?

2. Szene

8 Wie spät ist es jetzt?
9 Mit was für einem Schein bezahlt Aldo?
10 Warum bekommt er so viel Kleingeld?
11 Was haben die Jungen verpaßt?
12 Warum können sie den Brief nicht in den Briefkasten stecken?

Vocabulary

da drüben over there
der Schalter counter
die Briefmarke stamp
der Automat machine
funktionieren work
das Kleingeld (small) change
würde would
anstehen queue up
verpassen miss
keineswegs not at all; 'no way'

der Schein (bank)note
das Wechselgeld (money given as) change
der Brief letter
schreiben write
der Umschlag envelope
stecken put
vergessen forget

4 Have we missed it or haven't we?

ABFAHRT

1 Es ist zehn Uhr. Wir haben den Zug verpaßt.
— Ja, das stimmt, wir haben ihn verpaßt!
— Aber nein, wir haben ihn noch nicht verpaßt!

2 Es ist neun Uhr zehn. Wir haben den Bus verpaßt.

3	sieben Uhr zwanzig	das Schiff
4	Viertel vor acht	die Bahn
5	elf Uhr zwölf	das Flugzeug
6	Viertel nach zwei	das Luftkissenfahrzeug
7	halb zwölf	die letzte U-bahn

5 Yesterday was worse than ever!

1 Ich verliere alles. Gestern ...... meine Hose ......
— Gestern habe ich meine Hose verloren.

2 Ich warte schon zwanzig Minuten. Gestern ...... stundenlang ......

3 Ich verpasse manchmal die Bahn. Gestern ...... drei Bahnen ......

4 Ich schreibe viele Briefe. Gestern ...... fünfzehn ......

5 Ich vergesse alles. Gestern ...... meinen eigenen Namen ......

6 Ich stecke meine Briefe oft ohne Briefmarken in den Briefkasten. Gestern ...... ohne Umschlag ......

6

Here is a **Briefmarkenautomat** (a double one, actually). It's very simple. What do you think **Einwurf** means? **Bei Versagen** means *in case of non-functioning*. What do you think **Knopf drücken** means?

Now explain exactly what you have to do, what you get, where you get it.

3 Auf der Post

1. Szene

Aldo	Mensch, sieh nur die Schlange da drüben am Schalter! Und ich will bloß eine Briefmarke kaufen.
Daniel	Du, da draußen ist ein Briefmarkenautomat.
Aldo	Das weiß ich, den hab' ich auch schon gesehen. Er funktioniert aber nicht, er ist kaputt. Außerdem hab' ich kein Kleingeld.
Daniel	Tja, ich auch nicht. Frag mal die alte Dame dort: die steht als zweite in der Schlange. Sie sieht sehr nett aus – sie kauft dir bestimmt eine Briefmarke.
Aldo	Gute Idee. – Entschuldigung, ich brauche bloß eine Briefmarke zu einer Mark. Würden Sie bitte so nett sein und mir eine kaufen?
Verschiedene Leute	He, junger Mann, kommen Sie zurück! Hier steht man an! Wir haben auch lange gewartet! Wir kaufen auch nur Briefmarken! Sie müssen warten, wie wir!
Alte Dame	Ach, sehen Sie, junger Mann, das darf ich nicht.
Aldo	(*kommt zum Ende der Schlange zurück*) Alberne Idee von dir. Typisch! Und sieh mal die Uhr – schon fünf vor drei: die nächste Leerung ist um fünfzehn Uhr – wir verpassen sie bestimmt.
Daniel	Nein, keineswegs! Wir verpassen sie nicht!

2. Szene

Aldo	(*zehn Minuten später*) Na, siehst du, fünf Minuten nach. Nun haben wir die Leerung doch verpaßt!
Daniel	Du bist aber der nächste am Schalter.
Aldo	Das hilft mir nicht mehr! Um fünf Minuten nach! Das nächste Mal telefoniere ich!
Postbeamter	Na, junger Mann, was soll es sein? So viel Zeit hab' ich nicht.
Aldo	Was? Ach, ja, eine Briefmarke zu einer Mark, bitte.
Postbeamter	Ein Fünfzigmarkschein? Naja, ich habe im Moment keine Zehnmarkscheine. Ihr Wechselgeld muß ich Ihnen leider klein geben. Neunundvierzig Mark. Bitte.
Aldo	Danke sehr!
Daniel	Mensch, jetzt hast du aber Kleingeld genug.
Aldo	Ja, und wir haben die Leerung verpaßt. Wo ist denn der Brief?
Daniel	Der Brief? Du hast doch den Brief. Oder hast du ihn verloren?
Aldo	Ich? Aber nein, den Brief hab' ich nicht. D u hast ihn!
Daniel	Aber keineswegs. Es ist d e i n Brief. Du hast ihn geschrieben, du hast ihn in den Umschlag gesteckt, du hast die Adresse darauf geschrieben, und –
Aldo	Und?
Daniel	Und, Mensch, du hast nicht nur die Leerung verpaßt, du hast auch deinen Brief zu Hause vergessen!

UNIT 54

1 Einkaufen

Jeden Samstag fahren Herr und Frau Gruber in die Stadt, um einkaufen zu gehen. Sie haben meistens ziemlich viel zu kaufen. Frau Gruber macht zwei Listen, bringt vier Einkaufstaschen und jeder macht allein die Hälfte der Einkäufe. So geht es schneller.

Herr Gruber hat das Auto diesen Samstagmorgen im Parkhaus geparkt, und Frau Gruber hat ihm seine Liste und seine Taschen gegeben.

einkaufen shop
meistens mostly
ziemlich rather
die Einkaufstasche shopping bag
die Hälfte half
das Parkhaus multi-storey car park

„Und bitte vergiß nichts diese Woche. Letzten Samstag hast du die Kartoffeln vergessen."

die Kartoffel potato

„Ja, eben, das war schlimm. Wir haben das ganze Wochenende Reis gegessen. Und Reis mag ich nicht!"

„Na gut, also paß auf die Liste auf. Alles steht drauf. Vergiß nichts. Und mach schnell!"

aufpassen auf pay attention to

„Schön. In einer Dreiviertelstunde bin ich zurück."

Fünfzig Minuten später sitzt Frau Gruber wieder im Parkhaus im Wagen und wartet auf ihren Mann. Sie hat alles auf ihrer Liste gekauft: zwei volle Taschen stehen im Kofferraum des Autos. Jetzt kommt Herr Gruber mit seinen Taschen zurück. Er stellt sie auf den Rücksitz des Autos.

der Kofferraum boot
stellen put
der Rücksitz back seat

„Nun, gib mir deine Liste. Komm, gib sie mir." Herr Gruber gibt sie seiner Frau. „Nun also: Kartoffeln. Hast du Kartoffeln gekauft?"

„Ja."

„Und Butter, Eier, Fleisch?"

„Ja, das habe ich auch gekauft."

„Und Zucker? Und das Gemüse?"

der Zucker sugar

„Ja, Zucker hab' ich auch gekauft, und Gemüse."

„Und Schlagsahne von der Konditorei?"

„Und auch Schlagsahne."

die Schlagsahne whipped cream
die Konditorei cake shop

„Salz und Pfeffer hast du nicht vergessen?"

„Nein. Und die Dose Milch hab' ich auch gekauft. Und die Schachtel Streichhölzer."

die Dose tin
die Schachtel box
das Streichholz match

„Na! Alles andere hab' ich. Diese Woche hast du anscheinend nichts vergessen."

„Richtig. Und ich habe auch ein paar Blumen für dich gekauft." Und Herr Gruber überreicht seiner Frau einen schönen Blumenstrauß.

die Blume flower
überreichen present with
der Blumenstrauß bunch of flowers

„Na, das ist aber wirklich nett von dir. Komm, wir fahren jetzt nach Hause."

Herr Gruber steckt den Schlüssel in das Zündschloß des Autos und dreht ihn um. Nichts passiert. Er dreht ihn wieder um. Der Motor startet nicht. Er versucht es ein drittes Mal. Nichts. Dann sieht er auf die Benzinuhr.

das Zündschloß ignition
die Benzinuhr petrol gauge

„Liebling . . ." sagt er. „Ich habe leider auch diese Woche etwas vergessen."

„Wieso?" sagt Frau Gruber; sie sieht auf Herrn Grubers Liste.

„Liebling, es tut mir leid . . . wir haben kein Benzin mehr im Tank!"

Du bist Herr Gruber. Antworte:

1 Was machst du jeden Samstag?
2 Wie machst du und deine Frau die Einkäufe?
3 Wo parkst du heute?
4 Was hast du letzten Samstag vergessen?
5 Wie lange soll das Einkaufen heute dauern?
6 Wohin legt deine Frau ihre vollen Einkaufstaschen?
7 Was hast du gekauft?
8 Was noch?
9 Was tust du mit dem Zündschlüssel?
10 Was passiert?
11 Warum?

2 Herr Gruber geht einkaufen

Was hat er hier gekauft?   Und hier?   ......

3 Hand it all over!

Ich hab eine Liste. — Gib mir die Liste, komm, gib sie mir.

Kartoffeln
Milch
Gemüse
Salz
Eier
Fleisch
das Wechselgeld

4 Weihnachtsgeschenke

Herr Gruber gibt seiner Mutter einen Schirm? — Nein, er gibt ihn seiner Frau.
seiner Schwester ...... — Nein, er gibt ....
seinem Vater ...... — ......
seiner Tante Gertrud ......
seinem Sohn
Onkel Willi
seiner Urgroßmutter
......

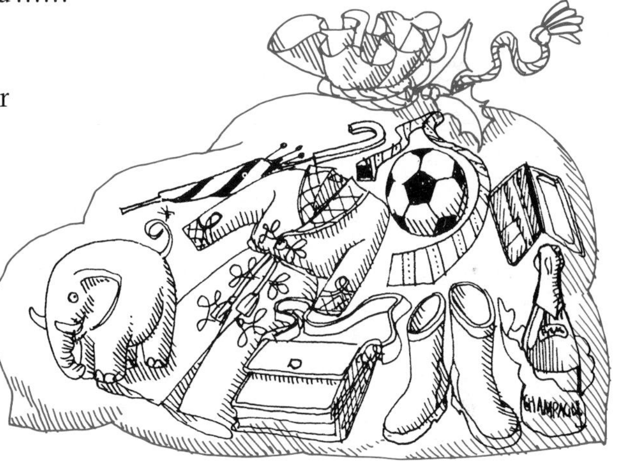

5 In pairs, play the Grubers

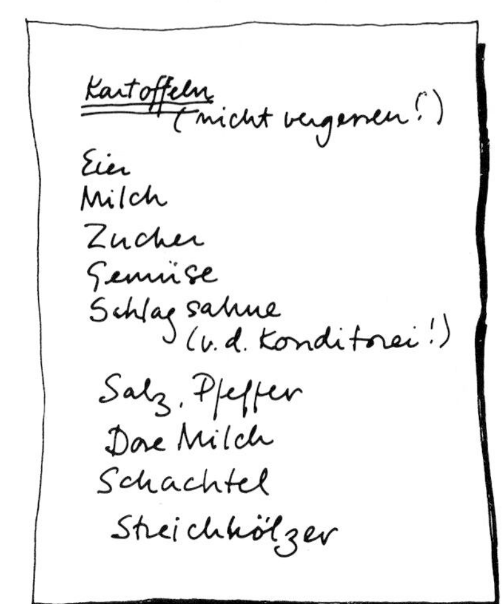

Kartoffeln (nicht vergessen!)
Eier
Milch
Zucker
Gemüse
Schlagsahne (v.d. Konditorei!)
Salz, Pfeffer
Dose Milch
Schachtel Streichhölzer

UNIT 55

1 Volltanken

Erste Szene
Günter kommt herein, zieht den Mantel aus.

Günter Wie spät ist es?
Marisa Fünf Minuten nach acht.
Günter Ach, Mensch, ich habe die Nachrichten im Fernsehen verpaßt. Schalt' mal schnell ein!
Marisa OK, OK. Du hast nur fünf Minuten verpaßt.
Sprecher . . . fünfundzwanzig prozentige Erhöhung der Benzinpreise heute ab zwanzig Uhr. – In Bonn hat der Arbeitsminister gesagt, . . .
Günter Mensch, hab' ich das richtig kapiert? Fünfundzwanzig Prozent Erhöhung! Ab zwanzig Uhr?
Marisa Das hat er gesagt. Warte nur, gleich kommt das Bild.
Günter Fünfundzwanzig Prozent! Und der Tank ist ganz leer. Du, ich fahre schnell zur Tankstelle, vielleicht bekomme ich das Benzin noch zum alten Preis.
Marisa Wie du willst. Lohnt es sich denn?
Günter Sicher lohnt es sich!

die Nachrichten news
das Fernsehen television
einschalten switch on
prozentig per cent
die Erhöhung rise
ab from
kapieren get (= *understand*)
das Bild picture
sich lohnen be worth it

1 Was hat Günter verpaßt?
2 Hat er alles verpaßt?
3 Was hört er?
4 Was tut er?
5 Warum?

Zweite Szene
Günter hält vor der Tankstelle, steigt aus, öffnet den Tank. Der Tankwart kommt herüber.

Günter Volltanken, bitte! Super.
Tankwart Bitte sehr. Soll ich auch nach dem Öl sehen?
Günter Nein, nein, kein Öl, kein Wasser, keine Luft. Nur Benzin. Und voll, ja?

der Tankwart petrol station attendant
sehen nach check
das Öl oil
die Luft air

Tankwart Der Tank war bestimmt leer, es geht so viel hinein. Für hundert Mark etwa.

etwa about; approximately

Günter Macht nichts! Morgen kostet es noch viel mehr als hundert Mark.

Tankwart Meinen Sie? Woher wissen Sie denn d a s ?

Günter Sie haben doch ein Radio da – hören Sie mal die nächsten Nachrichten!

hören listen

Tankwart Na. Fünfundneunzig Mark, bitte.

Günter Großartig! Bitte sehr!

großartig great

1 Was sagt Günter zum Tankwart?
2 Wieviel Benzin geht in den Tank hinein, meint der Tankwart?
3 Wieviel geht wirklich hinein?
4 Weiß der Tankwart von der Preiserhöhung?
5 Was schlägt Günter vor?

Dritte Szene
Günter kommt herein.

Günter Prima! Ich habe fünfundzwanzig Mark gespart!

sparen save

Marisa So. Und was hat dein Benzin gekostet?

Günter Fünfundneunzig Mark. Ich hatte einen fast leeren Tank. Und ich habe es noch zum alten Preis bekommen – morgen kostet es hundertzwanzig.

hatte had

Marisa In Warschau vielleicht. Ich habe eben die Schlagzeilen am Ende der Nachrichten gehört: die Preiserhöhung war in Polen, nicht hier. Morgen kostet es fünfundneunzig Mark, wie heute!

die Schlagzeile headline

1 Wieviel Geld hat Günter gespart, meint er?
2 Wo kostet es morgen hundertzwanzig Mark, meint seine Frau?
3 Wo war die Preiserhöhung?
4 Woher weiß Marisa das?

2 Gudrun doesn't speak English . . .

1 Ask her to turn the telly on.
— Wollen Sie ......

2 Tell her you don't like the programme.
— Diese Sendung ......

3 Ask her to change channels.
— ...... umschalten.

4 Tell her you don't like this programme either.
— ...... auch nicht.

5 Ask her to turn it off again.
— ...... wieder ausschalten.

3 There I was, standing on the landing, when in flew this bird

Copy out this diagram, then add the rest of the arrows, numbered like this one, to indicate where the bird went.

1 Der Vogel fliegt herein.
2 Er fliegt hinunter.
3 Er fliegt herauf.
4 Er fliegt hinauf.
5 Er fliegt herunter.
6 Er fliegt hinaus.

4 An der Tankstelle

Use these prices to buy petrol from your partner.

— { Volltanken, bitte. Super.
Für fünfzig Mark Diesel, bitte.
Zwanzig Liter Normal, bitte. }

— Bitte sehr. ...... Mark ...... bitte.
Sonst noch etwas?

— { Ja, bitte. Wollen Sie bitte nach	dem Öl	sehen?
Nein, danke. }	dem Kühlwasser	
	der Batterie	
	den Reifen	

— Ja gerne. . . In Ordnung.
— Danke schön.
— Auf Wiedersehen.

UNIT 56 REVISION

Grammar

1 The perfect tense

We express the past in at least four different ways in English: *I put, I was putting, I have put, I have been putting.* In spoken German for most verbs the past is expressed in one way only: the perfect tense, formed with **haben** + past participle:

stellen → ich habe gestellt.

The past participle must go at the end of the clause:

Ich habe die Taschen in den Kofferraum gestellt.

The form of the past participle may be:

ge . . t (most verbs), e.g. stellen → gestellt
ge . . en } (strong verbs) e.g. sehen → gesehen
ge . . en + vowel change } (strong verbs) e.g. schreiben → geschrieben

Most verbs are spoken with the stress on the first syllable.
Those that have the stress later have no **ge-** in their past participles:

ka*pie*ren → kapiert
ver*ges*sen → vergessen
ver*lie*ren → verloren.

Sein (ich war) and **haben (ich hatte)** use a different, one-word tense to express the past. We shall be learning more about the past tenses at the beginning of Book 2.

2 Order of objects

Gib *mir die Liste* – give *me the list*: pronoun before noun
Gib *Sie mir* – give *it me*: two pronouns, accusative first
Gib *deiner Schwester die Tasche* – give *your sister the bag*: two nouns, dative first.

This order is identical with the normal English order.

3 hin, her

Hin means *away from the speaker*, **her** means *towards the speaker*.

They are used with separable verbs, in which case they form part of the prefix:

Kommen Sie herein!

They are also used as prefixes in their own right:

der Schein (-e) (bank)note
der Moment (-e) moment
der Brief (-e) letter
der Umschlag (¨-e) envelope
der Schalter (-) counter
der Automat (-en) (vending) machine
der Knopf (¨-e) button
der Einkauf (¨-e) purchase
der Kofferraum (¨-e) (car) boot
der Rücksitz (-e) back seat
der Zucker sugar
der Blumenstrauß (¨-e) bunch of flowers
der Motor (-en) engine
der Tank (-s) tank
der Tabakladen (¨) tobacconist's
der Liter (-) litre
der Reifen (-) tyre
der Sprecher (-) newsreader
der Tankwart (-e) petrol station attendant
der Vogel (¨) bird

die Briefmarke (-n) stamp
die Einkaufstasche (-n) shopping bag
die Hälfte (-n) half
die Kartoffel (-n) potato
eine Dreiviertelstunde three quarters of an hour
die Bahn (-en) train
die Schlagsahne whipped cream
die Konditorei (-en) cake shop
die Dose (-n) tin
die Schachtel (-n) box
die Blume (-n) flower
die Gemüsehandlung (-en) greengrocer's
die Metzgerei (-en) butcher's
die Schlagzeile (-n) headline
die Batterie (-n) battery
die Ordnung order
die Nachrichten (*f.pl.*) news
die Erhöhung (-en) rise
die Luft air
die Sendung (-en) broadcast

das Wechselgeld change (*given*)
das Kleingeld change (= *coins*)
das Ende (-n) end
das Parkhaus (¨-er) multi-storey car park
das Wochenende (-n) weekend

Bring es her, stell es hin!

Hin by itself often means *down*.

4 **Verbal nouns** (e.g. *shopping, bringing, writing*)

English forms these with *-ing*, German with the infinitive with a capital letter. They are always neuter:

das Einkaufen, das Mitbringen, das Schreiben.

5 New strong verbs we have met, present tense:

halten: du hältst, er hält
vergessen: du vergißt, er vergißt
vorschlagen: du schlägst vor, er schlägt vor.

A A trip to town

Was hast du hier gemacht?

— Ich habe T......
g......

1

2

(eine Bahn; nehmen → genommen)

das Salz(-e) salt
das Streichholz (¨-er) match
das Benzin petrol
das Lebensmittelgeschäft(-e) grocer's
das Wirtshaus (¨-er) pub; inn
das Weihnachtsgeschenk (-e) Christmas present
das Fernsehen television
das Prozent percent
das Bild (-er) picture
das Öl(-e) oil
das Radio (-s) radio

bitten ask
telefonieren telephone
vergessen forget
stecken put (in)
schreiben write
funktionieren work
anstehen queue up
verpassen miss
drücken press
einkaufen shop
aufpassen auf pay attention to
schnell machen be quick
stellen put
überreichen present with
antworten answer
dauern last
sparen save
einschalten switch on
umschalten switch over
ausschalten switch off
kapieren (*colloq.*) understand
sich lohnen be worth (it)
halten stop
volltanken fill up
sehen nach check
vorschlagen suggest

da drüben over there
verschieden various
keineswegs not at all
stundenlang for hours
manchmal sometimes
meistens mostly
ziemlich rather
prozentig per cent
etwa about; approximately
ab from
großartig great

3

4

(einen Film)
5

6

7
(warten auf + *acc.*)

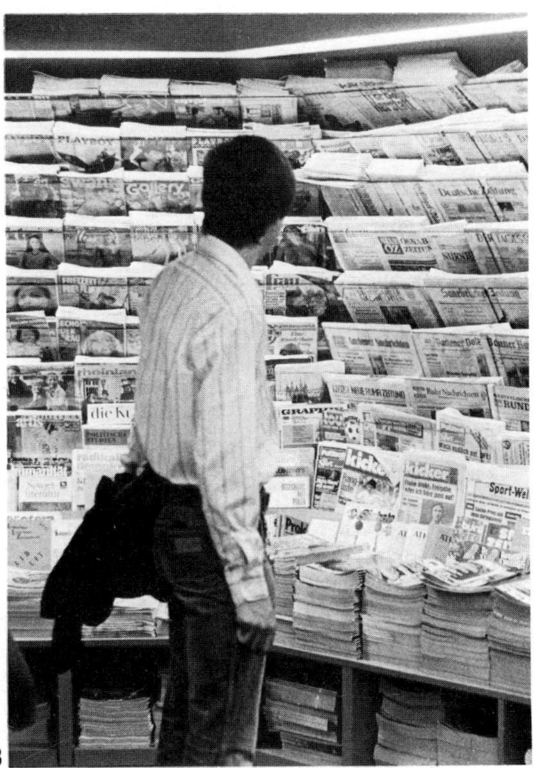

8

B 1 Soll ich deinem Bruder das Geld geben?
— Ja, gib es ihm!

2 dieser Dame das Salz reichen?
3 den Schmidts ihr Weihnachtsgeschenk geben?
4 dem Wachtmeister meinen Namen sagen?
5 Mutter den Wein reichen?
6 ihren Freunden die Blumen geben?
7 dem Tankwart das Kleingeld geben?

C I can't stand any of it!

1 Tapezierst du gern?
— Ach nein, das Tapezieren hasse ich!

2 Schreibst du gern?
3 Kaufst du gern ein?
4 Sparst du gern?
5 Baust du gern um?
6 Denkst du gern?
7 Stehst du gern auf?
8 Wäscht du gern ab?

D *In pairs:* Play customer and post-office counter clerk. Buy the following combinations of stamps (make sure you get your currencies right!)

POSTWERTZEICHEN (BRIEFMARKEN)

Ich hätte gern . . .

1 2 × 20 Pf, 4 × M 1.00, 1 × M 1.20
2 7 × 80 Pf, 1 × 40 Pf, 2 × DM 2.00
3 2 × 10 Sch, 1 × 12 Sch, 9 × 5 Sch
4 1 × SF 0.50, 3 × SF 1.00, 2 × SF 0.75

E Die Grubers gehen einkaufen

Listen to the story in unit 54:1 again, then write it in your own words, shortening it by cutting out unnecessary detail. Follow this plan:

Jeden Samstag – einkaufen gehen – zwei Listen, vier Einkaufstaschen, jeder macht die Hälfte – diesen Samstagmorgen – im Parkhaus – „Vergiß nichts! – schnell machen" – fünfzig Minuten später – warten auf – zwei Taschen im Kofferraum – alles auf der Liste gekauft – auch Blumen – Schlüssel ins Zündschloß des Autos stecken – umdrehen – nichts passiert – wieder – ein drittes Mal – auf die Benzinuhr sehen – wieder etwas vergessen – kein Benzin mehr im Tank.

F Buying petrol

Zapfsäule

Motor abschalten! **Rauchen verboten!**

1. **Zapfventil abheben** und in Tank einführen.
2. **Zapfventil betätigen.** Im vollen Tank schließt Zapfventil selbsttätig. Füllgeschwindigkeit kann am Handhebel reguliert werden.
3. **Zapfventil bitte sorgfältig einhängen.**
4. **Tank wieder schließen.**
5. **Beleg entnehmen** und an der Kasse vorlegen.

Many West German petrol stations are **SB** (= **Selbstbedienung**, *self-service*). Use the vocabulary to explain in detail how you operate this pump.

die Zapfsäule petrol pump
das Zapfventil nozzle
betätigen operate
selbsttätig automatically
die Geschwindigkeit speed
der Hebel lever
der Beleg voucher
vorlegen present

Only a very limited number of petrol stations in the DDR, like this one, sell petrol of a quality that can be used in Western cars. They have the sign **Intertank**, and you must pay either in Western currency, or with vouchers like this one bought with Western currency before your visit.

INTERNATIONALER TANKDIENST
des VEB Minol
Berechtigt zum Bezug von Kraft- und Schmierstoffen und anderen Erzeugnissen
im Werte von DM 5,–
an allen öffentlichen Tankstellen der DDR
VI 030162 /5

Present tense and past participle of irregular verbs

All verbs we have met showing irregularities are included.
Only irregular parts of the present are given.
Only past participles we have met are given.

dürfen	**ich/er darf, du darfst**
essen	**du/er ißt**; p.p. **gegessen**
fahren	**du fährst, er fährt**
fallen	**du fällst, er fällt**
geben	**du gibst, er gibt**; p.p. **gegeben**
gefallen	→ fallen
haben	**du hast, er hat**
halten	**du hältst, er hält**
helfen	**du hilfst, er hilft**
können	**ich/er kann, du kannst**
lassen	**du/er läßt**
laufen	**du läufst, er läuft**
lesen	**du/er liest**
mögen	**ich/er mag, du magst**
müssen	**ich/er muß, du mußt**
nehmen	**du nimmst, er nimmt**; p.p. **genommen**
schlafen	**du schläfst, er schläft**
schreiben	p.p. **geschrieben**
sehen	**du siehst, er sieht**; p.p. **gesehen**
sein	**ich bin, du bist, er ist, wir/sie/Sie sind, ihr seid**
sollen	**ich/er soll, du sollst**
sprechen	**du sprichst, er spricht**
tragen	**du trägst, er trägt**
treffen	**du triffst, er trifft**
treten	**du trittst, er tritt**
tun	**ich tue, du tust, er/ihr tut, wir/sie/Sie tun**
vergessen	→ essen; p.p. **vergessen**
verlieren	p.p. **verloren**
vorschlagen	**du schlägst vor, er schlägt vor**
waschen	**du/er wäscht**
werden	**du wirst, er wird**
wissen	**ich/er weiß, du weißt**
wollen	**ich/er will, du willst**

German – English Vocabulary

Plurals are given in brackets. Irregular verbs are marked*; their irregularities can be found in the verb list on p. 180. Numbers after the English meaning of a word indicate the first unit in which it appears with this meaning.
a.n. = adjective used as noun: takes capital letter and adjective endings.

ab, from 55
der **Abend** (-e), evening 35
das **Abendbrot** (-e), evening meal 7
das **Abendessen** (-), dinner 29
abends, in the evening 8
aber, though 3; but 9
der **Abgeordnete** (a.n.), deputy; M.P. 49
abholen, call for 29
abmachen, remove 38
abnehmen, take off 46
absetzen, take off 37
abwaschen, wash up 39
ach!, oh! 3
acht, eight 6
achte, eighth 27
Achtung!, look out! 44
achtzehn, eighteen 7
achtzig, eighty 6
die **Adresse** (-n), address 43
affenteuer, horribly dear 51
albern, silly 13
alle (*colloq.*), finished; all gone 3
alles, everything 6
  alles Gute, all the best 29
als, than 45
also, so 1
alt, old 32
(das) **Amerika,** America 35
amerikanisch, American 47
an, on 22
andere, other 37
andersrum, the other way round 51
angenehm, pleasant
  sehr angenehm!, pleased to meet you 31
ankommen:
  es kommt d(a)rauf an, it depends 39
die **Ankunft,** arrival 34
die **Anmeldung,** reception 44
anscheinend, apparently 46
anstehen, queue up 53
antworten, answer 54
anziehen, put on 37
der **Anzug** (¨-e), suit 11
der **Apfel** (¨), apple 45
der **Apfelsaft,** apple juice 29
die **Apotheke** (-n), chemist's 21
der **Apparat** (-e):
  am Apparat, on the phone; 'speaking' 41
der **April,** April 27
die **Arbeit,** work 49
arbeiten, work 49
die **Arbeitsgruppe** (-n), working party 49
die **Arbeitslosigkeit,** unemployment 49
der **Arbeitsminister,** Minister of Labour 49
arm, poor 45
der **Arm** (-e), arm 46
der **Arzt** (¨-e), doctor 46
das **Aspirin,** aspirin 39
atlantisch, Atlantic 50
au!, ouch! 39
auch, also; as well 2
auf, open 19; on 23
  auf haben, be open 19
aufgehen, open 43
aufmachen, open 37
aufpassen auf (+ *acc.*), pay attention to 54
aufschreiben, write down 43
aufsetzen, put on 37
aufstehen, get up 37
aufwachen, wake up 37
das **Auge** (-n), eye 17
der **August,** August 27
aus, out of 23
der **Ausgang** (¨-e), exit 44
ausnahmslos, without exception 52
ausschalten, switch off 55
aussehen, look like 46
außer, except 22
außerdem, apart from that 51
die **Aussicht,** view 33
aussteigen, get out 38
aussuchen, choose 37
ausziehen, take off 37
das **Auto** (-s), car 10
der **Automat** (-en), (vending) machine 53

die **Bäckerei** (-en), baker's 21
das **Bad** (¨-er), bath 25
der **Bademantel** (¨), dressing gown 37
die **Badewanne** (-n), bath 51
das **Badezimmer** (-), bathroom 37
die **Bahn** (-en), train 53

der **Bahnhof** (-̈e), station 35
bald, soon 33
der **Balkon** (-e), balcony 42
die **Banane** (-n), banana 6
die **Bank** (-en), bank 21
der **Baron** (-e), baron 18
die **Baronin** (-nen), baroness 18
Basel, Basle 34
die **Batterie** (-n), battery 55
bauen, build 51
der **Baum** (-̈e), tree 23
(das) **Bayern,** Bavaria 34
bedauerlich, unfortunate 43
sich **befinden,** be (situated) 38
beginnen, begin 36
bei, at the house of; at . . .'s 28
beide, both 49
das **Bein** (-e), leg 46
bekommen, get 20
der **Beleg** (-e), voucher 56
(das) **Belgien,** Belgium 50
belgisch, Belgian 50
das **Benzin,** petrol 54
die **Benzinuhr** (-en), petrol gauge 54
der **Berg** (-e), mountain 50
beschreiben, describe 17
besser, better 9
beste, best 43
am **besten,** best 35
bestimmt, certainly; bound to be 30
betätigen, operate 56
das **Bett** (-en), bed 42
bezahlen, pay 13
das **Bier,** beer 1
der **Bikini** (-s), bikini 27
das **Bild** (-er), picture 55
billig, cheap 51
der **Bindestrich** (-e), hyphen 41
die **Birne** (-n), pear 6
bis, until 25; by 25
bis morgen, see you tomorrow 13
ein **bißchen,** a bit 33
bissig, savage 52
bitte, please 1; there you are 6; don't mention it 6
bitten, ask (= request) 53
blaß, pale 46
blau, blue 11
bleiben, stay 13
blitzen, lighten 27
blond, blonde; fair 33
der/die **Blonde** (a.n.), blond(e) 50
bloß, merely; simply 46
die **Blume** (-n), flower 54
der **Blumenstrauß** (-̈e), bunch of flowers 54
die **Bluse** (-n), blouse 11
der **Boden,** floor 43
die **Bratwurst** (-̈e), fried sausage 13
brauchen, need 25
braun, brown 11
der **Brief** (-e), letter 53
der **Briefkasten** (-̈), letter box 22
die **Briefmarke** (-n), stamp 53
der **Briefmarkenautomat** (-en), stamp machine 53
die **Brieftasche** (-n), wallet 29
die **Brille** (-n), (pair of) spectacles 9
das **Brot,** bread 7
das **Brötchen** (-), bread roll 14
die **Brücke** (-n), bridge 45
der **Bruder** (-̈), brother 31
Brüssel, Brussels 51
das **Buch** (-̈er), book 13
das **Bücherregal** (-e), book case 42
der **Buchstabe** (-n), letter 46
buchstabieren, spell 41
die **Bundesbahn,** Federal Railways 43
die **Bundesrepublik,** Federal Republic (= W. Germany) 45
bunt, brightly coloured 46
das **Büro** (-s), office 19
der **Bus** (-sse), bus 48
der **Busbahnhof** (-̈e), bus/coach station 35
die **Butter,** butter 7

der **Champagner,** champagne 10
der **Champignon** (-s), mushroom 29
die **Cola,** cola 1

da, there 8; then 19
dafür, for it 46
dagegen, against it 46
dahin, to there 34
die **Dame** (-n), lady 22
meine Dame, madam 29
danach, after that 43
(das) **Dänemark,** Denmark 50
Dank:
recht vielen Dank, thank you very much 29
danke, thank you 6
danke schön, thank you very much 6
dann, then 13
das, that 3
die **Dauer,** period 40
dauern, last 54
dazu, to that 35
die **DDR** (= Deutsche Demokratische Republik), GDR (= E. Germany) 45
der **Deckel** (-), lid 38
dein, your 17
die **Delikateßwaren** (*pl.*), (goods sold in) delicatessen 9
denken, think 43
denken an (+ *acc.*), think of 51
denn, then 13; for 49
deutlich, clearly 37
deutsch, German 41
Deutsch, German (language) 48
der **Deutsche** (a.n.), German 47

(das) **Deutschland,** Germany 34
der **Dezember,** December 27
dich, you 29
der **Dienstag,** Tuesday 22
der **Dienstraum** (¨e), office 52
der **Diesel,** diesel (fuel) 55
dieser, this 14
diesmal, this time 43
dir, (to) you 29
die **Diskothek** (-en), disco 22
doch, after all 1; yes (in contradiction) 10
der **Dollar** (-s), dollar 47
der **Dom** (-e), cathedral 29
donnern, thunder 27
der **Donnerstag,** Thursday 22
das **Doppelzimmer,** double room 25
dort, there 5
die **Dose** (-n), tin 54
draußen, outside 25
sich **drehen,** turn 33
drei, three 1
dreißig, thirty 6
eine **Dreiviertelstunde,** three quarters of an hour 54
dreizehn, thirteen 7
drin, in it 43
dritte, third 27
da **drüben,** over there 53
drücken, press 53
du, you 2; (*exclamation*) hey; come on 33
dumm, stupid 45
dunkel, dark 37
durch, through 35
das **Durcheinander,** mess 51
***dürfen,** may 25
die **Dusche** (-n), shower 25

eben, exactly; quite right 38; just 39
der **Edamer,** Edam cheese 5
das **Ei** (-er), egg 14
eigen, own 52
eigentlich, in fact 33
die **Eile,** hurry 33
der **Eimer** (-), bucket 49
ein(s), a 1; one 1
der **Eingang** (¨e), entrance 49
einige, some 49
der **Einkauf** (¨e), purchase 54
einkaufen, shop 54
das **Einkaufen,** shopping 54
die **Einkaufstasche** (-n), shopping bag 54
einladen, invite 29
die **Einlage** (-n), filling, garnish 29
einschalten, switch on 55
einschließlich, inclusive of 25
eintreten, enter 44
einundzwanzig, twenty-one 7
der **Einwurf,** amount to be inserted 53
das **Einzelzimmer** (-), single room 23
das **Eis,** ice 13
der **Elefant** (-en), elephant 38
elf, eleven 7
das **Ende** (-n), end 53
endlich, finally 36
der **Endpreis** (-e), final price (*i.e. including VAT and service*) 29
(das) **England,** England 33
der **Engländer** (-), Englishman 33
englisch, English 47
der **Enkel** (-), grandson 31
die **Enkelin** (-nen), granddaughter 31
das **Enkelkind** (-er), grandchild 31
entlang, along 35
Entschuldigung!, excuse me 6
er, he 5
die **Erde,** earth; ground 33
sich **ergießen,** pour 49
die **Erhöhung** (-en), rise 55
erlaubt, allowed 40
erschossen, shot 52
erst, only (*time*) 13
erste, first 27
zum **erstenmal,** for the first time 33
der **Esel** (-), ass; donkey 49
***essen,** eat 13
das **Essen,** food 29; meal 40
etwa, about; approximately 55
etwas, something 39
euer, your 18
(das) **Europa,** Europe 36
europäisch, European 50

fabelhaft, fabulous 18
***fahren,** travel; go by vehicle 22
das **Fahrzeug** (-e), vehicle 40
fallen, fall 49
falsch, wrong 41
das **Familienfoto** (-s), family photo 31
fantastisch, fantastic 18
die **Farbe** (-n), colour 11
fast, nearly 49
der **Februar,** February 27
der **Fehler** (-), error 33
das **Fenster** (-), window 26
der **Fensterputzer** (-), window cleaner 49
die **Ferien** (*pl.*), holidays 28
der **Ferienort** (-e), holiday resort 51
das **Fernsehen,** television 55
der **Fernsehturm** (¨e), television tower 45
fertig, ready 39
das **Filetsteak** (-s), fillet steak 27
der **Film** (-e), film 56
finden, find 18
flach, flat 50
die **Flasche** (-n), bottle 5
das **Fleisch,** meat 30
fliegen, fly 33
der **Flughafen** (¨), airport 34
das **Flugzeug** (-e), aircraft 34
der **Flur** (-e), hall 42

die **Folge** (-n), consequence 49
das **Formular** (-e), form 47
fragen, ask 38
der **Franken** (-), (Swiss) franc 47
(das) **Frankreich,** France 36
französisch, French 36
die **Frau** (-en), Mrs 7; wife 25; woman; lady 43
das **Fräulein** (-), girl 14; Miss 29
frei, free 25
der **Freitag,** Friday 22
der **Freund** (-e), friend 31
die **Freundin** (-nen), (girl) friend 33
frieren, freeze 27
früh, early 34
der **Frühling** (-e), spring 27
das **Frühstück** (-e), breakfast 25
führen, lead 52
das **Fundbüro** (-s), lost property office 43
fünf, five 3
fünfzehn, fifteen 5
fünfzig, fifty 6
funktionieren, work 53
für, for 1
der **Fuß** (¨e), foot 46
der **Fußball,** football 40
der **Fußballspieler** (-) footballer 48

ganz, right; quite 9; all; the whole of 33
gar . . ., . . . at all 31
die **Garage** (-n), garage 21
die **Garderobe,** hats and coats 44
der **Garten** (¨), garden 51
das **Gästezimmer** (-), spare room 42
das **Gebäude** (-), building 49
***geben,** give 31
es gibt, there is 14
der **Geburtstag** (-e), birthday 28
geduldig, patient 33
gefährlich, dangerous 33
***gefallen** (+ *dat.*), please (be pleasing to) 49
der **Geflügelsalat,** chicken salad 29
gegen, towards 29
der **Gegenstand** (¨e), object 43
gegenüber, opposite 49
gehen, go 7; be OK 25
gelb, yellow 11
das **Geld** (-er) money 13
gemeinsam, common 31
gemischt, mixed 29
das **Gemüse,** vegetable(s) 32
die **Gemüsehandlung** (-en), greengrocer's 54
genau, exactly 25
Genf, Geneva 34
genug, enough 35
geöffnet, open 19
gern(e), gladly 10
ich hätte gern, I should like 6
einen gern haben, like someone 39
wir trinken gern, we like (drinking) 10
wie **gesagt,** as I said 50

das **Geschenk** (-e), present 12
geschlossen, closed 22
die **Geschwindigkeit** (-en), speed 56
das **Gesicht** (-er), face 17
gestattet, allowed 52
gestern, yesterday 22
gestohlen, stolen 43
gestorben, dead 41
gesund, healthy 26
die **Getränkekarte** (-n), wine (drinks) list 29
das **Glas** (¨er), glass 2; jar 38
die **Glasscherbe** (-n), broken bit of glass 23
glauben, believe 33
gleich, straight away 13
das **Gleichgewicht,** balance 49
glücklich, happy 52
glücklicherweise, luckily 49
gnädig:
gnädige Frau, madam 43
die **Gondel** (-n), gondola; car 33
Gott:
Gott sei Dank!, thank goodness 29
grau, grey 11
groß, big 17
großartig!, great! 55
die **Großeltern** (*pl.*), grandparents 31
die **Großmutter** (¨), grandmother 31
der **Großvater** (¨), grandfather 31
grün, green 11
das **Gulasch,** goulash 50
der **Gummistiefel** (-), wellington (boot) 27
die **Gurke** (-n), gherkin 38
gut, good 5

das **Haar** (-e), hair 17
***haben,** have 5
halb, half 7
halblang, of medium length 17
die **Hälfte** (-n), half 54
hallo!, hello! 25
der **Hals** (¨e), throat 46
***halten,** stop 5
die **Hand** (¨e), hand 46
die **Handtasche** (-n), handbag 29
hängen, hang 51
hassen, hate 42
häßlich, ugly; hideous 16
hastig, hastily 37
hatte (from **haben**), had 55
hätte gern, should like 6
der **Haupteingang** (¨), main entrance 49
die **Hauptstadt** (¨), capital 43
das **Haus** (¨er), house 9
nach Hause, home 13
zu Hause, at home 29
die **Hausarbeit,** housework 7
der **Hebel** (-), lever 56
heiß, hot 27
heißen, be called 31
***helfen** (+ *dat.*), help 43

(das) **Helgoland,** Heligoland 34
das **Hemd** (-en), shirt 5
der **Herbst** (-e), autumn 27
hereinkommen, come in 43
(der) **Herr,** Mr 7
  mein Herr, sir 29
die **Herrenhose** (-n), men's trousers 22
meine **Herrschaften,** sir, madam; ladies and gentlemen 29
herunterkommen, come down 49
heute, today 2
  heute abend, tonight 14
hier, here 5
Himmel:
  um Himmels willen, for heaven's sake 31
sich **hinauslehnen,** lean out 49
sich **hinlegen,** lie down 38
hinstellen, put (down) 42
hinten, at the back 9
hinter, behind 21
hoch, high; big 29
höchste, highest; greatest 40
(das) **Holland,** Holland 36
der **Holländer** (-), Dutchman 50
holländisch, Dutch 50
hören, hear 30; listen 55
die **Hose** (-n), (pair of) trousers 9
das **Hotel** (-s), hotel 21
hübsch, pretty 43
das **Huhn** (¨er), chicken 29
die **Hühnerbrühe,** chicken broth 29
der **Hund** (-e), dog 23
hundert, hundred 7
der **Hunger,** hunger 13
  ich habe Hunger, I'm hungry 13
der **Hustenbonbon** (-s), cough sweet 46
der **Hut** (¨e), hat 11

ich, I 2
die **Idee** (-n), idea 13
ihr, you 10; her 17; their 18
Ihr, your 18
immer, always 2
immer noch, still 19
in, in 21
der **Ingenieur** (-e), engineer 33
die **Insel** (-n), island 41
insgesamt, all together 29
sich **interessieren für,** be interested in 38
der **Ire** (-n), Irishman 50
irgendein, any (at all) 50
irgendwo(hin), (to) somewhere 34
irisch, Irish 50
(das) **Irland,** Ireland 50
ist, is 3
(das) **Italien,** Italy 50
der **Italiener** (-), Italian 50
italienisch, Italian 50

ja, yes 1; (*intensifying adverb*) perfectly well 17
die **Jacke** (-n), jacket 11
das **Jahr** (-e), year 27
die **Jahreszeit** (-en), season 27
der **Januar,** January 27
jawohl, yes indeed 29
die **Jeans** (*pl.*), (pair of) jeans 9
jeder, every 22
jetzt, now 18
der **Jugoslawe** (-n), Jugoslav 50
(das) **Jugoslawien,** Jugoslavia 50
jugoslawisch, Jugoslav 50
der **Juli,** July 27
jung, young 43
der **Junge** (-n), boy 39
der **Juni,** June 27

der **Kabeljau** (-e), cod 32
der **Kaffee,** coffee 7
kalt, cold 27
kapieren (*colloq.*), understand; 'get' 55
kaputt, broken 18
die **Karte** (-n), ticket 33; card 46
die **Kartoffel** (-n), potato 54
der **Käse,** cheese 5
die **Kasse** (-n), cash-desk 47
Kasseler, cured; smoked (*of pork*) 29
die **Kassenstunden** (*pl.*), banking hours 22
die **Kassette** (-n), cassette 5
der **Kater** (-), hangover 37
die **Katze** (-n), cat 23
kaufen, buy 5
kein, no; not a 13
keineswegs, not at all; 'no way' 53
kennen, know 31
die **Kette** (-n), chain 44
das **Kilo,** kilo 6
das **Kind** (-er), child 13
das **Kino** (-s), cinema 31
der **Klappstuhl** (¨e), folding chair 42
Klasse!, great 18
das **Kleid** (-er), dress 13
die **Kleidung** (*sing.*), clothes 37
klein, small 17
das **Kleingeld,** (small) change 53
klopfen, knock 33
klug, clever 45
der **Knopf** (¨e), button 53
der **Kofferraum** (¨e), (car) boot 54
Köln, Cologne 29
das **Kölsch,** *Cologne beer* 29
kommen, come 7
die **Konditorei** (-en), cake shop 54
***können,** can 13
  könnte, could; might 37
der **Kopf** (¨e), head 37
kosten, cost 9
krank, ill 7

die **Kreditkarte** (-n), credit card 29
der **Kreis** (-e), circle 46
der **Krimi** (-s), thriller 13
die **Krone** (-n), crown 54
die **Küche** (-n), kitchen 37
der **Kuchen** (-), cake 28
der **Kugelschreiber** (-), ball point 17
kühl, cool 27
das **Kühlwasser,** coolant; radiator water (*car*) 55
kümmerlich, miserable 42
der **Kunde** (-n), customer 34
das **Kurkonzert** (-e), spa concert 52
kurz, short 17
die **Kusine** (-n), (female) cousin 35

der **Lachs** (-e), salmon 50
der **Laden** (¨), shop 22
die **Lampe** (-n), lamp 42
das **Land** (¨er), country 48
lang (*adj.*), long 17
lange (*adv.*), long 13
länger, longer 13
langsam, slow(ly) 32
sich **langweilen,** be bored 43
der **Lärm,** noise 39
***lassen,** leave 13
der **Lastkraftwagen (LKW)** (-), heavy goods vehicle 40
***laufen,** run 33
der **Lautsprecher** (-), loudspeaker 33
das **Lebensmittelgeschäft** (-e), grocer's 54
ledern, leather 42
leer, empty 23
die **Leerung** (-en), (postal) collection 22
leicht, easy 38
leid:
es tut mir leid, I'm sorry 18
leider, unfortunately 3
leihen, lend 18; borrow 28
der **Leiter** (-), leader 49
***lesen,** read 13
letzt, last 51
die **Leute** (*pl.*), people 33
das **Licht** (-er), light 44
lieber, for preference; rather 10
ich trinke lieber, I prefer to drink 10
der **Liebling** (-e), darling 18
liegen, lie 23
die **Limonade,** lemonade; 'pop' 2
die **Linie** (-n), line 46
links, on the left 9
die **Liste** (-n), list 54
der **Liter** (-), litre 55
locker, loose 38
sich **lohnen,** be worth (it), 55
löschen, put out 44
die **Luft,** air 55
das **Luftkissenfahrzeug** (-e), hovercraft 51

machen, make; come to 6; do 13
es macht nichts, it doesn't matter 29
das **Mädchen** (-), girl 30
mag (*from* **mögen**), like 54
der **Magen** (¨), stomach 26
der **Mai,** May 27
mal, just 29
das **Mal** (-e), time (= *occasion*) 43
-mal, times 8
man, one 22
manchmal, sometimes 53
der **Mann** (¨er), man 24; husband 31
der **Mantel** (¨), coat 9
die **Mark,** mark 3
die **Marmelade,** jam 14
der **März,** March 27
das **Meerschweinchen** (-), guinea pig 43
mehr, more; longer 23
mein, my 10
meinen, think 13
meist, most 47
meistens, mostly 54
melden, report 43
der **Meldezettel** (-), report form 43
die **Melone** (-n), melon 45
eine **Menge,** a lot 51
Mensch!, good heavens! 14
die **Metzgerei** (-en), butcher's 54
mich, me 17
die **Milch,** milk 2
der **Minister** (-), minister 49
die **Minute** (-), minute 8
mir, (to) me 29
mit, with (me, etc.) 9
das **Mitbringen,** bringing 52
der **Mittag,** midday; noon 8
das **Mittagessen,** lunch 7
die **Mittagspause,** lunch break 9
die **Mitte,** middle 46
mittelgroß, medium sized 17
das **Mittelmeer,** Mediterranean 50
die **Mitternacht,** midnight 8
der **Mittwoch,** Wednesday 22
die **Möbel** (*pl*), furniture 42
möchte (*from* **mögen**), would like 25
die **Mode** (-n), fashion 22
***mögen,** like 25
möglich, possible 35
die **Molkerei** (-en), dairy 54
der **Moment** (-e), moment 53
der **Monat** (-e), month 27
der **Montag,** Monday 22
der **Morgen** (-), morning 5
morgen, tomorrow 13
morgen früh, tomorrow morning 29
Moskau, Moscow 51
der **Motor** (-en), motor; engine 54
müde, tired 7
München, Munich 34
der **Mund** (-e), mouth 17

die **Münze** (-n), coin 48
das **Musikgeschäft** (-e), music shop 30
***müssen**, must 13
die **Mutter** (¨), mother 5
Mutti, mother (*familiar*) 52

na, well 19
na, so was!, well, would you believe it! 3
nach, after 7; to (+ *name of town*) 22
der **Nachbar** (-n), neighbour 31
nachmittags, in the afternoon 8
die **Nachricht** (-en), piece of news; (*pl.*) news (*TV, radio*) 55
nächst, next; nearest 22
die **Nacht** (¨e), night 22
nachts, at night 8
die **Nähe**:
in der Nähe von, near 21
der **Name** (-n), name 11
die **Nase** (-n), nose 17
natürlich, naturally 39
neben, near 33
nebenan, next door 47
neblig, foggy 27
der **Neffe** (-n), nephew 31
***nehmen**, take 25
nein, no 1
nennen, name 50
nett, nice 22
neu, new 30
neun, nine 6
neunzehn, nineteen 7
neunzig, ninety 6
nicht, not 3
nicht?, isn't it? 17
die **Nichte** (-n), niece 31
nichts, nothing 19
nie, never 14
niedrig, low 45
niemand, nobody 41
noch, else 6; more 13; still 25
noch ein, another 13
noch nicht, not yet 30
nochmal, again 37
der **Norden**, north 34
nördlich, north 50
die **Nordsee**, North Sea 50
das **Normal**, regular (*grade of petrol*) 55
(das) **Norwegen**, Norway 50
der **Norweger** (-), Norwegian 50
norwegisch, Norwegian 50
nötig, necessary 38
der **November**, November 27
null, nought; zero 8
die **Nummer** (-n), number 11
nun, (well) now 39
nur, only 5

o weh, oh dear 37
ob, whether 44
oben, above; at the top 33
der **Ober**, waiter 29
Herr Ober!, waiter! 29
ober, upper 49
oder, or 1
öffnen, open 22
ohne, without 23
der **Oktober**, October 27
das **Öl** (-e), oil 55
der **Onkel** (-), uncle 31
der **Optiker** (-), optician 46
die **Orange** (-n), orange 6
der **Ordner** (-), file 17
die **Ordnung**, order 55
Ost-, east 34
der **Osten**, east 34
(das) **Österreich**, Austria 34
der **Österreicher**, Austrian 47
österreichisch, Austrian 50
östlich, east 50
die **Ostsee**, Baltic 50
oval, oval 17
die **Ozean** (-e), ocean 50

ein **paar**, a few 13
der **Pariser** (-), Parisian 51
parken, park 21
das **Parkhaus** (¨er), multi-storey car park 54
der **Parkplatz** (¨e), car park 40
der **Paß** (¨e), passport 47
der/die **Patient (-in)** (-e; -nen), patient 46
das **Penicillin**, penicillin 46
die **Person** (-en), person 25
der **Pfeffer**, pepper 32
der **Pfirsich** (-e), peach 32
die **Pflanze** (-n), plant 42
die **Pflaume** (-n), plum 6
das **Pfund**, pound 6
der **Pilot** (-en), pilot 35
die **Platte** (-n), record 5
Platz nehmen, take a seat 46
plötzlich, suddenly 36
(das) **Polen**, Poland 50
die **Polizei**, police 43
die **Polizeiwache** (-n), police station 43
die **Pommes frites** (*pl.*), chips 13
(das) **Portugal**, Portugal 50
das **Postamt** (¨er), post office 21
das **Postwertzeichen** (-), stamp 56
der **Preis** (-e), price 25
prima!, very good; super 14
privat, private 44
prost!, cheers! 3
das **Prozent**, per cent 55
prozentig, per cent 55
der **Pullover** (-), pullover 9
das **Püree**, mashed potatoes 29
putzen, clean 7
der **Pyjama** (-s), pyjamas 37

das **Quadrat** (-e), square 46

das **Rad** (¨er), bike 13
das **Radio** (-s), radio 55
sich **rasieren,** shave 37
rauchen, smoke 44
die **Rechnung** (-en), bill 29
recht vielen Dank, thank you very much 29
rechts, to, on the right 9
der **Regenmantel** (¨), raincoat 14
regnen, rain 27
der **Reifen** (-), tyre 55
der **Reis,** rice 29
das **Reisebüro** (-s), travel agency 28
die **Reisegruppe** (-n), package tour 51
der **Reisescheck** (-s), traveller's check 47
das **Restaurant** (-s), restaurant 19
der **Rhein,** Rhine 50
das **Rheinland,** Rhineland 34
richtig, right 12
das **Riesenrad,** big wheel 33
der **Rock** (¨e), skirt 11
Rom, Rome 51
rot, red 11
der **Rotwein** (-e), red wine 3
der **Rücksitz** (-e), back seat 54
ruhig, quiet 51
rund, round 17
der **Russe** (-n), Russian 50
russisch, Russian 29
(das) **Rußland,** Russia 50

die **Sache** (-n), thing 19
sagen, say 9
sag mal, tell me 19
der **Salat** (-e), salad 29
das **Salz** (-e), salt 54
die **Salzkartoffel** (-n), boiled potato 29
der **Samstag** (*S. German*), Saturday 22
sauberhalten, keep clean 10
das **Sauerkraut,** sauerkraut (*pickled white cabbage, cooked*) 29
die **Schachtel** (-n), box 54
schaffen, manage 35
der **Schal** (-e), scarf 27
der **Schalter** (-), counter 53
der **Scheck** (-s), cheque 47
die **Scheibe** (-n), slice 14
der **Schein** (-e), (bank)note 53
scheinen, shine 27
das **Schiff** (-e), ship 51
der **Schilling** (-e), (Austrian) schilling 47
der **Schinken,** ham 14
der **Schirm** (-e), umbrella 14
der **Schlaf,** sleep 37
***schlafen,** sleep 22
das **Schlafzimmer** (-), bedroom 37
das **Schlagobers** (*Austrian*), whipped cream 33
die **Schlagsahne,** whipped cream 54
die **Schlagzeile** (-n), headline 55
die **Schlange** (-n), queue 33
schließen, shut 22
schlimm, bad 46
der **Schlips** (-e), tie 18
der **Schlüssel** (-), key 25
schmecken, taste 29
schmeckt es?, are you enjoying it? 29
der **Schmuck,** jewellery 22
schmutzig, dirty 23
der **Schnaps,** brandy; spirits 5
schneien, snow 27
schnell, quickly 13
schnell machen, be quick 54
der **Schnellimbiß,** snack bar 32
der **Schnitzel** (-), escalope 29
die **Schokolade,** chocolate 52
schon, already 13; just 29
schön, nice 5
bitte schön, there you are 6; don't mention it 6
danke schön, thank you very much 6
der **Schotte** (-n), Scot 50
schottisch, Scottish 50
(das) **Schottland,** Scotland 50
***schreiben,** write 53
der **Schuh** (-e), shoe 18
die **Schulter** (-n), shoulder 49
der **Schuppen** (-), shed 51
schwach, weak 45
schwarz, black 11
das **Schwarzbrot,** black bread 29
(das) **Schweden,** Sweden 50
das **Schweinefleisch,** pork 30
das **Schweineschnitzel** (-), pork escalope 29
die **Schweiz,** Switzerland 36
der **Schweizer** (-), Swiss 50
der **Schweizer Käse,** Swiss cheese 29
schweizerisch, Swiss 47
schwer, difficult; hard 49
die **Schwester** (-n), sister 32
sechs, six 3
sechzehn, sixteen 7
sechzig, sixty 6
***sehen,** see 13; look 30
sehen auf (+ *acc.*), look at 43
sehen nach, check 55
sehr, very 7
die **Seife,** soap 5
***sein,** be 3
sein, his; its 17
seit, for (+ *time*) 33
die **Seite** (-n), side 49
die **Sekretärin** (-nen), secretary 41
die **Selbstbedienung,** self-service 56
selbsttätig, automatic 56
die **Semmel** (-n) (*S. German*), bread roll 13
die **Sendung** (-en), programme 55
der **Senf,** mustard 32

die **Tüte** (-n), paper bag 23
typisch, typical 19

die **U-Bahn** (-en), underground (*railway*) 51
über, over 33
überall, everywhere 43
überhaupt nicht, not at all 38
übermorgen, the day after tomorrow 28
überreichen, present with 54
übrigens, by the way 29
die **UdSSR,** USSR 48
(die) **Uhr,** o'clock 7
um, at 7
  um . . . zu, in order to 39
umbauen, rebuild 51
umschalten, switch over 55
der **Umschlag** (¨e), envelope 53
unbedingt, absolutely 19
unberechtigt, unauthorized 44
und, and 1
ungarisch, Hungarian 50
(das) **Ungarn,** Hungary 50
ungeduldig, impatient 33
unmöglich, impossible 33
unser, our 18
unten, below; at the bottom 33
unter, under 23
unterschreiben, sign 43
die **Unterschrift** (-en), signature 43
die **Urgroßeltern** (*pl.*), great-grandparents 51
der **Urlaub,** holiday 33
  auf Urlaub, on holiday 33

der **Vater** (¨), father 13
Vati, father (*familiar*) 2
Venedig, Venice 51
verbinden, connect 41
  falsch verbunden, wrongly connected; 'wrong number' 41
verboten, forbidden 40
verbringen, spend (*time*) 50
* **vergessen,** forget 53
der **Verkäufer** (-), shop assistant 34
* **verlieren,** lose 43
  verloren, lost 43
verpassen, miss 53
verschieden, various 53
versuchen, try 38
viel, much 9; many 11
vielleicht, perhaps 13
vier, four 3
das **Viertel** (-), quarter 7
vierzehn, fourteen 7
vierzig, forty 6
der **Vogel** (¨), bird 55
die **Volkskammer,** 'People's Chamber' (*DDR, = House of Commons*) 49
voll, full (of) 49
völlig, completely 38
volltanken, fill up (*car*) 55
vom = von dem 21
von, of 18
vor, before 7; in front of 21
  vor allem, especially 29
die **Vorderseite** (-n), front 49
vorgestern, the day before yesterday 22
vorlegen, present 56
vormittags, in the morning 8
der **Vorname** (-n), Christian name 31
vorn(e), at the front 9
* **vorschlagen,** suggest 55
Vorsicht!, beware 52
die **Vorspeise** (-n), starter 29

der **Wachtmeister** (-), constable 43
der **Wagen** (-), car 18
wahrscheinlich, probably 43
(das) **Wales,** Wales 50
der **Waliser** (-), Welshman 50
walisisch, Welsh 50
die **Wand** (¨e), wall 46
wann, when 7
wäre (*from* **sein**), would be 51
warm, warm 27
die **Warnung** (-en), warning 44
warten auf (+ *acc.*), wait for 29
warum, why 14
was, what 2
  was für, what sort of 13
sich * **waschen,** wash 37
das **Wasser,** water 2
das **Wechselgeld** (-er), (money given as) change 53
wechseln, change 47
weg, away 13; gone 41
weh tun, hurt 39
weichgekocht, soft boiled 14
das **Weihnachtsgeschenk** (-e), Christmas present 54
der **Wein** (-e), wine 2
weiß (*from* **wissen**):
  ich weiß nicht, I don't know 5
weiß, white 11
der **Weißwein** (-e), white wine 3
weit, far 21
  weiter, further 33
weitsichtig, long-sighted 37
welcher, which 9
weniger, less 49
wer?, who? 13
* **werden,** become; get 27
werktags, on weekdays 40
der **Wert** (-e), value 47
wertvoll, valuable 48
West-, west 34
der **Westen,** west 34
westlich, west 50
das **Wetter,** weather 27
der **Whisky,** whisky 50

Grammar index